I0794374

Crossing the Atlantic

Number Forty-two:
The Walter Prescott Webb Memorial Lectures

A list of other titles in this series appears at the back of the book.

Contributors:

Ashley Sides
Whitney Walton
Dieter K. Buse
Andrew Lees
James Ross-Nazzal

Crossing the Atlantic

Travel and Travel Writing in Modern Times

Edited by
Thomas Adam *and* Nils H. Roemer
With an Introduction by Frank Trommler

Published for the University of Texas at Arlington
by Texas A&M University Press
College Station

Copyright © 2011 by The University of Texas at Arlington
Manufactured in the United States of America
All rights reserved
First edition

This paper meets the requirements of ANSI/NISO Z39.48-1992 (Permanence of Paper).
Binding materials have been chosen for durability.

Library of Congress Cataloging-in-Publication Data

Crossing the Atlantic : travel and travel writing in modern times / edited by Thomas Adam and Nils H. Roemer ; with an introduction by Frank Trommler ; contributors: Ashley Sides . . . [et al.]. — 1st ed.
p. cm. — (The Walter Prescott Webb memorial lectures ; no. 42)
Includes index.
ISBN-13: 978-1-60344-265-7 (cloth : alk. paper)
ISBN-10: 1-60344-265-0 (cloth : alk. paper)
ISBN-13: 978-1-60344-292-3 (e-book)
ISBN-10: 1-60344-292-8 (e-book)
1. Travel writing—United States—History—19th century. 2. Travel writing—United States—History—20th century. 3. Travel writing—Germany—History—19th century. 4. Travel writing—Germany—History—20th century. 5. Travelers' writings, American—History and criticism. 6. Travelers' writings, German—History and criticism. 7. Women travelers—History—19th century. 8. Travel writing—Middle East—History—19th century. I. Adam, Thomas, 1968– II. Roemer, Nils H. III. Sides, Ashley. IV. Series: Walter Prescott Webb memorial lectures ; 42.
G220.C76 2011
917.3—dc22 2010034083

CONTENTS

Preface vii
Introduction by Frank Trommler 1

PART 1
American Travelers in Europe

"That Humane and Advanced Civilization": Interpreting Americans' Values from Their Praise of Saxony, 1800–1850—*Ashley Sides* 11
Internationalism, Travel Writing, and Franco-American Educational Travel, 1898–1939—*Whitney Walton* 50

PART 2
German Travelers in the United States

Social Crossings: German Leftists View "Amerika" and Reflect Themselves, 1870–1914—*Dieter K. Buse* 81
Mapping Modernity: Jews and Other German Travelers —*Nils H. Roemer* 131
Between Modernity and Antimodernity: From Enthusiasm to Hostility in German Perceptions of Big Cities in America, 1870s–1930s —*Andrew Lees* 149

PART 3
Gender and Travel

Travel, Gender, and Identity: George and Anna Ticknor's Travel Journals from Their 1835–36 Journey to Dresden —*Thomas Adam* 189
The Women of Palestine in American Women's Travel Writing —*James Ross-Nazzal* 210

Contributors 249
Index 251

PREFACE

The Walter Prescott Webb Memorial Lecture series was inaugurated in 1965 by professors Will Holmes, Harold Hollingsworth, and E. C. Barksdale. In the 1970s and 1980s, under the leadership of Richard G. Miller, Stanley Palmer, and Kenneth R. Phil (successors to Barksdale as chair of the department of history of the University of Texas at Arlington), the lecture series and concomitant publications grew in stature and have gained a national reputation. The presentations are published by means of a generous endowment from C. B. Smith Sr. of Austin, a graduate of the University of Texas at Arlington and a former student of Walter Prescott Webb at the University of Texas at Austin. Smith also provided funds for the annual prize given for the best essay on the year's theme.

The Walter Prescott Webb Memorial Lectures held at the University of Texas at Arlington on March 12, 2009, explored the travel writing of Germans and Americans who crossed the Atlantic in the nineteenth and twentieth centuries. The chapters in this book by Dieter K. Buse (Laurentian University), Andrew Lees (Rutgers University), Nils Roemer (University of Texas at Dallas), and Thomas Adam (University of Texas at Arlington) are based on the talks they gave as part of these lectures. Lynne Fallwell, (Texas Tech University), Frank Trommler (University of Pennsylvania), Dennis Kratz (University of Texas at Dallas), and Beth Wright (University of Texas at Arlington) introduced the four speakers and offered helpful comments. The chapters by Whitney Walton (Purdue University), and James Ross-Nazzal (Houston Community College) were chosen from a number of essays submitted for our Webb-Smith Essay Competition. We decided also to include the chapter by Ashley Sides who is a graduate of the master's program in history at the University of Texas at Arlington. In March 2008, Sides defended a remarkable master's thesis on American travel to Germany in the course of the nineteenth century. His chapter is based upon this thesis. We are very grateful to Frank Trommler for agreeing to write the introduction to this volume.

The success of the Webb Lecture series depends on the support of many people. First we would like to thank our colleagues from the department of history at the University of Texas at Arlington for their assistance and generous support. Joyce Goldberg, who has chaired the Webb Lectures Committee for several years, and Mylynka Kilgore, a doctoral student in our transatlantic PhD program and assistant to the Webb Lectures Committee, were of immense help in organizing the conference. We would also like to thank Ben Huseman, our Special Collections librarian and specialist in German-American history, for organizing the tour of the cartographic special collection at our university and the behind-the-scenes tour at the Amon Carter Museum in Fort Worth. Without his help and expertise the event would not have been as successful as it was. Lynne Fallwell and Imre Demhardt (University of Texas at Arlington) also helped with the logistics of the event and supported the organizers in their attempt to make all visitors feel at home.

This volume is dedicated to Beth Wright (dean of the College of Liberal Arts at the University of Texas at Arlington) and Dennis Kratz (dean of the School of Arts and Humanities at the University of Texas at Dallas) who supported and encouraged the collaboration between our two universities.

Crossing the Atlantic

INTRODUCTION

Frank Trommler

One of the more appealing fruits of the immense literature about Kafka in recent years was the discovery of the writer Franz Kafka as traveler. Examining Kafka's intense exploration of exotic landscapes, travels, and experiences, John Zilcosky found that the image of the sedentary bureaucrat in Prague does not do justice to Kafka's engagement with travels to foreign places in such works as *Amerika* (*Der Verschollene*) and "In the Penal Colony."[1] The context of turn-of-the-century colonialism is easily evoked if one follows Kafka's obsession with the pulp fiction series Schaffsteins Grüne Bändchen in which the French and British colonial empires foreground blustery adventure stories abroad that resonate in some of his disturbing narratives. As pointed out in this volume by Nils Roemer, Kafka, in his projection of a rather sinister America, used a widely publicized travel book on the United States, Arthur Holitscher's *Amerika heute und morgen: Reiseerlebnisse* (1912), about which Andrew Lees reports in another essay. In Kafka's writing, traveling does not necessarily mean traversing other continents in person but rather conjuring the exotic, reporting travels that occur in the realm of fantasy yet have the accoutrements of real-life observations. Kafka's writing is but one—though prominent—example of the open boundaries between real and imagined travel literature. It also documents that even an author who sees himself in a highly unusual way as an explorer always responds to an already scripted setting.

As open as the boundaries between fiction and travel writing have been for centuries, as ubiquitous have been the signs of scriptedness, even writing that seems to focus on the unfamiliar already responds to a textual predicament, and not just in the case of Kafka. Holitscher himself took basic arguments of his critical descriptions of the trip from New York to San

Francisco from earlier observers, negotiating an informed stance toward the often-stated optimistic promise of America as a new world. Like many twentieth-century travel writers about America, he guided the reader toward the conclusion that the reality of life in the United States did not match the promise, a conclusion that, again, had been formulated many decades before, though under different circumstances and with many distinct and not at all similar observations. What Dieter Buse in his chapter illuminates in socialist writers such as Wilhelm and Karl Liebknecht, Friedrich Engels, Edward Aveling, and Carl Legien, who visited the industrialized cities and explored the chances for socialism in the United States, gains its full significance only in the context of established liberal and middle-class travel writing about America. In his exhaustive analysis of their reports, Buse points to their difficulties of emancipating themselves from the travel-specific stereotypes that hinder a sharper look at social conditions, although the step from Wilhelm Liebknecht, the cofounder of the German Social Democratic Party who traveled in 1886, to his son Karl who visited in 1910, illustrates well the evolution of the ideological baggage. It gives insights into the general transformation of the curious, well-meaning, and optimistic travel images in the nineteenth century to a more professional and critical note-taking about American industrialization and modernization that was increasingly seen as the future of Europe—and not always loved for it.

Of course, crossing the Atlantic meant, at least since the nineteenth century, also going east, traveling to Europe, accompanied by a similarly intricate web of images, prejudice, and textual references within which American travel writing developed its distinct profile. What James Buzard chose as the title for his book about "European Tourism, Literature, and the Ways to Culture, 1800–1918"—*The Beaten Track* (1993)—already summarizes the predicament of American travel writers who had to appeal to and overcome a deeply clichéd knowledge about the Old Continent. Established by a plethora of travel books, novels, essays, poems, letters, and diaries, this predicament was, as Buzard emphasizes, never forgotten by the writers. He explains: "Two main observations recur frequently in their accounts: first, that the Continental tour seemed to be surrounded and regulated by a variety of guiding texts; and second, that by writing one's own travel record one had to work within the boundaries mapped out by those prior texts or somehow to stake out new territories with one's own text."[2] Buzard accounts both for the confirmation of stereotyped travel texts on the beaten track and the aspiration to overcome them. What this means is exemplified by the studies in which Ashley Sides and Thomas Adam unearth an unusual deviation of the grand tour which included England, France, Italy, Switzerland, and the Rhine valley but not Berlin and Saxony: George and Anna Ticknor's 1835–1836 travelogues of their journey to Dresden. The interest of American travelers in Germany, almost zero until Napoleon's demise in 1815, was triggered by a group of New England academics—George Ticknor, Edward Everett, Joseph Green Cogswell, and George Bancroft—who studied at German universities, setting off a trend to cast the encounter with the quaint, at times rough German life in terms of a student excursion—a widely successful narrative that accompanied thousands of young Americans in their studies at the universities in Göttingen, Heidelberg, Berlin, Halle, and Leipzig in subsequent decades. When George Ticknor returned with his wife Anna and their two children to Germany in 1835–1836, taking residence in Dresden, the capital of the small Kingdom of Saxony, he became, as Sides lays out in detail in his contribution, a promoter of a somewhat different experience in cultural education: culture in a monarchical garb yet with happy and intelligent citizens. And with great museums, libraries, and music, as Washington Irving, James Fenimore Cooper, and other prominent Americans learned in their sojourns off the beaten track. Dresden off the beaten track? How much it was indeed has been documented by Buzard himself. Saxony does not even appear in his book on the American tourism in Europe in the nineteenth century. Taking the contributions of the Ticknors at face value, there is no better illustration of the fact that perceptive travelers were able to stake out "new territories."

Looking more closely at the conditioning of travel writing on both sides of the Atlantic, one cannot but notice a fundamental difference in the kinds of information set up in America and Europe. As the learning about European culture constituted a part of the education of the middle classes that became institutionalized in U.S. colleges and universities at the end of the nineteenth century, travel to Europe was motivated by seeing in reality what had been studied, often with the additional investment in the languages. Instituting foreign language departments was made possible by breaking the dominance of Latin and classical antiquity; language instruction brought a more intense engagement with various countries. This predicament prevailed throughout the twentieth century. Given the cultural stereotypes of Europe as America's past, a new "story" could only result from a recovery of family histories that had been forgotten in the great migration, or from participation in the two world wars. At any rate, built on knowledge that was accumulated as part of a liberal arts education, travel to Europe meant for many a continuation of searching for an identity as educated Americans. The internationalism that Whitney Walton describes as an important aim of Franco-American educational travel between 1898 and 1939 did not represent a static layer of worldliness above traditional national identity but rather a constant process of mediating other nations and cultures, a process in which the spirit of adventure in young people was put to good use. While the American college had encouraged study abroad for a long time, prestigious fellowships like Albert Kahn's Around-the-World Scholarships, the David-Weill Travel Scholarships, and the fellowships of the Institute of International Education helped integrate study abroad into the structures of institutionalized cooperation that shaped international politics after the devastating world war. In the business of transatlantic travel after 1918, the notion of American isolationism was visibly absent.

In contrast to the institutionalized study of Europe in the American system of higher education, the study of the United States was hardly present in the canon of European learning in primary and secondary education. Knowledge about the United States was seldom academically grounded. It constituted part of European self-definition but drew mostly on secondhand information spiced up by reports, narratives, novels, emigrant stories, and personal impressions, aside from encounters with traveling Americans who filled a relatively narrow spectrum of tourist stereotypes. For a long time the most consistent information, especially in the German lands, Italy, Ireland, and eastern Europe, had been the experience of emigrants which led to the fact that "America" was more present among lower classes where migration often constituted the only alternative to a dreadful everyday existence. Migration as a condition that did not expire by settling in some American village or city but often meant more movement, even return to the homeland, kept the United States intensely present in Europe without reference to travel writing. Traveling to America as a matter of pleasure or professional curiosity, in turn, remained mostly in the hand of self-styled adventurers or middle-class tourists and professionals for whom the world exhibitions in Philadelphia in 1876, Chicago in 1893, and St. Louis in 1904 became magnets. Since the late nineteenth century a steady stream of businessmen and engineers established the image of America as the harbinger of modernization. All this helped transform the reference to America as the truly new world to which any travel would yield insights into the future of Europe. And yet, lacking the accoutrements of a grand culture—newness by itself was not accepted as a culture—the United States hardly rose to a topic of academic study. Travel writing and migration stories remained, together with journalistic reporting, the basic source of information. Its educational value was short-lived, often thinned out to mere slogans like "the land of unlimited possibilities," as in the title of Ludwig Max Goldberger's travel book of 1903.[3]

In this context, the chapter by Andrew Lees opens the eyes not just toward the changing reaction to American big cities but also toward the function of travel writing for the internal German discussion about modernization and urbanization. The absence of formalized studies of America allowed travel reports about the United States to become a forum for discourse on modernity. So strong was the urge to draw a general conclusion from the encounter with America that the voyage itself often did not deliver more than legitimacy for generalizing assessments about the future course of European culture, cities, and industry. Lees shows how these generalizations about U.S. cities comprise crucial factors of the internal German discussion, triggering vehement anti-Americanism once the niceties of tourist visits evaporated. In a similar setup, Nils Roemer locates in Jewish travel writing about America discourses about modernity that helped define the specifics of Jewish alienation and integration in the prevailing culture. The ups and downs of America's reputation as a haven of freedom and entrepreneurship are closely observed with critical attention to growing restrictions in immigration policies and racism. Roemer's overview, from the "German period" in American Jewish history (1825–1870) to the 1930s, resonates with the insights of Lees into the ways in which the story of modernity is embedded in cultural losses, reflecting a central European point of view that only the look at Nazi barbarism keeps from becoming hypocritical, as Stefan Zweig documents in his famous memoir, *The World of Yesterday.*

While this volume concentrates on transatlantic travel that undoubtedly produced the richest harvest of travel books, diaries, novels, and journalistic reports, it extends the perspective on voyages to a geographical area that generated travel writing of almost equal density: what was called the Holy Land, nowadays the Middle East. The number of travel and guide books about this area since the nineteenth century is indeed stupendous, though explainable by the fact that the first of these books was not the famous Murray or Baedeker who shaped the travel experience of European and American travelers, but the Holy book itself, the Bible. It is telling that the most literary response to the canonization of guide books was set off by texts about the Holy Land: Mark Twain's *The Innocents Abroad, or The New Pilgrim's Progress* (1869), probably the most popular travel book in American literature, "the quintessentially American burlesque of Holy-Land travel books and irreverent send-up of smug sanctimoniousness."[4] Twain identifies how established opinions predetermine the traveler's reactions: "I can almost tell, in set phrase, what [travelers] will say when they see Tabor, Nazareth, Jericho and Jerusalem—because I have the books they will 'smouch' their ideas from . . . The pilgrims will tell of Palestine, when they get home, not as it appeared to them, but as it appeared to Thompson and Robinson and Grimes—with the tints varied to suit each pilgrim's creed."[5]

James Ross-Nazzal overcomes the redundancy of Holy Land books as he concentrates on the perspective of female travelers in Palestine between 1832 and 1899. As part of a growing wave of research into travel writing by women, Ross-Nazzal and Thomas Adam add important insights into the gender-specific responses of American women travelers. Based on the travel writings of fifty-one American women, Ross-Nazzal unearths a rich harvest of anthropological observations into the facets of female life in nineteenth-century Palestine that were generally closed to male travelers—especially the harem and other parts of domestic life—or had their roots in the subservient role of women in the paternalistic society, aside from the different religious customs between Muslims, Jews, and Christians. Deeply troubled by the sad condition of these women, the American visitors usually went beyond passing moral judgments, trying to disentangle their obligations to their gender from those to their race, in many cases overstating the degree of female equality in the United States. Thomas Adam's focus is much narrower in his exploration of female observations of "the other"—reading Anna Ticknor's diary about the Dresden sojourn side by side with that of her husband—but especially fruitful for understanding the conditioning of these observations. Being totally private, though more distant than necessary, these diaries hold their own against the clichés of the "European tour," illuminating in different ways the charm and flaws of life in a small German residence where the king not only welcomes the American visitors but makes them part of the social life of the court. Only Anna, however, saw beyond the social circles and included observations of the common people in her diary.

These essays, though diverse, have in common a rather straightforward concept of travel as an exploration of "the other" which becomes an exploration of the self, at times a confirmation of identity. They offer significant illustrations of the question that Terry Caesar raises in his summarizing view of travel versus fictional literature, *Forgiving the Boundaries*—"What is a travel book?"—a question that Caesar answers: "The central prescription is that the writer not be abstract or heedless of circumstance. . . . The genre's mode of knowing does not change. Knowledge in each text remains saturated by the experience of observation."[6] The collection hardly touches on the border areas of nonfiction travel writing and novel writing—with the exception of Kafka—yet provides some examples for Terry Caesar's assessment: "My sense is that authors choose to write travel rather than fiction (especially the many, like [Paul] Theroux, who write both) because they want to try to *embed* a 'self' in a certain way."[7] As the travel texts about America, Europe, and Palestine are evaluated in the following essays, they interconnect well under the patronage of one of the oldest literary devices, one based on the premise that subjectivity in the pursuit of objectivity anchors realism better than an attempted and failed objectivity. The only problem in travel writing, however, is to give this subjectivity its original voice. Mark Twain's groan about the scripted nature of travelers' experiences reverberates more than ever in our age of unlimited textual, acoustic, and visual reproduction.

NOTES

1. John Zilcosky, *Kafka's Travels: Exoticism, Colonialism, and the Traffic of Writing* (New York: Palgrave Macmillan, 2003).

2. James Buzard, *The Beaten Track: European Tourism, Literature, and the Ways to Culture, 1800–1918* (Oxford: Clarendon Press, 1993), 156.

3. Ludwig Max Goldberger, *Das Land der unbegrenzten Möglichkeiten: Beobachtungen über das Wirtschaftsleben der Vereinigten Staaten von Amerika* (Berlin: F. Fontane, 1903).

4. Hilton Obenzinger, "Americans in the Holy Land, Israel, and Palestine." In *The Cambridge Companion to American Travel Writing*, ed. Alfred Bendixen and Judith Hamera (Cambridge: Cambridge University Press, 2009), 146.

5. Mark Twain, *The Innocents Abroad, or The New Pilgrim's Progress* (Hartford: American Publishing, 1869), 511 and following pages, quoted after ibid., 146 and following pages.

6. Terry Caesar, *Forgiving the Boundaries: Home as Abroad in American Travel Writing* (Athens: University of Georgia Press, 1995), 143.

7. Ibid., 144.

PART I

American Travelers in Europe

“That Humane and Advanced Civilization”: Interpreting Americans’ Values from Their Praise of Saxony, 1800–1850

Ashley Sides

As travel to Europe became increasingly fashionable and possible for privileged Americans in the early to mid-nineteenth century, the little German Kingdom of Saxony turned into a beloved destination. American travel literature from this period contains glowing praise for Saxony and its people. In comparison to other German lands like Prussia and Austria, Saxony fared particularly well in Americans’ attitudes. Just what made Saxony so special in the hearts of these visitors? It was actually a combination of factors—cultural, aesthetic, social—that elite Americans were predisposed to perceive in Saxony and appreciate. They admired the Saxons’ cultivation and social responsibility, their enlightened government, and their scenic and fertile country, and they respected their resilience in the face of adversities. In other words, these elite Americans loved Saxony because it reminded them of what they valued in their own nation.[1]

Before exploring these American impressions of Saxony, however, it will be useful to understand the context of American travel to Germany and Europe in general. The Americans in this study are Anglo-Americans, not of German extraction. During the first four decades of the United States, Germany as a whole was a relatively unknown land among New Englanders and other non-German Americans, especially in comparison to their familiarity with England and France.[2] Before 1815, only a handful of Americans had ever found their way to Germany, and their travels up to that time did not represent a larger trend, nor did their pursuits there awaken a general awareness of Germany among Americans back home.

Nineteenth-Century American Travel to Europe

The end of the Napoleonic Wars in 1815 marked the beginning of a long American tradition of traveling to Germany for educational and cultural self-improvement. This was part of a broad increase in American travel to Europe in general, due to more safety on the continent after Napoleon's exile, to the establishment of regular transatlantic passenger sailing routes, and to peace and rising affluence in the United States.[3] The rise in American economic prosperity during the nineteenth century greatly expanded a privileged class who had money, leisure time, and an interest in traveling. When transatlantic steamships came into service in the 1840s, they made travel abroad much faster and more convenient. Before long they also began to offer second-class fares, which greatly reduced the cost of an overseas voyage, making it more accessible to a wider range of people. Whereas only a few thousand Americans were going abroad annually before this time, steam travel allowed as many as thirty thousand per year in the 1840s, and up to one hundred thousand in the 1890s. Though travel on the continent was revolutionized by the expansion of railroads, this effect did not happen until after mid-century.[4] Prior to that, travelers still faced slow travel by diligence, or stagecoach.[5]

Some travelers went to Europe for business. Paris, Rome, and Florence lured art students. Churches often sent their clergymen for inspiration and rest. Some people hoped to regain health in one of the famous spas. And many sought cultural education, personal improvement, and social status by making a pilgrimage to the Old World.[6] Since America was also believed to lack the cultural refinements and treasures of Europe, many in the growing upper class traveled to Europe to claim the prestigious cultural and social advantages associated with it.[7] In other words, "a European trip provided many a pilgrim with a pedigree by association."[8] Sufficient numbers of these travelers stayed abroad long enough that American expatriate communities grew in major European cities. For most of these travelers (especially the early ones), Germany was not the main destination. The traditional grand tour required them to spend time in England, Paris, and Italy, with maybe a swing through picturesque Switzerland and then up the romantic Rhine valley and out through the Low Countries, and in the early days, "only a few of the more venturesome went farther afield to northern Germany, Spain, or other parts of the Continent."[9] Saxony, tucked away in the interior of central Europe, appeared on very few American itineraries in these early days.

The United Kingdom and France proved enduringly the most popular places for American travel and travel writing, because of their longtime traditional connections with North America and because of their geographical location. An additional factor that fostered close bonds was language. Most Americans spoke English, and the well-educated of them also spoke French.[10] Therefore, due to familiarity with Britain and France and their respective languages, it was natural that most American travelers to Europe probably intentionally planned visits to those countries. But even if their destination was farther inland and they had no interest in Britain and France, transatlantic travelers would likely have docked in Liverpool or Le Havre first anyway, before being able to continue to other countries, so a visit to Britain or France may have been in some cases unavoidable. Italy also enjoyed well-established popularity due to its renown for art and its classical past. In addition to cultural travelers on the grand tour, Italy especially attracted artists. For aspiring American artists in the nineteenth century, the United States did not offer adequate training in their craft, so they had to go to Europe. From the late eighteenth century through about 1820, American artists often received training in England, but Italy then became the destination of choice, due to its artistic heritage, picturesque ruins, and affordable living. Rome and Florence attracted colonies of over one hundred American artists from 1830 to 1875.[11]

American Travel to Germany

In addition to the traditional attractions of art, culture, and history that Europe (especially Britain, France, and Italy) had long been famous for, Americans also quickly developed an enthusiasm for German university education. In 1815, George Ticknor and fellow Bostonian Edward Everett arrived in Europe to study at the University of Göttingen. They were joined there by Joseph Green Cogswell in 1816 and followed by George Bancroft in 1818, both also of Massachusetts. The return of these men a few years later from their successful studies in Europe sparked an American trend of studying in Germany. They began to awaken the American elite society—especially in New England—to Germany's intellectual and cultural offerings. These four were really the first and most influential apostles of the new idea that Germany was the place to go for men of letters who wanted to advance their education beyond what the United States could offer. Though a couple of isolated individuals had preceded them in Göttingen, these were the first in a snowballing trend that saw thousands of American students flocking to German universities throughout the rest of the nineteenth century and beyond.[12]

Americans began studying at German universities in ever-increasing numbers. From the handful of pioneers at Göttingen prior to 1820, American registrations at German universities increased dramatically each decade into at least the 1870s, so that by 1900—or the latest 1920—nearly nine thousand Americans had studied in Germany.[13] During the first half of the nineteenth century, New England was the biggest contributor to this growing trend.[14] Study abroad—and increasingly in Germany—became an important part of a privileged American education.[15]

Students made up an important part of the ranks of American travelers in Germany, but they were not the only ones discovering the appeals of the various German lands—perhaps just some of the best-documented ones. Ticknor and his early Göttingen companions probably had a smaller influence over the variety of other travelers to Germany than they did over the students who went there. The ever-growing hordes of American travelers to Europe were driven by a complex array of factors like those mentioned above (some of which, of course, would have applied to the students as well). Although the primary destinations generally remained the United Kingdom, France, and Italy, increasing numbers of Americans traveling in Europe under improving travel conditions surely meant that Germany would have eventually received its share of American visitors regardless of whether it appealed to students or not. The mass American "discovery" of Germany toward mid-century seems to have coincided with a similar boom in travel to other countries, and travel to all was probably fueled by these same factors.

The main difference is that the well-known United Kingdom, France, and Italy were already receiving a greater degree of American travel interest in the 1810s and 1820s before Germany started coming into its own as a destination in the 1830s and after.

Although Germany was relatively unknown among Anglo-American societal elites at the start of the nineteenth century, it gained popularity after the 1820s when growing numbers of Americans began traveling deeper into the Continent and writing home about it. As the attractions of Germany became better known, it was able to compete with the other time-honored destinations of Europe as the century progressed. The first Americans to discover it after 1815 began to recommend it to students and to publish books about its people and places. Especially from the 1830s on, as more Americans began to flood the continent, and as travel to and within Europe became more efficient, more of these travelers began to push farther into Germany and to write about it, perpetuating the cycle that helped to familiarize Anglo-Americans with Germany. This is probably also more or less the pattern that acquainted Americans with the Kingdom of Saxony and led to its eventual popularity as a travel destination.

American Travel to Saxony

Saxony was not a great, well-known military or political power in central Europe, as its neighbors Prussia and Austria were. And, located relatively deep in the heart of the continent—nowhere near the travel routes between England, France, and Italy—it was quite out of the way for American travelers primarily interested in visiting the classic highlights of the grand tour. It would have to wait for the rising tide of American travel to wash these crowds of transatlantic visitors farther into the European continent, while its growing reputation based on reports from its early American visitors would provide the current that directed a flow of travelers onto its soil.

At the beginning of the nineteenth century, if Anglo-Americans knew anything about Saxony at all, it probably had to do with Martin Luther and the Reformation, the Battle of Leipzig where Napoleon was defeated in 1813, the Leipzig trade fairs, and possibly the Dresden art gallery or Meißen porcelain (or both). But as increasing numbers of Americans traveled there in successive decades, Saxony's fame grew and distinct images emerged in the growing body of travel writings. Saxony developed a reputation for fertile soil and lovely scenery, highly cultivated citizens (who bore up admirably in the face of injustices from abroad), enlightened rulers, and the cultural treasures of Dresden and Leipzig. These perceived characteristics reflect some of the values of the Americans who observed and praised them.

John Quincy Adams's "Letters on Silesia," published in 1801 in the *Port Folio,* provided American readers some of their earliest imagery of what was then the Electorate of Saxony, but most of Adams's comments as he passed through the region were brief and matter-of-fact.[16] George Ticknor, traveling with Edward Everett fifteen years later, made a much more thorough exploration of Saxony and commented insightfully on many features of the country that would be echoed by subsequent American travelers over the next several decades as Saxony's reputation grew. The letters and journals that Ticknor sent back to friends and family in 1816 must have been some of the first such detailed accounts of the region that his audience had read from the pen of a countryman. But the Kingdom of Saxony that Ticknor visited in 1816 was already different from the Electorate of Saxony that Adams had visited in 1800. Having fought on Napoleon's side at the Battle of Leipzig, Saxony, seen as a traitor to the victorious powers, was forced by the Congress of Vienna in 1815 to cede 58 percent of its territory with 42 percent of its population to neighboring states (mostly Prussia) as punishment.[17] As another early American traveler, Timothy Dwight, said, Saxony "was so diminished in its territory by the Congress of Vienna, that it now forms one of the weakest European monarchies."[18]

Saxons as Noble Victims

Visiting the area just the following year, Ticknor was in a unique position to observe some of the effects of the recent changes. During a semester break from studies at the University of Göttingen, he and Everett made a trip of a few weeks through Prussia and Saxony, where they researched important educational institutions and visited cities, scholars, and battlefields. Tick-

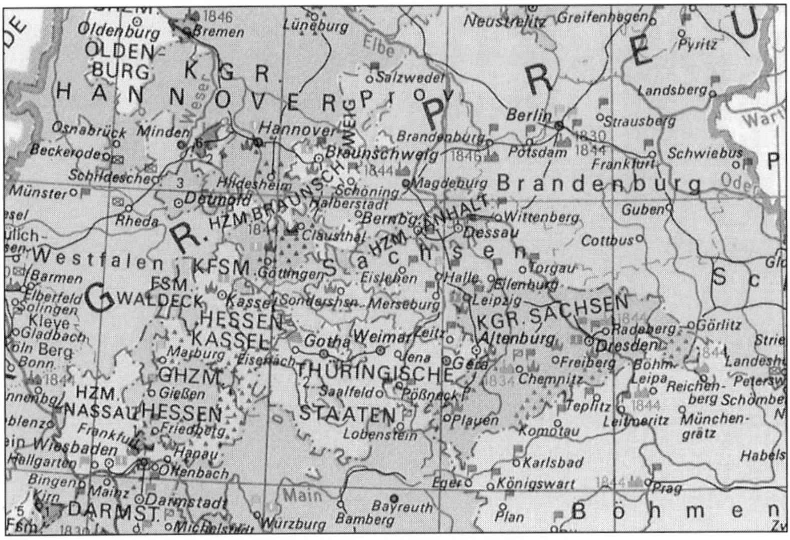

Map of the German Confederation, 1815–1847. The Kingdom of Saxony bordered with the Kingdom of Prussia to the north and the Empire of Austria and the Kingdom of Bavaria to the south. Reprinted from Atlas zur Geschichte vol. 1, VEB Hermann Haack, Geographisch-Kartographische Anstalt Gotha / Leipzig 1981, 87, with the courtesy of Ernst Klett Verlag GmbH, Zweigniederlassung Gotha

nor used every opportunity possible to study as much as he could about the countries. The things he learned aroused his empathy for the diminished little Kingdom of Saxony. Heading toward Leipzig via Weimar in September 1816, they first had to cross through a section of Prussian territory that, until the Congress of Vienna just the previous year, had belonged to Saxony. Interested in the local perspective on the change of government, Ticknor wrote, "From Eckartsberg to beyond Lützen, we were in that part of Saxony, which was given up to Prufsia, and I was curious to see what was the feeling of the people on their new transfer. I therefore spoke freely with all I met, on the point, and I found that all, even the lowest of clafses, who generally feel so little here, felt a bitter regret and sometimes indignation at the change, and two, in particular, in speaking of the days of the Saxon Government, called them 'their golden times.'—Two or three miles from Lützen we, at last, entered Saxony, shorn of its glories & strength."[19]

The people with whom Ticknor spoke were subjects of the King of Prussia, but there was no doubt that they were still Saxons at heart. This was

Ticknor's first introduction to the Saxon homeland, and it must have made an impression.[20] A few days later, Ticknor wrote that a "true Saxon—hates the Pruſsians & Buonaparte with rival animosity—and loves his own little enlightened & industrious country with all his heart & strength."[21] And a few days after that, Ticknor referred to "the animosity" toward the Prussian "nation from all parts of Saxony," explaining that "the disputes & bitterneſs between Saxony & Pruſsia are ~~now extremely~~ rancorous."[22] Finding that "ye Saxon peasants are more communicative than those of Pruſsia or Hannover," Ticknor interviewed a few more of them as he and Everett, making their way from Dresden to Berlin, crossed the northern border of Saxony and once again entered Prussian territory that had formerly been Saxon. He recorded that they "entered the ceded part of Saxony at Elsterwerda." As they passed through the region, "I took ~~great~~ pains to speak with every man I met in the ceded part of Saxony, on the subject of the ceſsion. Without a single exception, I found a decided dislike of Pruſsia openly expreſsed even by those in Pruſsian pay—and as open an attachment to Saxony. The number of persons was not, to be sure, above six or seven; but so distinct an expreſsion of their feelings to a stranger showed a ~~very~~ rooted ~~abhorrence~~ dislike of their present masters in a country, where it is so rare to hear an opinion expreſsed on politicks as it is in Germany."[23]

Ticknor was getting the unequivocal message that the proud Saxons loved their native land and despised the Prussians for taking much of their territory and people. And though he realized that Saxony's cession to Prussia was a form of punishment for Saxony's alliance with Napoleon during the war, he felt that dismembering this state without regard to the character of the people or their needs for resources was extraordinarily unfair.[24] In a section titled "Injustice to Saxony," Ticknor wrote in his journal on the three-year anniversary of Napoleon's great defeat at the Battle of Leipzig, and he expressed remarkable solidarity with the Saxon people over their losses:

> The three last days, which I have paſsed in Leipzig are the most memorable in its memorable history and yet they are an anniversary which they Leipzig people do not notice. It was ye emancipation

> of Europe; but it was partly by the ruin of Saxony, that this great battle was won; & therefore no true Saxon ~~will~~ now rejoices in it. Indeed, I have seen many, who could not quite conceal their regret that ye French times were gone by, and spoke of coming troubles & revolutions in Europe with a kind of ~~concealed~~ suppreſsed satisfaction, which showed how bitterly yy. feel their wrongs. In this feeling all Europe, except ye two countries yt. have profited by the unjust division sympathizes with them. England & France, who agreed on almost no other point at ye congreſs of Vienna agreed in protesting against this violence—Spain & portugal, tho' so distant from y^{e} ~~instant~~ interest were not indifferent—& even all ye little states of Germany, who, on common occasions are glad eno' to pull one another down united generally against this ~~palpable~~ piece of injustice. Glad, therefore, as I should be to see ye battle of Leipzig celebrated with all pomp & thanksgiving, I cannot claim it at ye hands of ye Saxons.[25]

For Ticknor, part of Saxony's image seems to have been that of the noble victim, worthy of sympathy. And this image was not limited to Ticknor; he was merely one of the first to show it. The same attitudes are evident in Dwight a decade later. In the ceded part of Saxony (which now under Prussia was called the Province of Saxony), Dwight found the same Saxon hostility toward Prussia, fresh as it ever was, and explained that splitting Saxony had broken ancient bonds formed by intermarriages, institutions, and history. Furthermore, the Saxon government, Dwight wrote, "has for many years, and almost for ages been so mild and so enlightened, that the Saxons have long felt an enthusiastic attachment to their sovereign. The Saxon Prussians, in addition to these evils, are now compelled to pay much heavier taxes tham [*sic*] their brethren in Saxony; and at the present time they are no more reconciled to this union, than when it took place."[26]

The picture Dwight painted makes it very clear that to be a Saxon, subject to the government of Saxony, was a real blessing, while subjection to Prussia was, in comparison, a state of misery:

> Although most of that part of Prussia, over which I have passed since leaving Trauenbrietzen, (Halle however is excepted,) was separated from Saxony and united to Prussia more than ten years since, at the Congress of Vienna, it has lost as yet very little of the Saxon, and acquired very little of the Prussian character. Its dialect is Saxon, much of its territory is in fertility genuine Saxony, and it is much more proud of its Saxon fame during the Reformation, than of the prowess of the armies of Frederick and Blucher. Besides the glorious recollections awakened by the part their ancestors sustained in freeing the human mind from the bondage of superstition, they have other reasons for desiring to remain Saxons, which are more immediately operative. One of the most important is, that the taxes of Saxony are much lighter than those of Prussia. The latter country, hemmed in as she is by France, Russia, and Austria, is under the necessity of maintaining a standing army, larger in proportion to her resources, than any other power in Europe. The southern part of Prussia, particularly Silesia and a part of Saxon Prussia, is fertile; while the northern half, with the exception of a few small tracts of land, is by nature excessively poor. The greatest proportion of taxes consequently falls on the south, and the inhabitants groan under their burdens. 'Because our taxes are so much heavier than they formerly were, and than those of Saxony now are;' was the reason every one gave me, in answer to the inquiries why they did not like the Prussian as well as the Saxon government. The Prussians, in this part of the kingdom, speak with a freedom about their monarch and his government, that forms a contrast to the sealed lips or the whispers of the inhabitants of the metropolis. It reminded me more of the freedom of political conversation in France, than any thing I have heard in Germany.[27]

Dwight presented the Saxon subjects of Prussia as victims, and named several reasons why it was better to belong to Saxony than to Prussia. These reasons happened to be issues that many Americans of the time—especially

New Englanders—would have strongly identified with based on their own nation's history: association with Protestant faith, limited military and taxation, and free speech. It is true that Prussians were also Protestant, and that the rulers of Saxony, in fact, were Catholic. But Saxony claimed a pivotal place in the Protestant Reformation, which Dwight says had freed "the human mind from the bondage of superstition" (Martin Luther's city Wittenberg had been part of Saxony until it was ceded to Prussia, and Americans continued to associate Saxony with Protestantism); Saxony did not keep the kind of standing army that Prussia did; its taxes were thought to be much lower; and Saxon people seemed more inclined to free speech than most other Germans. Thus, Saxons were people that Americans felt they could identify with in many respects, at least to a greater extent than with other Germans. This also made it easy for Americans to see Saxons as victims of injustice, inclining them to feel empathy for this people and its truncated land. This empathy would not have been enough by itself to create an ongoing American interest in Saxony, but it does seem to have formed a part of Saxony's image in the American mind. By regarding Saxons as noble victims and feeling compassion for these good, honest, unfortunate folk, Americans may have predisposed themselves to perceive Saxony more favorably than Prussia—that big, proud, militaristic, bullying neighbor to the north. The underdog image is an endearing one.

Another reason for the "noble victim" image is that Saxony had suffered many devastations from being caught between outside warring powers. The scars from the most recent war were still visible to American visitors in the first several years after 1815. Ticknor himself heard firsthand accounts of the horrors, as in this interview with a peasant woman near the damaged town of Stötteritz in 1816:

> She said that she never left ye village during the battle and spent most of the time in a cellar to keep out of ye way of ye balls & bombs;—that she did not know but the country had gained by the victory and she hoped it had, for she had lost enough by it—that she had two sons killed in ye battle—and that her husband and

> remaining son had died of the hospital fever, wh. immediately after ye campaign ravaged Saxony—and that now she was left quite alone in the world to get her bread as she could. The village which is ~~very~~ small, suffered terribly she said, during ye battle & it was easy to see that many houses had been burnt down; but this was nothing she went on, to the times, when they all had ye hospital fever, that came out of Leipzig and there were not well ones enough left to take care of ye sick or to bury the dead, so that in one house, which she pointed out to me, a man and his wife remained many days unburied till aſsistance came from Leipzig.[28]

But Napoleon's were just the latest in a long history of wars that had ravaged the land, and this contributed to Saxony's victim image. Dwight called Saxony "the great battle-ground of Germany, and Germany more than any other country, the battle-ground of Europe."[29] Not only, he pointed out, was it sandwiched between the two great German rivals, Prussia and Austria, it was also in the direct warpath of French and Russian armies whenever they fought each other. It faced ruin and destruction in the Thirty Years' War and the Seven Years' War, as well as the recent Napoleonic Wars.[30] Dwight felt it was a credit to the Saxon character that they persevered through all these catastrophes: "It has been not merely the great scene of conflict, but has been compelled to nourish foreign armies, as well as to feel the devastations which they spread around them. Still, so fruitful is the soil, so great the industry of the inhabitants, so universal their intelligence, and I should also add, so wise has been the administration of the government, that Saxony has entirely recovered from these repeated and terrible ravages, in a shorter period than any other country which has been equally afflicted. The inhabitants often spoke of these calamities, and of the dangers to which they were exposed, with a feeling awakened only by sad experience."[31]Dwight saw that, although Saxons were victims, they were neither helpless nor hopeless. He was impressed at how quickly they were able to recover, and attributed this resilience to their fertile soil, their industry and intelligence, and their wise government. The image of these hard-working people pulling themselves up by their bootstraps seems to have appealed to early American travelers.

The Fertility of Saxon Soil

As the early nineteenth-century American traveler passed through the former Saxon lands and into Saxony proper, the Kingdom of Saxony, what other images would he or she have formed of this land and its people? One of the first impressions was usually the quality of the soil and the appearance of the landscape. Soil was a feature that many early-nineteenth-century Americans observed carefully as they traveled throughout Europe, apparently out of a general belief that the quality of a civilization was in large part due to the quality of the soil that it inhabited.[32] As was often the case, well-informed American travelers already had an expectation of this land based on their European sources. And in this case, sight confirmed reputation: Saxony was one of the most fertile places in Europe. Many travelers, including George and Anna Ticknor, John Adams, and John Quincy Adams, commented on the fertility of Saxon soil.[33] Dwight especially effused about "the celebrity which Saxony has so long enjoyed, for the fertility of its soil," to the extent that "the word Saxony, to the ears of the Germans, and to those of all travellers who have associated much with them, is synonymous with fertility."[34] He also boldly pointed out the direct connection he saw between quality of land and quality of inhabitants:

> Its soil is surpassed by none in Europe of a similar extent, with the exception of Lombardy and the Netherlands, and is equalled by none in Germany, unless by that part of Baden immediately bordering the Rhine. It is almost literally filled with inhabitants; but so rich is the soil, and so comparatively light are the taxes, that the peasants here are better clad, better educated, and enjoy more of the comforts of life, than in any part of Europe I have seen. They can universally read and write, while some of them take one or more newspapers, and have some knowledge of the literature of Germany. A few of them have libraries, and in this respect, as well as in the amount of their incomes, and in the comforts of life, they resemble our farmers of the northern states, more than any of the peasantry of the continent, many of whom are but little elevated

> above the blacks of the southern states. The villages here are much larger, cleaner, and better built, than any others in Europe, and are truly gladdening to the eye of the traveller, so long accustomed to the dirty villages of France and to the miserable-looking houses of the peasantry of sandy Prussia.[35]

For Dwight, rich soil and light governance were prerequisites for a productive, educated, healthy population. Under these conditions, even peasants could rise to a high level of civilization, almost on par with American farmers. Again, here is an example of a nineteenth-century American rating his own people toward the top of a hierarchy of human civilization. Dwight's American traveler is happy to finally find in Europe such an advanced, refined population where the villages look good and even the people of the land are cultured. In other words, Saxony gladdens the American traveler's eye by being more like home than other places in Europe.

The High Quality of the Population

Saxony's reputation as a well-educated, cultured nation was a significant aspect of American travelers' image of it. Dwight called Saxony and Prussia "the two most enlightened countries on the continent, . . . both rapidly advancing in knowledge and science."[36] He said that Saxons consider Prussians inferior to themselves in that "love of learning, which has for so long a period distinguished Saxony, even in Germany," and though this claim had historical merit, Dwight saw the coming day when Saxony would no longer enjoy intellectual superiority over certain regions of an ascendant Prussia.[37] But at least for the time being, Dwight could still speak of Saxony's "learning and intelligence, which now elevates that little state above every other."[38] George Bancroft, in fact, a few years before Dwight, wrote that Prussian education was already the best in Germany.[39] But often, Americans named Saxon and Prussian education together as among the best in Germany or even Europe, like Horace Mann did in 1843.[40] Saxony's intimate association with the Protestant Reformation provided the foundation for much of its enduring educational repute. Protestants made the expansion of education a priority from the very beginning.[41] Then an extensive school reform law in 1835 propelled Saxon education to the cutting edge of modernity, and made it a model for later foreign reformers—like American Horace Mann and Briton John Bashford—to study in hopes of improving education in their own countries.[42] Even as early as 1816, George Ticknor took a break from Göttingen to roam Saxon (and former Saxon) lands and study various exemplary local educational institutions.

Another quality about Saxony that struck American travelers, especially the Ticknors, was the contented, quiet, orderly way in which inhabitants seemed to live their lives. In many cases, this observation was made of the peasantry or artisans, though it was also often claimed for the population at large. To an extent, George Ticknor considered this a trait of Saxons in general—not just the inhabitants of the Kingdom of Saxony, but also those of other Saxon states ruled by the Ernestine branch of the Wettin dynasty, which were clustered in the region of Thuringia to the west of the Kingdom of Saxony.[43] In the Grand Duchy of Saxe-Weimar-Eisenach, for example, he "found every where traces of that humane and advanced civilization, which does so much credit to the Saxon character, and renders the Saxon population so contented and moral."[44] But usually he spoke of the Kingdom of Saxony. This "pleasant, quiet land of Saxony," he said, has a population that "inspires more confidence, & seems more contented & comfortable" than that of Prussia.[45] Anna Ticknor seemed even more impressed by this quiet, contented spirit, which was especially manifest in the city of Dresden. She repeatedly commented on it. Two days after arriving in Dresden, she wrote in her journal, "We are much struck with the good order & quiet of this pleasant city. Perhaps they are too quiet, for much gaiety of spirits, for I have not heard a shout, nor even a loud voice from the streets, since I have been here."[46] It was pleasant to be among such a mild people, even if they were less exciting than one might wish. A person could feel safe in Dresden, whether in the market crowds or leaving a theater at night.[47] Anna Ticknor attributed this to the character of the people more than to the presence of security forces:

> The lowest class of hard working shop keepers, mechanics, and those, who fill the streets, at their various employments, strike me very much, they have so quiet, contented and industrious an appearance.... There are no urgent solicitations, no teasing to buy, but all try to gain an honest penny; and they live so simply, are so contented with light fare, and so thankful, cheerfully, agreeably thankful for your patronage, it is a pleasure to buy.... There is, I am told, terrible poverty among the peasantry, in some parts of the country, but quiet and order are still universal. There is no beggary in the streets.
>
> There is to be sure, a vigilant police, and sentinels before the palaces and public buildings, are hints not to be disregarded; but there is nothing to repress, no symptoms of mischief, or ill-temper or rudeness.... It is a kind-hearted, gentle, industrious people, giving a stranger the pleasant sensation of confidence in their honesty and good intentions, & affording the pleasure of a sort of sympathy.[48]

Although Anna Ticknor claimed that "quiet and order are still universal" throughout the country of Saxony, these qualities were most often observed in Dresden. They may indeed have been common to Saxons in general, but Leipzig could make a different impression. After one night there, Anna Ticknor did not find the same kind of quiet order that she was used to in the capital: "Leipsic is certainly an unsavoury and uninteresting place, to a visiter of one night. I was waked this morning, with a rattling and clattering of tongues, as if of an army of monkeys; such as is never heard in my good refined city of Dresden, and, looking out upon the narrow street below, found a butter and egg market, beneath the windows, vegetables, flowers and all sorts of things stretching away in the distance, there being certainly more women and tongues than any thing else."[49] Then again, this may not have accurately reflected the normal local temperament, since Anna Ticknor also mentioned that Leipzig on that day "looks very busy & active, the impulse of the great fair has not yet passed away, for it is but just over."[50] Even if quietness was not quite as universal in Saxony as some thought, American visitors still admired Saxons for their overall contentedness. Bayard Taylor observed, "As far as I have yet seen, Saxony is a prosperous and happy country. The people are noted all over Germany for their honest, social character, which is written on their cheerful, open countenances."[51]

The Respectable Royal Family

Much of Saxony's contentedness was perceived to be related to benevolent government. "The people," Anna Ticknor wrote, "are notoriously contented with their rulers."[52] American travelers frequently commented on the qualities of the royal family that made them respectable in the eyes of their subjects and foreign visitors. Specifically, the Americans pointed out their piety, humility, intellectual cultivation, and relative "liberality." Dwight directly linked the happy state of the Saxon people to the wise administration of King Frederick Augustus I (who reigned 1806–1827):

> When he looks around him, and beholds the poverty of Prussia, the semicivilization of the Russians, the physical character of the Austrians, and contrasts them with the prosperous and intelligent Saxons, he finds at least in times of peace, a satisfaction, which his neighbours may look for in vain. I can scarcely conceive of a more enviable situation, . . . than that of a monarch, who like Frederick Augustus, can look upon his people with the feelings of a parent, and discover wherever he goes, that they regard him with the strongest affection; who in looking around him, sees prosperity blessing the labours of his industrious subjects, and finds them continually rising in the scale of existence; who in traversing his dominions, learns that there is not a village where the means of instruction are not provided for every peasant, and that scarce an individual exists, who has reached adult years, that has not availed himself of the opportunities which have been afforded to him, to gain knowledge; who, at the same time, perceives a literary enthusiasm and research

> among the enlightened men of his nation, by which the boundaries of the human mind are enlarged, and discovers that the happiness of the world has been greatly augmented by the institutions he has founded and patronised, remembering as he does, that prayers are continually ascending from the hearts of his subjects, that he may long be continued to them, as the greatest earthly blessing which they can receive.[53]

Frederick Augustus's successor, Anthony (who reigned 1827–1836), and his family, were almost as highly praised by American observers, although the Ticknors admired Anthony more for his character than for his administrative abilities. Anna Ticknor called him a "puppet," but wrote that "he has been harmless, civil, and honest, and I have been told so often, that he is loved here, that I begin to believe it."[54] George Ticknor said that Anthony was honored for his "mere honesty & good intentions," since he had, in Ticknor's opinion, "no other attractive qualities whatever."[55] But Henry Wikoff recalled, "There was not a more popular man in Germany than Anthony, the reigning King of Saxony."[56]

In fact, the character of the entire royal family impressed American visitors. George Ticknor asserted that "nothing can be more respectable, than the private character of the whole of the royal family—they seem, too, to be much respected and valued by their subjects—especially the old King [Anthony], who is perfectly honest and well-meaning, and the co-regent [Frederick Augustus II], who is looked upon as a capable and efficient governor of the state."[57] Some of them were distinguished for their genuine literary accomplishments. Princess Amalia wrote and published a popular play, "Der Oheim" ("The Uncle"), under the pseudonym Amalie Heiter in 1835. Her brother, Prince John (who later reigned as king from 1854 to 1873), was a renowned translator of Dante under the pseudonym Philalethes.[58] Growing out of a shared love of Dante and literary interests in general, George Ticknor and Prince John formed a friendship that survived from 1836 until Ticknor's death in 1871.[59] But not only was Prince John admirable for his intellect, Ticknor was also pleased with his humility, remarking that "nothing could be more simple and unpretending than his manner."[60]

The benevolent administration of the monarchy, the civilized population that it provided for, and the richness of the nation in culture if not in revenue, were united in a description by Anna Ticknor:

> It is in the character of the people, the gentle and humane tone of its government, and its public institutions, that the little kingdom of Saxony finds its distinction now. Education is carefully provided for, laws are strictly and impartially enforced, and therefore observed, and great attention is now beginning to be paid, to the regulation of prisons, and the best modes of punishment. The more I have seen of the poverty of the peasantry, and known of the circumscribed means of the nobility, the more wonder I feel at the splendour and riches of the collections in art, and for instruction; for the contrast grows constantly stronger to me.
>
> The reigning family are very rich by long inheritance; they do what can be done to increase the prosperity of the people, and their private liberality is honourable to them. At the same time, they are able to preserve these beautiful collections, and to add some treasures to them; and, having had the good sense to place over each, men fitted by science & taste, to preserve and improve the articles and arrangement, the justice done to such treasures is as gratifying as the information gained by them, and the pleasure from their intrinsic beauty.[61]

The Cultural Appeals of Dresden and Leipzig

Most of the early nineteenth-century American travelers were highly educated societal elites, and one of the big reasons for traveling to Europe was to advance their education in ways that the United States could not provide.[62] Many were seeking the best universities, the most important museums, and the locations where the great events of Western history actually happened. The Ticknors represented this group at its education-seeking extreme. As a student, George Ticknor announced, "The whole tour in Europe I consider a sacrifice of enjoyment to improvement," and then made good on this statement by doing almost nothing but learning.[63] When not in university classes, he was methodically researching educational institutions, cities, and art, even during his "vacations." Back in Europe two decades later with his family, Ticknor was less intensely studious, but there was no doubt that this sojourn was also meant to be an "improving" experience. Little Anna (the oldest daughter) was provided with tutors in music, art, and language the moment the family settled in a city, while the parents established themselves in the best society, attending theater, opera, balls, and museums. But they were not interested in superficial glamour; they privately scorned people they considered stupid, while pursuing intelligent interactions with those whose character and learning they respected. In their quiet moments at home, George Ticknor would read Dante and Shakespeare to the family, and Anna Ticknor would write in her journal religiously. Even when she was too tired to do much else, she still "lounged industriously."[64] For travelers like this, who wanted to use every experience for self-improvement, a destination needed to have a high level of quality educational and cultural offerings. Saxony earned a reputation for providing some of the best of these experiences that money could buy, especially in relation to its small size.

Most of this opportunity for American cultural education was found in Dresden. For this reason and others, Dresden was the main attraction for Americans coming to Saxony in the first half of the nineteenth century.[65] It was one of the most important places Washington Irving, James Fenimore Cooper and his family, the Ticknors, and countless others later in the century came to reside for months or more. It also made a worthwhile stop for those whose main destination was somewhere else (for example, as they traveled between Prussia and Austria); some of these short-term visitors wished they could stay longer.[66] Dresden was not an especially large capital, like Paris, London, Berlin, or Rome, but it was a pleasant city that boasted world-class galleries and collections, a welcoming royal court and high society (welcoming to the right people), and a low cost of living. This combination of factors strongly appealed to educated American travelers looking for opportunities for improvement. According to George Ticknor, "Dresden attracts strangers, I think, chiefly by its remarkable publick institutions & collections in the arts; and by the state of society which such institutions & collections naturally create.—Among these the first place is to be given, no doubt, to the Gallery of Pictures."[67] This picture gallery, the Gemäldegalerie, was by far the Americans' favorite collection. Every visitor to Dresden absolutely had to make a pilgrimage to this museum. In fact, it was this gallery that Americans most knew Dresden for, and which gave the city the nickname "Florence on the Elbe."[68] Americans were also impressed by collections of engravings, porcelain, armor, jewelry and other treasures, and casts of the great sculptures of classical antiquity. They also marveled at the Royal Library, which was "beyond all praise," for "its order is as perfect as anything well can be" and its "administration as liberal as can be asked."[69] Americans recognized the role that these institutions played in the relatively enlightened and cultivated Kingdom of Saxony. Anna Ticknor wrote that these collections "are well used, and enjoyed too, for the Saxons have taste, and they visit all these establishments, with attention and pleasure."[70] Dwight reversed the causality, believing that these institutions did not just reflect fine local taste, but argued that the Saxons' taste and knowledge had been *formed* (at least in part) by these establishments: "Two such institutions as the [picture] gallery and library of Dresden, you will easily suppose, exert a most auspicious influence on the taste and intellect of the inhabitants, and to this influence is this metropolis not a little indebted, for the superior cultivation of its citizens to those of any other town in Germany."[71]

After Dresden, Leipzig stood in second place in the American perception of Saxony.[72] In most respects, however, it had a different image than Dresden. In fact, it had many different facets to its image, and it variously attracted and repelled different Americans for different reasons throughout different periods of the nineteenth century. In certain negative ways, it almost seemed like Dresden's antithesis. In other, more positive ways, it shared in the high reputation of Saxony, while also offering its own unique opportunities. Leipzig was not the seat of a royal court, nor did it boast collections of art and treasure like Dresden's. Some Americans considered its population less quiet and refined, giving the city an unpleasant atmosphere. At the same time, in good Saxon fashion, it had its own impressive claims to educational and literary achievement, as it was home to a major university and was the center of a thriving book trade. Furthermore, it was a world-renowned commercial center, due to its huge annual trade fairs. The other major aspect of Leipzig's image in the early nineteenth-century American mind was its association with Napoleon's great defeat in 1813. As Ticknor put it in an 1816 letter: "Leipsic is a very remarkable place, and presents itself to everybody who comes with a judicious acquaintance with it, under three distinct forms,—a city associated with many famous recollections in early history, and the Marathon of our own times, where the inroads of a tumultuous barbarism were finally stopped; as a trading city, for its size the most important in Europe; and as a University, one of the largest, most respectable, and ancient in the world. The second is, of course, the aspect in which it is first seen by a stranger."[73] Americans were divided on its appeal, however. The Ticknors, though they respected Leipzig's roles in letters and commerce, were overall unimpressed by the city. During his 1816 visit, George Ticknor had been fascinated by the trade fair and the battlefield, but upon returning with his family twenty years later, he dismissed Leipzig as a "merely commercial city," while Anna Ticknor judged, as already noted, that it was "certainly an unsavoury and uninteresting place, to a visiter of one night.[74] They preferred the courtly charms of Dresden to the traffic of Leipzig. Yet other Americans found Leipzig an enjoyable place because of its parks, promenades, fairs, and Napoleonic connections. [75]

Scenic Saxon Switzerland

Another place that contributed to Americans' concept of Saxony was the Saxon Switzerland. If the landscape of Saxony was considered pleasant enough simply because it was more varied and fertile than the barren sand plains of nearby parts of Prussia, the Saxon Switzerland added a much deeper dimension to Saxony's reputation for natural beauty. This scenic region straddled the Saxon-Bohemian border where the Elbe River carved dramatic sandstone formations out of the Ore Mountains. Dwight said of it,

> Among all the rambles which a traveller can enjoy in the north of Germany, there is none which is so much celebrated as the Saxon Switzerland. "Have you seen the Switzerland of Saxony," is the

> question which every one of your acquaintances in Dresden puts to you, before you have been here a week. "You must visit it," he tells you in reply to your answer in the negative. "I hope you will not leave this country until you have seen our Switzerland," says another. "You have of course visited our Alps?" says a third. To avoid the commiseration which always flows from your negative reply, you order a carriage, and tell the driver to conduct you to this fairy scenery, looking neither to the right nor the left.[76]

Of course, everyone realized these modest mountains did not truly resemble the Swiss Alps. But the fact remained that the Saxon Switzerland was breathtakingly beautiful. It inspired its visitors to pen pages describing the rocky cliffs, the wild forests, the dark hollows, the flowing rivers, and the panoramic vistas of mountain chains stretching off into the hazy blue distance. Whether reading Dwight, Taylor, or either of the Ticknors, the accounts sound remarkably similar.[77] The untamed romantic landscape refreshed the spirits of those who had become accustomed to urban society. The Saxon Switzerland was a significant reason why Americans (especially those Americans who traveled in northern Europe and did not see the real Switzerland) raved about the beauty of the Saxon landscape. As Mann said, "No one can have any adequate idea of the face of Saxony, who does not visit this miniature of Switzerland."[78]

The Complex Identity of the Saxon Cession to Prussia

Not all aspects of the American image of Saxony came from within the boundaries of the Kingdom of Saxony. Historically, the name "Saxony" had been associated in one way or another with several territories across large portions of northern Germany (not to mention the remote Saxon heritage in England). Over time, "Saxony" and "Saxon" have meant different things in different contexts, and some of these various vague connotations probably lurked in the background of nineteenth-century Americans' image of the Saxony of their day. Some of these associations—to the extent they existed—would likely be too subtle to study here, but at least one is fairly pronounced. The regions of the former Electorate of Saxony that had been ceded to Prussia at the Congress of Vienna continued to contribute complex associations to the American idea of Saxony in the first half of the nineteenth century, even though they were not a part of the Kingdom of Saxony. The case of Wittenberg illustrates both a positive and negative side to the image, and how Americans selectively attributed to Saxony the traits they saw most fit.

For centuries Wittenberg had been an important part of the Electorate of Saxony. Even though Saxony lost it to Prussia in 1815, in some respects Americans continued to identify it as Saxon. Of course, Wittenberg's main claim to fame was the Protestant reformer Martin Luther. Probably most of the Americans who traveled to Europe in the early 1800s—especially the many who hailed from New England—were Protestant, and their writings show that they held Luther in high regard. Luther, furthermore, was known to have been a Saxon. Henry Wheaton, the former U.S. minister to Prussia, in a speech at Brown University, attributed much of the achievement of Western civilization to this "Saxon reformer." He said that mankind was indebted to Germany "for two of the greatest promoters of their moral improvement. To Germany we owe that mechanical invention which lends wings to thought [Gutenberg's printing press], and that great moral revolution which has purified Christianity from its grossest corruptions, and adapted it to promote the onward progress of humanity. . . . Guttenberg and Luther—two immortal names—sufficient to give lustre to any age or nation!"[79] Wheaton called them "heroes of civilization, these conquerors in the realms of thought," and referred to Luther's city, "Wittemberg, where the Saxon reformer burnt the bulls of Leo, and kindled that mighty flame which can never be extinguished. American liberty is the daughter of British liberty, and they are both the children of the Reformation."[80] American travelers often shared this grateful view of Luther as the rescuer of Christianity and the emancipator of men's minds.[81] A visit to Wittenberg was often something of a pilgrimage for the more devout among them. As Dwight said, "To a Protestant, and to every one who loves mental freedom, it will long remain a hallowed spot, as it was once the scene of the labours, and now contains the ashes, of two of the greatest reformers [Luther and Melanchthon]."[82] Ticknor wrote about his and Everett's stop in the city in 1816:

> The first thing we went to see was the chh. of ye Virgin or, as a Protestant would rather call it, the chh. where Luther used to preach. . . .
>
> Luther's chamber, too, we saw, and it moved a very different clafs of feelings from those I had experienced in the apartments of Frederick & Voltaire at Sans Souci, for a moment after entering it I found myself without knowing it, uncovered. . . . I have seen few things in Europe that have more deeply moved me than this, and I came away with a higher trust in ye gratitude of the world, when I had seen yt. this humble & obscure room had been preserved three centuries & amid such tremendous revolutions, unchanged out of respect to the memory of ye great man, who had once lived in it.[83]

In 1836 Ticknor visited Luther's room again and said, "It is holy ground."[84] Hugh Swinton Legaré, U.S. chargé d'affaires in Brussels, upon a tour through Germany that same year, also sought Luther's memory in Wittenberg and made the historical Saxon connection: "Wittenberg is no longer Saxon, . . . the ashes of Luther lie in what may be called foreign ground. To be sure, the King of Saxony is a Catholic, and perhaps it is fit that the chief of Protestant Germany [the King of Prussia] should have the guardianship of its most precious and sacred shines [*sic*]. Potsdam, Frederick, Voltaire,—Wittenberg, the unfortunate Elector, Luther.—What a contrast."[85] Of course, depending on one's confession, not all Americans thought Luther was worth reverence. George Henry Calvert, traveling with relatives while on a break from his studies in Göttingen, related the internal struggle that his Catholic uncle faced upon viewing the bronze statue of Luther in Wittenberg's market square:

> To my uncle it was not permitted to know Luther. He regarded him with that stolid, insatiable, Romish aversion, whose unutterability is deepened by the fear that mingles with the hate. If at any time

> the mighty shadow of the Giant crossed the disk of his sensations, it was only to be thrust angrily down into the nameless pit, to be there the compeer of Lucifer, chewing forever, beside that prime rebel, the bitter cud of bootless remorse for an impious revolt. But my uncle being preëminently an æsthetic traveller, caring little for history, or geology, or ethnography, or statistics, could look with critical calmness, with judicial impartiality, upon a statue even of the apostate Augustinian monk; and so looking, he pronounced it good.[86]

For Protestant Americans, Wittenberg had a special appeal because there Luther had begun the Reformation. It was a moment in history worthy of—or even due to—Saxony's legendary love of enlightenment.

In another sense, however, Wittenberg did not fit the stereotypical American image of Saxony. It was ugly. Anna Ticknor was the most outspoken on this point: "[From Wörlitz] we drove off to Wittemberg, leaving all beauty behind us, and finding nothing but flat, sandy plains. . . . It is an ugly place, this Wittemberg. . . . My husband thought me sadly wanting in enthusiasm, and I know not why it excited me so little. . . . I was glad to get away from the ugly old place."[87] Anna Ticknor thought the city shabby, and she and others found the surrounding countryside dreary as well, more Prussian than Saxon. Americans were happy to count Wittenberg's spiritual and intellectual contributions as part of the Saxon heritage, but when it came to aesthetic considerations, sometimes they lumped it in with the rest of sandy Prussia from the Saxon kingdom's borders to Berlin.[88] Anna Ticknor did so when traveling from Potsdam to Dresden in 1836 and commenting on the route: "Herzberg is any thing but a pretty town. It is ancient, but neither venerable,—nor picturesque, and it has the cheerless, comfortless look so common in the villages of this part of Prussia. I have felt a certain satisfaction that every mile brought us nearer to Saxony, and, when we had absolutely passed the barrier, I found, or imagined that I found immediately, a great difference in the appearance of the people, as well as in the cultivation of the country. There is good reason for it, however, for the soil, in this part of Saxony is vastly superior to what we have seen in the adjacent part of Prussia, and the people are notoriously contented with their rulers."[89] For her, Herzberg (which was not especially far from Wittenberg) and its environs were clearly Prussian. Yet this region that she disdained for its "cheerless, comfortless look so common in the villages of this part of Prussia" had been a part of the Electorate of Saxony for centuries, only becoming Prussian scarcely more than twenty years before. For Anna Ticknor, in terms of appearance, the Kingdom of Saxony was the true Saxony. It was only when she crossed the 1815 border back into that kingdom that she noticed the landscape beginning to look more "Saxon." George Ticknor, meanwhile, also characterized the Saxon cession as Prussian, not only because of the quality of the soil, but also for its general military spirit. In Herzberg he saw a "warlike character, which is present through all the borders of Prufsia, and is, to strangers especially, very striking. We have found it every where, that we have been from Wittenberg round to the borders of Saxony again." And back in the Kingdom of Saxony he found peace again: "This forenoon, we found ourselves again in the pleasant, quiet land of Saxony—surrounded with more fertility, than we have seen before since we left it, & in the midst, if not of a better population, of one that inspires more confidence, & seems more contented & comfortable."[90] Despite Ticknor's survey of inhabitants of the cession in 1816, where he found that they still considered themselves and the land Saxon, twenty years later he believed that the people and the land of that region seemed more Prussian than Saxon.

Dwight was unlike the Ticknors in this regard, however. He considered this former Saxon region still Saxon, despite Prussian rule. And yet he also observed that its barren landscape did not fit the characteristic image of Saxony:

> In quitting Berlin with your face turned towards the south, you anticipate the pleasure of leaving the sands behind you; but not such is the reality. . . . The celebrity which Saxony has so long enjoyed, for the fertility of its soil, leads you to hope, that every mile you travel, in approaching this comparative land of promise, will present a fairer region, to your eye. After leaving Trauenbrietzen (half way between Berlin and Wittenberg) a few miles behind, you

> arrive at the boundary of Saxony, as it existed before the Congress of Vienna. The word Saxony, to the ears of the Germans, and to those of all travellers who have associated much with them, is synonymous with fertility, but no bright verdure exhibits to your eye a fairer land, and the walls and towers of Wittenberg rise from the sand, as if to remind you of Tadmor in the desert.[91]

A few pages later, however, Dwight amended his assessment of the soil in the Saxon cession, in order to better support his argument that the region's character was still more Saxon than Prussian: "Although most of that part of Prussia, over which I have passed since leaving Trauenbrietzen, (Halle however is excepted,) was separated from Saxony and united to Prussia more than ten years since, at the Congress of Vienna, it has lost as yet very little of the Saxon, and acquired very little of the Prussian character. Its dialect is Saxon [and] much of its territory is in fertility genuine Saxony."[92] Thus, Dwight seems to have contradicted himself. First he wrote that the cession was sandy, with "no bright verdure," and then he claimed that much of it was "in fertility genuine Saxony." Both times, though, he emphasized the point that Saxony was synonymous with fertility, and Prussia with the opposite. And in attributing opposing characteristics to the same territory, he manipulated the cession's image to underscore his stereotypes of Saxony and Prussia.

Clearly, Wittenberg and the rest of the territory that Saxony ceded to Prussia in 1815 posed a problem for Americans in defining their image of Saxony. Its intellectual spirit, as exemplified by Luther and the Protestant Reformation, was Saxon. Yet in a way, it was appropriate that it now belonged to Prussia, whose king was Protestant while Saxony's was not. Meanwhile, Saxony was reputed to be fertile and attractive, with citizens living in comfort and contentment, while Prussia (or at least Brandenburg, the province of Prussia to the north of Saxony, centered on the city of Berlin) was despised for its drab, infertile land and its impoverished peasants. For many Americans, the landscape of the cession more resembled the latter. Wittenberg and the cession were thus a complicated middle ground, Saxon in historical identity but Prussian in appearance. Americans like Dwight and the Ticknors struggled to categorize it. Regardless of whether they perceived it as more Saxon or more Prussian, their thoughts revealed that their underlying image of Saxony—in this case fertile land and enlightened, contented people—was a very strong one in their minds.

Conclusion

Early in the nineteenth century, Germany was in many ways a terra incognita to most Anglo Americans, perhaps especially those from New England. Saxony was probably even less known across the Atlantic. The downfall of Napoleon and the ensuing peace in Europe opened the door for a few illustrious American cultural pioneers to rediscover Europe beyond England, France, and Italy. George Ticknor and his generation popularized study in the German universities, which became an important way for men of means to gain the best education available and jump-start their careers. From a well-known handful of young men in the second and third decades of the nineteenth century to uncountable thousands making the academic overseas voyage at the end of the century, students were a significant part of America's general growing awareness of Germany. The concurrent travel trend of wealthy Americans seeking social prestige, health, or adventure abroad connected America even more firmly with Germany. Germany's popularity as a destination in this respect had less to do with any perceived superiority over other countries (as it may have had with regard to universities), and more to do with the fact that, as increasing thousands of Americans traveled to Europe each year, more and more of them were bound to come to Germany as a side effect. Initially the growth in American travel to Germany lagged behind the traditional, well-known destinations in western Europe, but as transportation improved and allowed faster travel to Europe and easier access to the interior of the continent, as a greater number of Americans became more prosperous and could afford to travel more, and as the appeals of Germany became more widely known in the United States through the proliferation of published travel accounts, Germany quickly became a popular destination in Europe. It never received as many visitors as the United Kingdom and France, mainly because sailing routes from America sent travelers to those countries first by default, because there were still important places to visit there, and because of America's dominant cultural kinship to England. As a landlocked destination deep within Germany, Saxony too had to wait until continental peace, increased American prosperity, improved transportation, and more widespread American awareness came about, before it saw a surge in American visitors. This belated surge in Saxon popularity in a way echoes the general trend of American travel to Germany overall.

Once American travelers began to discover Saxony, it developed a particularly favorable reputation among them. They praised it for the intellectual quality and good-natured spirit of its population and the respectable character of its rulers. Being a small kingdom sandwiched between the two ambitious powers of Prussia and Austria, and having been the site of numerous devastations from European wars, Americans were inclined to have an empathetic attitude toward it. The picturesque and fertile landscape of Saxony was a relief to the eyes of Americans who had been traveling in bleak Brandenburg, Prussia just across the border. With these stereotypes established in their minds, Americans were free to adjust their image of the 1815 Saxon cession to Prussia in ways that maintained the stereotypes: to the extent that the region was known for its enlightened population, it could be regarded as typically Saxon; to the extent that it showed a strong military spirit and its land was barren and drab, it reflected the image of Prussia. The Americans' favorite place to go in Saxony before 1850 was Dresden, because of its world-famous art gallery and other impressive collections, its pleasant and peaceful atmosphere, and its royal court and high society that Americans could associate with if they had the right credentials. It was an ideal place to reside a while for cultural and social self-improvement, as exemplified by the Ticknors. Leipzig was a distant second favorite among pre-1850 American travelers to Saxony.[93] Its appeals were mainly its association with Napoleonic War history and its unparalleled annual international trade fairs (which to some people were actually more of an inconvenience than an excitement). It, too, had a pleasant city atmosphere, but it was not as quiet as Dresden. Its fine educational institutions upheld the Saxon reputation for literacy. Finally, Americans in Saxony enjoyed getting away from the cities to marvel at the natural wonders of the Saxon Switzerland, which they considered one of the most scenic areas in all of northern Europe.

These preferences and prejudices of American travelers, and the perceptions recorded in their writings, tell us something about these individuals. These early visitors to Saxony were essentially all from the privileged classes, were well-educated, and often from New England. Their visits to Saxony—and Europe in general—were meant to improve them socially, culturally, and physically, and to prepare them for better opportunities in the United States. They all found much to love in Europe. Often what they appreciated most were things they felt would be useful in elevating their own country to a higher level of educational and cultural perfection (like museums and libraries). But no matter how much they loved certain aspects of Europe, they remained committed American republicans, proud to feel that their nation was the freest and purest nation in the world, with the strongest potential for great achievements. Self-improvement was a key concept with these Americans, on both the personal and national levels. These attitudes are probably some of the most important reasons why they loved Saxony. Or perhaps the other way around: these are the attitudes of the types of Americans that Saxony attracted. Regardless, early-nineteenth-century American images of Saxony as a culturally and agriculturally cultivated land, with intellectual and humane rulers, who were well-loved by their enlightened and contented subjects, highlight some of elite Americans' own ideals and dreams for their own budding nation striving toward utopia.

NOTES

1. For a fuller analysis of American perceptions of Saxony, as well as a deeper study of the historical context and development of American travel to Saxony and Germany in general, see Ashley Sides, "What Americans Said about Saxony, and What This Says about Them: Interpreting Travel Writings of the Ticknors and Other Privileged Americans, 1800–1850," master's thesis, University of Texas at Arlington, 2008.

2. Both George Ticknor (1816) and Henry Dwight (1829) used the term "terra incognita" about Germany and its literature to describe how little Americans knew about it, though they probably spoke more for New Englanders than for Americans in other parts of the nation. See Orie William Long, *Thomas Jefferson and George Ticknor: A Chapter in American Scholarship* (Williamstown, Mass.: McClelland Press, 1933), 13; and Henry E. Dwight, *Travels in the North of Germany, in the Years 1825 and 1826* (New York: G. & C. & H. Carvill, 1829), iii. For more discussion of American knowledge of Germany in the early 1800s, see Hermann Wellenreuther, "'Germans Make Cows and Women Work': American Perceptions of Germans as Reported in American Travel Books, 1800–1840," in *Transatlantic Images and Perceptions: Germany and America Since 1776*, ed. David E. Barclay and Elisabeth Glaser-Schmidt (Washington, D.C.: German Historical Institute; Cambridge: Cambridge University Press, 1997), 44–45; Henry A. Pochmann, *German Culture in America: Philosophical and Literary Influences, 1600–1900* (Madison, Wis.: University of Wisconsin Press, 1957; reprint, Westport, Conn.: Greenwood Press, 1978), 41, 49–56, 62–63; Dirk Voss, "National Stereotypes about Germans in American Travel Writings, 1815–1914," (PhD diss., University of Oklahoma, 2000), 11–12; and Sides, "What Americans Said about Saxony, and What This Says about Them," 10–24.

3. Foster Rhea Dulles, "A Historical View of Americans Abroad," *Annals of the American Academy of Political and Social Science* 368 (November 1966): 12.

4. In 1836, George Ticknor, traveling by coach between Meißen and Leipzig, commented on seeing the construction of the first long-distance railway line in Germany: "We crofsed the Mulda, by a beautifully constructed stone bridge erected in 1831, where, twenty years ago, I crofsed it by a clumsy ferry; & on our left hand saw, as we also saw at several other places in the course of our ride, the beginnings of the rail-road, which is now constructing between Leipzig & Dresden & in whose stock, the most absurd speculations have been made during the last winter."

See George Ticknor, *Microfilm Edition of the Travel Journals of George and Anna Ticknor: In the Years 1816–1819 and 1835–1838*, vol. 4 (Ann Arbor, Mich.: Xerox University Microfilms, 1974), May 13, 1836.

5. Dulles, "Historical View of Americans Abroad," 13–14.

6. Ibid., 12–14.

7. William W. Stowe, *Going Abroad: European Travel in Nineteenth-Century American Culture* (Princeton, N.J.: Princeton University Press, 1994), 5–6.

8. David B. Tyack, *George Ticknor and the Boston Brahmins* (Cambridge, Mass.: Harvard University Press, 1967), 164.

9. Dulles, "Historical View of Americans Abroad," 12–13.

10. The lingua franca of the European high society was French, and the Ticknors arrived in Europe already having a basic ability to speak it, as can be seen throughout all their European journals.

11. Cushing Strout, *The American Image of the Old World* (New York: Harper & Row, 1963), 68.

12. Jurgen Herbst, *The German Historical School in American Scholarship: A Study in the Transfer of Culture* (Ithaca, N.Y.: Cornell University Press, 1965), 9; John T. Krumpelmann, *Southern Scholars in Goethe's Germany* (Chapel Hill: University of North Carolina Press, 1965), xi; and Sides, "What Americans Said about Saxony, and What This Says about Them," 24–31.

13. Daniel Fallon, "German Influences on American Education," in *The German-American Encounter: Conflict and Cooperation between Two Cultures, 1800–2000,* ed. Frank Trommler and Elliott Shore (New York: Berghahn Books, 2001), 83, 85. Fallon writes that "careful scholarship counting the number of American scholars studying in Germany decade by decade from 1850 through 1930 has yet to be done," and accepts a total of nine thousand Americans in Germany by 1900, whereas Herbst accepts the figure of nine thousand by 1920. See Herbst, *German Historical School,* 1. Also see Carl Diehl, "Innocents Abroad: American Students in German Universities, 1810–1870," *History of Education Quarterly* 16, no. 3 (1976): 324–25.

14. Diehl, "Innocents Abroad," 331.

15. James Fenimore Cooper observed this phenomenon among doctors already in 1827 or 1828 while living in Europe: "Indeed, the well-educated American physician very commonly enjoys an advantage that is little known in Europe. After obtaining a degree in his own country, he passes a few years in London, Edinburgh, Paris, and frequently in Germany, and returns with his gleanings from their several schools. This is not the case with one

individual, but with many, annually. Indeed, there is so much of a fashion in it, and the custom is attended by so many positive advantages, that its neglect would be a serious obstacle to any very eminent success." See James Fenimore Cooper, *Notions of the Americans: Picked up by a Travelling Bachelor,* vol. 2 (London: Henry Colburn, 1828), 129.

16. As a matter of fact, though Adams has brief positive words for various parts of Saxony, the only thing he spends much time praising is the elector's collection of prints in Dresden. See John Quincy Adams, *Letters on Silesia, Written during a Tour through That Country, in the Years 1800, 1801* (London: J. Budd, 1804), 246–61.

17. Katrin Keller, *Landesgeschichte Sachsen* (Stuttgart: Ulmer, 2002), 24–27.

18. Dwight, *Travels in the North of Germany,* 339.

19. George Ticknor, *Travel Journals,* vol. 2, September 14, 1816. In order to preserve the flavor of the source documents referenced in this essay, I have attempted to reproduce the antiquarian handwriting conventions employed by the quoted sources.

20. For an analysis of the power of the local homeland (*Heimat*) in shaping the regional and national consciousness of Germans, see Celia Applegate, *A Nation of Provincials: The German Idea of Heimat* (Berkeley: University of California Press, 1990). Although Applegate focuses specifically on the Pfalz region in western Germany, the study suggests ways to interpret the real and significant aspects of *Heimat* identity in Saxony and other regions as well.

21. George Ticknor, *Travel Journals,* vol. 2, September 26, 1816.

22. Ibid., October 1816, "Dresden. Elgin Marbles. Mad. Brun.," "Dresden. Baron Oelsen, Mengs's Casts." This Saxon animosity toward Prussia actually went back at least to the Seven Years' War in a defeat by Prussia, and it was fueled over the next century by subsequent Saxon losses and Prussian gains, as Prussian power grew and Saxony's influence waned. Of course, Prussia's acquisition of most of Saxony in 1815 inflamed the passions to a new level. This rivalry with Prussia became a major part of Saxon identity. See Hartmut Zwahr, "Foreword," in *Saxony in German History: Culture, Soci-*

ety, and Politics, 1830–1933, ed. James Retallack (Ann Arbor: University of Michigan Press, 2000), xiv–xv.

23. George Ticknor, *Travel Journals,* vol. 2, October 6, 1816.

24. Ibid., vol. 1, September 6, 1815.

25. Ibid., vol. 3, October 18, 1816.

26. Dwight, *Travels in the North of Germany,* 154.

27. Ibid., 272–73.

28. George Ticknor, *Travel Journals,* vol. 3, October 17, 1816.

29. Dwight, *Travels in the North of Germany,* 339.

30. Ibid., 339–40.

31. Ibid., 340.

32. Among the various Americans who reported on the quality of local soil in their travel writings were George Ticknor, Anna Ticknor, Henry Dwight, George Rapelje, Aaron Burr, and John Quincy Adams.

33. George Ticknor, *Travel Journals,* vol. 4, May 31, 1836; John Adams, Braintree, Massachusetts, to the President of Congress, 4 August 1779, in Francis Wharton, ed. *Revolutionary Diplomatic Correspondence,* vol. 3 (Washington, D.C.: Government Printing Office, 1889), 284–85; John Quincy Adams, *Memoirs of John Quincy Adams Adams, Comprising Portions of His Diary from 1795 to 1848,* edited by Charles Francis Adams, vol. 1 (Philadelphia: J. B. Lippincott, 1874–1877; reprint, New York: AMS Press, 1970), 228 (page citation is to the reprint edition).

34. Dwight, *Travels in the North of Germany,* 258–59.

35. Ibid., 339.

36. Ibid., 347.

37. Ibid., 346–47.

38. Ibid., 347.

39. Mark Antony DeWolfe Howe, *The Life and Letters of George Bancroft,* vol. 1 (New York: Charles Scribner's Sons, 1908), 89–90.

40. Horace Mann, *Life and Works of Horace Mann,* vol. 3, ed. Mary Mann, Annual Reports on Education (Boston: Horace B. Fuller, 1868), 258.

41. John L. Bashford, *Elementary Education in Saxony* (London: Sampson Low, Marston, Searle, & Rivington, 1881), 2.

42. W. Pätzold, *Geschichte des Schulwesens im Königreich Sachsen* (Leipzig and Frankfurt: Kesselringsche Hofbuchandlung (E. v. Mayer) Verlag, 1908), 143.

43. These Saxon states were the Grand Duchy of Saxe-Weimar-Eisenach, the Duchy of Saxe-Meiningen, the Duchy of Saxe-Altenburg, and the Duchy of Saxe-Coburg and Gotha (the latter two were formed in 1826 by a reshuffling of territories after the breakup of the Duchy of Saxe-Gotha-Altenburg).

44. George Ticknor, *Travel Journals*, vol. 3, November 17, 1835.

45. Ibid., vol. 4, May 31, 1836.

46. Anna Ticknor, *Travel Journals*, vol. 3, November 22, 1835.

47. Ibid., vol. 3, January 1836, April 26, 1836.

48. Ibid., vol. 3, April 26, 1836; see also further description of the "good temper" of the Dresdeners in ibid., vol. 3, January 15, 1836. George Ticknor, too, made very similar observations in his *Travel Journals*, vol. 3, December 20, 1835.

49. Anna Ticknor, *Travel Journals*, vol. 3, May 14, 1836.

50. Ibid., vol. 3, May 13, 1836.

51. Bayard Taylor, *Views A-foot: Or, Europe Seen with a Knapsack and Staff*, 9th ed. (New York: George P. Putnam, 1850), 134.

52. Anna Ticknor, *Travel Journals*, vol. 4, May 31, 1836.

53. Dwight, *Travels in the North of Germany*, 357.

54. Anna Ticknor, *Travel Journals*, vol. 3, December 27, 1835.

55. George Ticknor, *Travel Journals*, vol. 3, December 27, 1835.

56. Henry Wikoff, *The Reminiscences of an Idler* (New York: Fords, Howard & Hulbert, 1880), 326.

57. George Ticknor, *Travel Journals*, vol. 3, December 26, 1835.

58. Roger Paulin, "An Unpublished Letter of King John of Saxony (Philalethes) to George Ticknor," *German Life and Letters* 41 (July 1988): 426–29.

59. For the exchange of letters that kept their friendship alive despite three and a half decades of living on different continents, see E. Daenell, ed., *Briefwechsel König Johanns von Sachsen mit George Ticknor* (Leipzig: B.G. Teubner, 1920); and Paulin, "Unpublished Letter." For an additional scholarly analysis of this relationship, see Eberhard Brüning, "König Johann von Sachsen

und sein amerikanischer Bewunderer und Freund," *Sächsische Heimatblätter* 38, no. 1 (January–February 1992): 48–52.

60. John Lothrop Motley, *The Correspondence of John Lothrop Motley,* ed. George William Curtis, vol. 1. (New York: Harper & Brothers, 1889), 144; George Ticknor, *Travel Journals,* vol. 3, January 8, 1836.

61. Anna Ticknor, *Travel Journals,* vol. 3, April 26, 1836.

62. Voss, "National Stereotypes," 21; Stowe, *Going Abroad,* 6.

63. George Ticknor, to Mr. Haven, Portsmouth, July 1814, in George Ticknor, *Life, Letters, and Journals of George Ticknor,* ed. Anna Ticknor and George S. Hillard, vol. 1 (Boston: James R. Osgood and Company, 1876), 23.

64. Anna Ticknor, *Travel Journals,* vol. 4, May 27, 1836.

65. In the second half of the century, in addition to Dresden, Leipzig was also a significant draw for Americans, as large numbers of them came to study at the university there.

66. Wikoff remarked, "I was so carried away by its attractions that I had half a notion to abandon [Edwin] Forrest, and let him proceed alone to Paris." See Wikoff, *Reminiscences of an Idler,* 325. Hugh Swinton Legaré also wished he could have stayed longer. See Hugh Swinton Legaré, *Writings of Hugh Swinton Legaré ... Consisting of a Diary of Brussels, and Journal of the Rhine; Extracts from his Private and Diplomatic Correspondence; Orations and Speeches; and Contributions to the New-York and Southern Reviews,* vol. 1, ed. Mary S. Legare (Charleston, S.C.: Burges & James, 1846), 142.

67. George Ticknor, *Travel Journals,* vol. 3, April 1836, "Dresden. Gallery of Pictures."

68. Eberhard Brüning, "'It is a glorious collection': Amerikanische Bildungsbürger des 19. Jahrhunderts auf 'Pilgerfahrt' zur Dresdner Gemäldegalerie," in *Jahrbuch der Staatlichen Kunstsammlungen Dresden 1996/1997,* 99–105.

69. Anna Ticknor, *Travel Journals,* vol. 3, April 26, 1836; George Ticknor, *Travel Journals,* vol. 2, September 23, 1816, and vol. 3, April 1836, "Dresden. Library.," "Dresden. Gallery of Antiques." See also Dwight, *Travels in the North of Germany,* 361.

70. Anna Ticknor, *Travel Journals,* vol. 3, April 26, 1836.

71. Dwight, *Travels in the North of Germany,* 360. For more in-depth discussion of American perspectives of Dresden, see Sides, "What Americans Said about Saxony, and What This Says about Them," 113–50.

72. Eberhard Brüning, "Entdeckung eines 'sehr bemerkenswerten Ortes.' Reiseeindrücke amerikanischer Bildungsbürger des 19. Jahrhunderts in und um Leipzig. Teil 1," *Stadtgeschichte: Mitteilungen des Leipziger Geschichtsvereins e.V.,* no. 1 (2001), 5.

73. George Ticknor, Leipzig, to Edward T. Channing, September 17, 1816, in George Ticknor, *Life, Letters, and Journals,* 1:107.

74. George Ticknor, *Travel Journals,* vol. 4, May 13, 1836; Anna Ticknor, *Travel Journals,* vol. 3, May 14, 1836.

75. Washington Irving, *Journals and Notebooks: Volume III, 1819–1827,* vol. 3, ed. Walter A. Reichart (Madison: University of Wisconsin Press, 1970), 189; Dwight, *Travels in the North of Germany,* 316; Taylor, *Views A-foot,* 125, 127; George Palmer Putnam, *The Tourist in Europe: or, A Concise Summary of the Various Routes, Objects of Interest, &c. in Great Britain, France, Switzerland, Italy, Germany, Belgium, and Holland; with Hints on Time, Expenses, Hotels, Conveyances, Passports, Coins, &c.* (New York: Wiley & Putnam, 1838), 244; Wikoff, *Reminiscences of an Idler,* 328. For more discussion of Americans' views of Leipzig, see Eberhard Brüning, "'Saxony Is a Prosperous and Happy Country': American Views of the Kingdom of Saxony in the Nineteenth Century," in *Traveling Between Worlds: German-American Encounters,* ed. Thomas Adam and Ruth Gross, 20–50 (College Station: Texas A&M University Press, 2006), 36–40; Anja Becker, "For the Sake of Old Leipzig Days . . . : Academic Networks of American Students at a German University, 1781–1914," PhD diss., University of Leipzig, 2006, passim; and Sides, "What Americans Said about Saxony, and What This Says about Them," 150–68.

76. Dwight, *Travels in the North of Germany,* 372–73.

77. Ibid., 372–81; Taylor, *Views A-foot,* 134–39; George Ticknor, *Travel Journals,* vol. 4, June 1–5, 1836; Anna Ticknor, *Travel Journals,* vol. 4, June 1–5, 1836.

78. Horace Mann, *Life and Works of Horace Mann,* ed. Mary Mann (Boston: Lee & Shepard Publishers, 1891), 206.

79. Henry Wheaton, *The Progress and Prospects of Germany: A Discourse Before the Phi Beta Kappa Society of Brown University, at Providence, R.I., September 1, 1847* (Boston: Charles C. Little and James Brown, 1847), 3–4.

80. Ibid., 4.

81. For a particularly dramatic example, see Dwight, *Travels in the North of Germany*, 262: "Luther conferred upon Northern Germany, and on the world, a greater blessing than has been imparted by any other individual during the last seventeen centuries." On page 77 he specifically attributes Germany's educational superiority to Protestantism: "Whence comes this difference between Germany and other nations? It doubtless results, in a very considerable degree, from the impulse which the Protestant religion gave to the public mind in the northern part of this country. The efforts of Luther and Melancthon to improve the schools and gymnasia, as well as the spirit of investigation which they excited, has been felt from age to age, and the effect will, probably, continue to the end of time."

82. Ibid., 259.

83. George Ticknor, *Travel Journals*, vol. 3, October 15, 1816. Ticknor's use of "uncovered" here refers to having taken off his hat.

84. Ibid., vol. 4, May 15, 1836.

85. Legaré, *Writings of Hugh Swinton Legaré*, 1:139.

86. George H. Calvert, *First Years in Europe* (Boston: William V. Spencer, 1866), 162–63.

87. Anna Ticknor, *Travel Journals*, vol. 3, May 15–16, 1836.

88. Prussia encompassed diverse territories over a large area of Germany, and not all of it was a sandy, barren wasteland. These American travelers who complained of the drabness of the Prussian landscape were usually referring to the province of Brandenburg, the region north of Saxony that surrounded the Prussian capitals of Potsdam and Berlin.

89. Anna Ticknor, *Travel Journals*, vol. 4, May 31, 1836.

90. George Ticknor, *Travel Journals*, vol. 4, May 30–31, 1836.

91. Dwight, *Travels in the North of Germany*, 260–61.

92. Ibid., 272–73.

93. Brüning, "'Saxony Is a Prosperous and Happy Country,'" 36–37.

Internationalism, Travel Writing, and Franco-American Educational Travel, 1898–1939

Whitney Walton

In 1928 a young French woman, Simone Téry, reported on her travels as a recipient of an Albert Kahn Around-the-World Scholarship. After visiting Europe, Asia, and the Americas for educational purposes, she offered these reflections on the philosophical condition of the traveler. Téry describes the effect of being torn from one's family and from all that is familiar: the traveler "finds himself alone, alone with himself." Being in foreign places makes a traveler feel like a shadow, "which causes a kind of uneasiness that sometimes extends to anxiety." According to Téry, the traveler seeks stability in himself, but to no avail, for he himself has changed. She concludes that travel confronts individuals with profound questions of existence: "I think that travel is what allows us to experience metaphysical anguish most acutely, and to feel the weight and the grandeur of these commonplaces—the eternal, insoluble problems."[1] Téry's reflections on the profound personal transformation that travel precipitates suggest the centrality of lived experience to a broader, internationalist view, a position that Albert Kahn, founder of the Around-the-World Scholarship, shared.

From 1898 through 1939, three philanthropic projects for educational travel originating in France and the United States—the Albert Kahn Around-the-World Scholarship, the David-Weill Travel Scholarship, and the Institute of International Education (IIE)—manifest a complex interplay of national interest and internationalist objectives through individual study abroad. The founders and leaders of these programs believed in the capacity of individuals to disseminate and acquire knowledge in other countries as a good in itself. Moreover, Albert Kahn and the founding figures of IIE were convinced that this intellectual and personal exchange could contribute to improved international relations, and also serve French and American national interests respectively. The recipients of this philanthropic largesse—fellows—fulfilled the founders' expectations, and their accounts of educational travel suggest a process of how knowledge is shared, mutual understanding is achieved, and personal and national identities are transformed through study abroad.

Although all three programs funded study abroad worldwide, I will focus on French and American educational relations. This essay examines the following issues regarding individual fellowships for educational travel between France and the United States in the first half of the twentieth century: the intentions and goals of the three philanthropic endeavors, the ways in which fellows articulated their study abroad experience, and some implications of this particular form of intellectual and personal exchange for the diffusion of knowledge, Franco-American relations, and internationalism.

Historical scholarship on travel provides important insights into class—mostly middle-class—formation, constructions of national identities, and the capacity of individuals to imagine new ways of being even in the age of mass tourism.[2] As a distinctive form of travel, study abroad contributes an internationalist perspective to this literature and links travel with international relations. Historians define "internationalism" in different ways, depending upon the particular historical context. Diplomatic historian Akira Iriye, among others, has examined primarily nongovernmental organizations (NGOs) that aspire to transnational cooperation and exchange as engaging in cultural internationalism, in contrast to the nation-state rivalries that usually constitute histories of international relations.[3] By contrast, for scholars of U.S. foreign relations in the twentieth century internationalism refers to various means by which political leaders, private enterprises, and other organizations and individuals sought to influence political, economic, and cultural practices in other parts of the world to conform with those in the United States.[4] While acknowledgement of national interest underlying or undermining more disinterested internationalism is often warranted, some scholarship suggests that internationalism and nationalism are antithetical.[5]

Scholarship on cosmopolitanism, usually by literary scholars, philosophers, and anthropologists, is more receptive to ambiguity, multiple allegiances, and complex identities relating to internationalism and nationalism. Bruce Robbins and Kwame Anthony Appiah, for instance, claim that cosmopolitanism, referring to a conscious commitment to humanity, can and often does coexist with nationalism, and that both are lived experiences or identities.[6] Appiah offers the term "rooted cosmopolitanism" or "cosmopolitan patriotism" to explain the condition of being at once identified with a region, a state, and humanity as a whole.[7] For this study I propose to modify the term "internationalism" as meaning transnational cooperation and exchange, and combine it with the more nuanced interrogation applied to cosmopolitanism to define the outcome of Franco-American educational travel. That is, "internationalism" here refers to understanding of and sympathy for national cultures and societies different from one's own derived from lived experience and compatible with national identity or loyalty. This essay emphasizes how French and American fellows' accounts of their experiences served both national interests and international aspirations. It also offers an alternative narrative of cooperation and exchange to the frameworks of Americanization and anti-Americanism in diplomatic and cultural histories of modern Franco-American relations.[8]

Motives and Goals

The turn of the nineteenth into the twentieth century was a time of increasingly militant nationalism, but internationalism also flourished in a variety of forms, including the establishment of transnational organizations to standardize weights, measures, time, transportation, and communication, as well as nongovernmental efforts to coordinate shared interests and concerns across national boundaries such as international women's groups, the socialist Second International, and peace movements.[9] Similar to Pierre de Coubertin, who revived the Olympic Games in 1896, and Cecil Rhodes, whose bequest started the Rhodes Scholarship to Oxford University in 1902, banker and philanthropist Albert Kahn (1860–1940) combined intense national pride with international and humanitarian ideals at this time.[10]

Born in Alsace, Kahn, like many Jews, left for France after Germany annexed Alsace and Lorraine in 1871. At the age of sixteen, he started working at the Goudchaux Bank of Paris, where he became an associate in 1892. He also made a fortune from investments in South African gold and diamond mines. While working at the bank and with the help of a tutor, Kahn earned his baccalaureate in both letters and science, along with a law degree, by 1884. In a letter of 1887 to his former tutor and friend Henri Bergson (1859–1941), Kahn suggested that his successful banking career was only a means to larger, more satisfying occupations. And indeed, the Around-the-World Scholarships were only the beginning of several varied, internationalist, philanthropic endeavors, including a Center of Social Documentation to promote the social sciences in France, the Archives of the Planet—a massive photographic collection from some fifty countries around the world, the National Committee for Social and Political Studies, and an offshoot of the scholarships, the Around-the-World Society.[11] These initiatives suggest a fascination with the unbounded possibilities offered by modern technology and science, similar to the fantastic voyages of the novels of Jules Verne (1828–1905), yet grounded in a Bergsonian faith in the positive growth and change inherent in individual experience.

The Around-the-World Scholarships, first announced in France in 1898, were to provide young *lycée* (secondary school) professors with experiences of the world that they were unlikely to have otherwise, with the expectation that this would make them better teachers.[12] Kahn also hoped that the knowledge gained from studying abroad might contribute to conflict resolution among countries: "We must seek to compile a precise understanding of the role that different nations play in the world, determine their different aspirations, see where these aspirations lead, if they incline nations toward violent shocks or if they can be reconciled with one another." Kahn thought that educated youth would be best suited to learn about other countries and cultures in a relationship of equal exchange: "To enter into friendly communication with the ideas, the feelings, indeed the life of different peoples, who better to do this than young [men] selected from the intellectual and moral elite of the nation, not old enough to have preconceived ideas, but mature enough to know how to observe and understand?" His ultimate goal was that fellows would meet and discuss what they had learned in order to identify some general trends "capable of usefully influencing the direction of our country's activity."[13]

For Kahn, France was a leader in world affairs, but he implied that developments elsewhere were challenging that leadership, and that part of the purpose of the scholarships was to analyze the strengths and weaknesses of France and other countries in order to benefit France. He explained: "The purpose of this travel [is] to allow these young professors to acquire an accurate idea of the situation of France in the world and a lively sense of the effort necessary to maintain France at a level worthy of her."[14] Kahn encouraged fellows to be open-minded and receptive to other cultures; he expected them to feel "invested with a sense of patriotic and humanitarian mission."[15]

In the following years Kahn established similar travel scholarships for young male teachers of different nationalities, including the Kahn Foundation for the Foreign Travel of American Teachers in 1911. By 1930, when he lost his fortune in the global financial collapse and the Around-the-World Scholarships ended, the Kahn fellows numbered seventy-two French men and women, and seventy-six men of other nationalities—British, Japanese, Russian, German, and American.[16]

The little information I have on the David-Weill Travel Scholarships suggests a more modest aim than Kahn's hopes for national competitiveness and international understanding. In 1910 the Council of the University of Paris accepted an anonymous donation of ten scholarships worth three thousand francs each for five years to fund travel and study at foreign institutions for holders of advanced degrees in medicine, pharmacy, law, and arts and sciences who were committed to teaching. The purpose of these scholarships was "to put young or future academics in the position to acquire the special cultivation that results from prolonged contact with a foreign civilization." Well over a hundred travel scholarships were granted to French men and women from the academic year 1910–1911 to 1939, and fellows pursued study and research in Europe and North America for the most part.[17]

The Carnegie Endowment for International Peace was also established in 1910, and World War I precipitated additional efforts by the Endowment and other American philanthropies to support war relief services, scientific research, and educational exchanges. Stephen P. Duggan (1870–1950), a professor of political science and diplomatic history, and chair of the Department of Education at City College of New York, proposed a plan in 1917 to address the call by Nicholas Murray Butler (1862–1947), then head of the Carnegie Endowment for International Peace, for "an institution devoted to the specific purpose of enabling our people to secure a better understanding of foreign nations and of enabling foreign nations to obtain accurate knowledge of the United States, its people, institutions, and culture." Waiting until after the war ended, the Endowment established the Institute of International Education (IIE) on February 1, 1919, "having for its general aim to develop international good will by means of educational agencies, and for its specific purpose to act as a clearing house of information and advice for Americans concerning things educational in foreign countries and for foreigners concerning things educational in the United States."[18] Duggan was appointed Director of the IIE, a post he held until 1946.[19]

When Duggan started his position in 1919 there were few fellowships available for study abroad, and one of the IIE's main functions became the administration of a rapidly increasing number of study and research fellowships. Some U.S. universities, like Harvard and Columbia, exchanged professors with European universities, notably French and German, before the war, but, according to Duggan, the poverty and losses from the conflict made it difficult for Europeans to send teachers abroad.[20] Even more difficult was funding for students. A partial solution to this problem involved cooperation between private institutions in the United States and the French government, an arrangement that became a model for student exchange fellowships between the United States and other countries.

Opportunities for educational exchanges between France and the United States multiplied in the immediate aftermath of World War I. Many American colleges and universities, mostly women's colleges, provided room, board, and tuition for over one hundred young French women to study in the United States (and to teach French) at the end of World War I. In response, the French government supported twenty young American women in French *lycées,* and four in higher institutions.[21] Additional posts for American men to teach and study in France soon followed. Moreover, in memory of the fallen volunteers of the American Field Service, survivors of this ambulance corps wanted to start a scholarship fund. As a result of a merger with the Society for American Fellowships in French Universities, started in 1915, the American Field Service Fellowships for French Universities awarded eight scholarships in 1919–1920 for young male American graduate students to pursue advanced research in France. By 1952 this program had funded 174 Americans to do research and advanced study in France, and 48 French men to pursue their studies in the United States.[22] The IIE took over the administration of these fellowships in 1924, whose purpose was "to create a better realization of the place of France in the leadership of the world in every field of science and learning," and "to foster international understanding."[23] Reports of the IIE from the 1920s reveal that fellowship support for Franco-American educational exchanges was particularly strong, and partly on that basis Duggan noted that "greater progress in the exchange of students with the United States has been made by France than by any other country."[24]

Unlike the Kahn Foundation or David-Weill, the IIE provided few scholarships of its own. Rather, it administered and publicized fellowships and exchange opportunities provided by private (mostly American) foundations and institutions of higher education and foreign governments. The increase in such fellowships and opportunities in the 1920s and 1930s is impressive and attests to a widespread faith in the benefits of educational exchange for international relations. Duggan noted that the IIE administered no fellowships in 1920, but was administering three hundred fellowships in 1930.[25] The preponderance of fellowships for Americans to study in France is also striking. In 1926 Duggan presented these figures of fellowships administered by the IIE:

Fellowships for Americans to Study Abroad

American Field Service Fellowships for French Universities—11
Franco-American Fellowships—21

American German Student Exchange Fellowships—20
American Czechoslovak Exchange Fellowships—5
American Hungarian Exchange Fellowships—5
Willard Straight Fellowship for China—1
Fellowships for Junior Year Abroad—5
Postes d'Assistant for French Universities—10
Total—78

Since at this time the Junior Year Abroad programs involved American undergraduates studying only in France, the number of opportunities for Americans to study in France represented forty-seven out of the seventy-eight fellowships listed.[26]

The main purpose of the IIE was to facilitate study abroad and academic exchanges between the United States and other countries, in order to "internationalize" Americans and to allow foreigners to understand the United States. Duggan credited "the intelligent American" with a desire "to cooperate with similar people in other countries in the material and spiritual reconstruction of a distracted world and in the development of international good will."[27] And he explicitly stated that a major benefit for foreign students in the United States was to learn about "American institutions and ways of looking at life," especially for those from newly formed democracies. He did caution that, "If [the foreign students] are to return to their home countries with a respect and admiration for things American, there must be no attitude of condescension upon our part."[28] An underlying assumption in Duggan's reports is that the United States emerged from World War I as a global power, and therefore its citizens had a responsibility to learn more about the world and to help other nationalities understand the United States.

The goals of the Kahn scholarships and of the IIE regarding educational travel were similar: the shared expectation was that study abroad would provide young people with a better understanding of the world, that they would communicate this new understanding to their compatriots after they returned home, and that such understanding would contribute to peaceful resolutions of tensions and conflicts among different nationalities. Additionally, Kahn hoped that French fellows would apply the knowledge gained about other countries toward buttressing France's global leadership position, and Duggan and his supporters believed that foreign students would take back with them positive views of the United States as an emerging world power. From their perspective, educational travel served national interests and internationalism simultaneously. How was this possible?

Travel Writing and Internationalism

Reports written by the fellows, and additional documentation such as surveys and fellows' publications, suggest a learning process whereby fellows compared and contrasted their own and another nation's values and practices (in this case, French and American), confronted various preconceptions and national stereotypes, and articulated strengths and weaknesses of different national cultures based on the travel experience. Many of the reports by David-Weill fellows adhere to this general pattern, and they also contain much specific knowledge gained in the fields of medical research, suggesting either that these scholarships were more focused on disciplinary and professional knowledge than on internationalism, or that fellows themselves emphasized professional practices. There is an inherent bias in such documentation, since fellows were predisposed to share the views of their sponsors, the study abroad experience generally fulfilled fellows' goals for personal enhancement and broader, international understanding, and fellows were grateful for the educational travel opportunity.[29] Nonetheless, fellows' accounts add an important dimension to travel writing and to understanding philanthropy-supported educational travel, for they show how individuals can at the same time be proud of their national identity and appreciate the value of other cultures.

A common response of French fellows to their educational travels in the United States was to compare and contrast particular strengths and weaknesses of France and the United States in the areas, for example, of education, international relations, cultural values, and social practices. In a 1904 volume of reports by thirteen of the first Kahn fellows, Georges Weulersse, a fellow in 1898, suggested that since the strengths and weaknesses of French and American education systems are exact opposites, a desirable education should combine the strengths of both, that is, the physical exercise, hygiene, and hands-on practicality of the United States with the more bookish, comprehensive, and abstract education of France.[30] Madeleine Mignon, who traveled to the United States in 1911, drew similar conclusions about the respective merits of French and especially American education systems, and she hoped that French educators could adopt certain American practices, such as equal scientific education for girls and boys, more attention to physical fitness and hygiene for pupils, and the cultivation of a social conscience among girls in school.[31] Overall, French *boursières* (women fellows) concluded that educated American women represented a positive example to French women. Rachel Allard wrote in 1911: "the cultivated American woman seemed to me more developed than ours, by her spirit of initiative and especially by her sense of social life, an example to propose to the French woman."[32]

The advent and the outbreak of World War I framed several fellows' outlooks on the United States and France in international relations. Ivan Linforth, an American professor of classics at the University of California at Berkeley, who traveled on a Kahn fellowship in 1912, deplored the nationalism and militarism that he witnessed in Europe, especially in Germany. This latent tribalism suggested to him that the United States, comprised of numerous European nationalities united in one country, had the opportunity and even obligation to steer clear of the conditions and practices that threatened to lead to war. He proposed that the United States fulfill this mission, in part, by refusing to fight: "To stop thinking of war; to stop planning for it; to stop spending money on army and navy,—these are the steps which will lead most surely to the reign of peace." Linforth believed that if the United States could halt its own "racial prejudice" and other failings, it might serve as a model for a less belligerent patriotism: "a new patriotism must be learned which can glory in the high calling of the country as leader in the salvation of the world."[33] According to Linforth, all countries could (and should) adopt this "true patriotism," serving both national and international interests through tolerance and cooperation.

Some French fellows were disappointed in the U.S. neutrality during the early years of World War I. French economist Emile Hovelaque, among the first Kahn fellows who traveled in 1898, later criticized the American tendency toward pacifism and avoidance of war, largely, in his opinion, out of economic interests. He charged American idealism with naïveté, a failure to discern the difference between executioner and victim in the European war, but in 1916 he was hopeful that the United States was gradually leaving its pacifist, non-interventionist position.[34] Similarly, Anne Main, who taught French in the United States in 1916 and 1917, attributed American neutrality to a lack of experience, history, and spiritual engagement, though she anticipated that this position would change: "We know things that the United States does not know yet, but that they will perhaps learn."[35]

The terrible slaughter of global warfare from 1914 through 1918 actually increased some of the fellows' hopes and efforts for peace through educational exchange in the two interwar decades. After the Around-the-World Scholarships ended in 1930, former fellows asserted the importance of this educational travel experience for promoting peace. In 1931 Félicien Challaye asserted that he and other fellows passed on the new insights gained as a result of their Around-the-World Scholarships through their teaching, public presentations, and writing, thereby perpetuating Kahn's goal of universal understanding and sympathy: "By bringing together all the great human races, the creation of the around-the-world travel scholarships perhaps prepares for the appearance of what [Rabindranath] Tagore calls *the infinite personality of man.*"[36]

Altering his original assessment of 1913 about the unique role of the United States in maintaining world peace, Ivan Linforth published another article in 1931 on internationalism, praising the many efforts by private organizations to foster cross-cultural exchange and understanding, of which Kahn's scholarship was an early example. Linforth acknowledged that ordinary citizens felt threatened by internationalism, fearing the loss of the "popular customs of their county, of their institutions and ideals, replaced by universal law, language, religion, and social organization to which they feel no attachment." But he was optimistic that educational and travel scholarships for students and professors would overcome this tendency, for they all shared "the goal of making men of different nations encounter one another and know one another." [37]

Subsequent positions and careers of both French and American fellows indicate that the internationalist perspective gained from the Around-the-World Scholarships was indeed lasting and incorporated into published works and involvement in various activities or causes (in addition to teaching), like journalism and publishing, education administration, the Around-the-World Society, anticolonialism, and the Center for Social Documentation.[38] Indeed, former fellows created the Around-the-World Society in 1906 (it lasted until 1949), a social and intellectual organization open to all internationalists, specifically for the purpose of "work[ing] to spread, in France, precise knowledge of foreign countries, abroad, knowledge of France, and to understand and foster all that one could call international civilization."[39] Challaye noted the value of Kahn's travel project in 1931 on the twenty-fifth anniversary of the scholarships: "All the joys of such voyages center around a superior satisfaction: the joy of intellectual liberation." Speaking of all fellows, he asserted, "Each of us drew from our travel some of the ideas that have subsequently directed our lives." For himself, that idea was the equality of all races: "each race has its value, originality, and charm, such that none is destined to be the eternal slave of another, and one day all the peoples of all races will be equally free and will unite in brotherhood in a peaceful world."[40]

Edmée Hitzel, among the last of the Albert Kahn fellows in 1929–1930, and perhaps familiar with André Siegfried's (and even Georges Duhamel's) popular critiques of the United States, mustered a spirited defense of American prosperity and energy.[41] Arriving in San Francisco after traveling in Asia, she praised the United States for its absence of hierarchies, servitude, and poverty characteristic of old civilizations. Recognizing that French imitation of the United States was out of the question, she concluded: "This danger of servile and inopportune imitation must be pushed away, not in awkwardly criticizing American civilization, which is justified and good in itself, as I have tried to show, but in trying to put into place an intelligent and sensitive collaboration between the Old World and the New."[42]

Kahn fellows from France learned to appreciate the culture and society of the United States in a way that differed from the disdainful fear of Georges Duhamel or other French travelers who wrote popular accounts of the United States for the general public in France, suggesting that American materialism, conformity, and uniformity would soon engulf French culture. Without denying the increasing influence of the United States, especially after World War I, many fellows (though by no means all) envisioned constructive exchanges of ideas and practices between the two countries. Additionally, Kahn fellows from the United States fulfilled their explicitly internationalist mission by trying to understand other national cultures and considering various means to promote transnational cooperation in the interest of peace.

Documentation from the IIE regarding Franco-American educational travel reveals similar patterns of national comparison and contrast and internationalist aspirations, and it also suggests what types of knowledge circulated in the transatlantic exchange.[43] Like the Kahn fellows, the majority of IIE fellows were graduate students and practicing professionals, a demographic that Duggan (like Kahn) believed was best suited to benefit from educational travel and to perpetuate those gains domestically and internationally.[44] Duggan's published reports based on confidential accounts by fellows suggest something of a balancing act between the two main purposes of study abroad: professional advancement and international goodwill, and a slight distinction between Europeans seeking more professional knowledge in the United States, and Americans oriented more toward academic careers.

In 1929–1930 the IIE surveyed 400 Americans who studied abroad on IIE-administered fellowships, and 450 foreigners who had studied in the United States. Among the Americans, 245 returned the survey, providing valuable information on their occupations and educational degrees, and evaluation of their contributions abroad and of the relevance of study abroad to their profession. Of the 245 American respondents, 197 of them had gone to France, 37 to Germany, and 11 to Czechoslovakia and Switzerland. The vast majority of them (73 percent) were professional educators at either secondary or post-secondary levels; 8 percent did research or professional work in business, industry, or nonprofit organizations; 6 percent were in the liberal professions (theology, medicine, law); and another 6 percent were in the arts. All earned either a master's degree or a PhD. The survey offered five categories of ways that fellows might have contributed to student life in a foreign university. Forty-four percent felt that their most important contribution was through "informal discussions with foreign students." Thirty-seven percent thought their greatest contribution was in helping foreign students learn English, and 10 percent evaluated scientific methods and research in their chosen fields as their most important contribution. The lowest percentage—4 percent considered "representing the American viewpoint" as their most important contribution to student life abroad. In terms of professional benefits of study abroad, the fellows' rankings were as follows: 34 percent valued most highly their familiarity with another language; 29 percent considered the personal and cultural benefits to be the greatest, without any bearing on their professions; 20 percent indicated that they thought study abroad contributed to their earning higher salaries.[45]

Beyond the categories supplied by the survey, the report of the survey notes that several fellows regarded the cultural and professional benefits to be so closely linked as to be almost inseparable. This was especially apparent among the majority of fellows who became teachers and academics. The survey report's interpretation is that understanding of another nationality and more avid interest in international affairs were results from study abroad that improved teaching effectiveness.[46]

Returns from foreign fellows who studied in the United States were fewer than those from Americans, which the IIE (probably accurately) attributed to the difficulty of locating the former fellows. Of the respondents, fifty-four were French, forty-three German, and sixteen were Czechoslovak, Hungarian, or Swiss. A notable difference in their responses from those of Americans is the distribution of occupations. Fifty-three percent were in education, and by far the greatest number in this category were French women. Twenty percent were in liberal professions, and 13 percent did research or professional work in business, industry, or nonprofit organizations. Slight differences occurred in the foreign fellows' evaluation of how they contributed to student life in the United States, with 32 percent saying that their greatest contribution was in helping Americans with another language, 31 percent opting for informal conversations, and 16 percent contributing most in their academic fields. In the area of benefits of foreign study, foreign fellows ranked most highly the personal and cultural benefits (33 percent), closely followed by familiarity with English (31 percent), then professional benefits *not* reflected in a better salary. The many foreign fellows who became teachers after studying in the United States indicated that the experience improved their ability to teach Americans abroad, and to teach English and American life to their compatriots. The report suggests that many foreign fellows took back with them ideas and practices from the United States in their fields and valued the dissolution of misperceptions and stereotypes about Americans and the United States from their experience. This suggests that Europeans thought they knew more about Americans than did Americans about Europeans, or that they were more willing to admit the error of their preconceptions.[47]

More details of cross-cultural exchange in the words of the fellows themselves appeared in 1933 when the IIE published selected excerpts from reports by American Field Service fellows, most of whom did advanced research in the humanities and social sciences in Paris (French language and literature, comparative literature, history, political science, and economics). It is important to remember that the purpose of American Field Service Fellowships was "to create a better realization of the place of France in the leadership of the world in every field of science and learning." The reports do indeed express admiration for French culture and education, praising the intellectual vibrancy of the University of Paris, the intense interaction between professors and students in the method known as *explication de textes,* the close links between *lycée* and university education, and the democratic learning that occurred in the Bibliothèque Nationale. One report summarized points made by several fellows regarding the quality of higher education in France: "Above all the serious atmosphere of the classes, the limitation of the university proper to the bare essential of adequate classrooms, and the maintenance by the professors of a fixed and superior attitude have contributed to make Paris seem more of an ideal university than the American."[48]

Fellows also noted features of French higher education that they considered less successful or just different from the United States. One thought that the seminars at the Ecole des Hautes Etudes were not as helpful as lectures and *explication de textes* at the University of Paris, and a few noted French students' and professors' engagement in politics, which they found interesting but perhaps detrimental to an ideal, pure educational or intellectual atmosphere. Several cautioned about the adjustments and challenges American students confronted in France: "To those who are not habituated to working independently, the French academic life may seem to suffer by comparison with that of many American universities."[49] Learning the language well enough to benefit from classes and social conversations took time, and finding adequate housing in Paris was not easy. But overwhelmingly, fellows reported that the experience was worthwhile in both Paris and provincial cities.

Fellows indicated that they learned a lot about their particular areas of study and about French culture and people. Being disabused of preconceptions was a first step in this learning process: "Any false preconceptions that [a fellow] may entertain about France, accumulated from a mass of unofficial information in America, are soon rudely smothered in the actualities of the French milieu." Another fellow asserted: "It is curious to me to note how my early attitude towards French civilization has changed with time. I have not found my first judgments wrong, but they have ceased to seem important to me." He went on to offer a nuanced understanding of the art of conversation in France, and an appreciation for what he calls "the fixity of French character" in contrast to the "intangibility and elasticity of" American natures. One went so far as to say that he learned internationalism by living in France: "I feel that by far the greatest advantage which I have derived from my two years of study in France is an international viewpoint." He credits meeting French people and those of other nationalities for this new outlook, and he mentions his reappraisal of his own national identity: "Above all, by considering my own country in perspective in the light of these new ideas, I have a much better conception and understanding of her problems."[50]

The results of the IIE survey, as well as Duggan's observations and the reports by David-Weill fellows, indicate that Europeans were more likely to come to the United States for study and research in the sciences and professions, while Americans pursued humanistic disciplines in Europe and especially France. Even before the statement of purpose by the American Field Service Fellowships for French Universities asserting French "leadership of the world in every field of science and learning," French scientists were questioning certain aspects of scientific education and practice in France, and acknowledging the merits of those in the United States. After spending a semester at Harvard University as an exchange professor, French biologist Maurice Caullery published his views about American universities and scientific life in 1917. He noted that a striking difference between French and American universities was the intense individualism characteristic of France in contrast to the sense of community cultivated in higher education in the United States. Caullery, along with French academics who reviewed his book, suggested reforms to improve and modernize French universities, reforms similar to American practices but appropriate for France, like establishing research centers in Paris so that academics could share ideas, integrating applied sciences into university science studies, and forming alumni associations to foster institutional loyalty.[51] In 1927 an American employee of the American University Union in Paris echoed Caullery's suggestion that French scientific education and training should be more collaborative and cooperative. Gary N. Calkins professed to having "the greatest respect and the warmest personal friendliness" for French scientists, but he believed that science in France was declining for lack of government and popular support, and because the French were out of step with modern science that required "concerted action and cooperation of many minds working from different angles on the same general problem" to make real progress.[52]

Issues of funding and collaboration appeared also in reports by David-Weill fellows who traveled to the United States in the 1920s and 1930s, most of whom were involved in medical research. For example, Dr. Pierre

Wertheimer, a neurological surgeon in Lyon, visited several hospitals in North America in 1930 and reported that collaborative research in the United States contributed to good experimental surgery. In 1931 Dr. Pierre Woringer interpreted the high level of private funding for medical research in the United States to be reflection of a general public faith in egalitarianism and research; given the opportunity in the form of funding, ordinary people will do scientific and medical research. Some fellows asserted that American hospitals were better organized (even Taylorized) than those in France, though this did not necessarily mean that treatment was better. Many noted that the competitive examination system in France was detrimental to good training of doctors and to their attitudes toward patients, in contrast to the larger scope for choice in medical appointments in the United States. Like the Kahn fellows, the David-Weill fellows discerned strengths and weaknesses in both French and American medical education, research, and practice, and they were grateful for the opportunity to learn from and share ideas with their American counterparts.[53]

Although the Kahn scholarships ended in 1930, the David-Weill Travel Scholarships continued through 1939, and the IIE continued to function and even flourish in the 1930s despite the global depression, increasing nationalism and militarism in Europe, and nationalism and isolationism in the United States. The growing (or, during the Depression, still substantial) numbers of Americans studying abroad and foreigners studying in the United States must surely be considered a measure of the success of the privately funded IIE. And no doubt Duggan's steadfast commitment to international education kept the project afloat despite the rise of fascist dictatorships in Europe. Although Duggan condemned totalitarian regimes, he continued to believe that there was something beneficial to learn from living and studying in another country, whether it was a democracy or a dictatorship.[54] He asserted in 1934 that "we [Americans] have lessons to learn from dictatorships which have great value," namely their focused sense of purpose and appeal to youth. But he also thought that "a sojourn in one of the educational institutions of our country may teach their young people something of the meaning of freedom."[55]

Published testimonials from students or exchange academics as well as Duggan's reports are similar to evidence from the Kahn fellows in the sense that they show a belief that the exchange of knowledge, better understanding of another culture and people, and reflection upon one's own personal and national identity from study abroad led toward improved international relations. Comparisons and contrasts between one's own culture and that of another are probably the only means for articulating understanding.[56] Those who studied abroad identified strengths and weaknesses of two different cultures, and saw merits, or at least justification, of both. Another part of the process of cultural understanding or internationalism is the dissolution of stereotypes or preconceptions. Duggan asserted that student reports frequently revealed that overcoming stereotypes was a major outcome of study abroad. For foreigners studying in the United States, he wrote, "America is revealed as a place which has something more vital to offer than its skyscrapers, vast factories, bootleggers, racketeers, and all the other 'American' products set forth in the movies, novels, and newspapers." He then quoted an American student on the result of study abroad for a sense of internationalism and nationalism as typical: "Perhaps the essential value of a year in a foreign country is a love of two countries, and proud consciousness of belonging to one of them."[57]

An account by a French economics professor, who was both a Kahn fellow and a visiting IIE-sponsored scholar to western and plains states in the United States in 1935–1936, showed a deep appreciation for American isolationism, higher education in the United States, and American students in this region. Etienne Dennery maintained that economic concerns among Great Plains wheat farmers explained the region's mistrust of international relations and organizations, as well as the optimism of students there who found a refuge from economic insecurity at the university and hope for the future. Dennery was modest in his assessment of the impact of his presence on Americans: "I am ignorant of what my public has retained of my lectures." But he was expansive on what he learned from his visit, notably about the "extreme diversity" of the region as well as of the United States in general: "Henceforth I shall always hesitate to speak of American tendencies as though they were unified." Dennery concluded: "This contact, though so rapid, with the professors and the students of the Northwest, has not only afforded me a better knowledge of the United States but it has given me that indispensable element of all true knowledge: sympathy."[58]

The outbreak of war in 1939 severely disrupted IIE activities in Europe, and marked the beginning of United States government involvement with the IIE and international cultural relations. Starting in the late 1930s and continuing through World War II, the U.S. Department of State became interested in cultural and educational exchanges as a means of combating fascist propaganda.[59] The IIE accepted money from the U.S. government during the war to fund its many and expanding activities, but Duggan insisted that it "remain[ed] a private organization," and that its success depended on its being "regarded abroad as a representative of the American people . . . rather than of the government."[60] At the end of the war and with the onset of the Cold War a new phase in the history of transatlantic educational travel began in which the United States government was heavily involved.

Conclusion

Even as transatlantic travel and communication accelerated and improved over the course of the twentieth century, information from hearsay or the media still could not replace or reproduce the kind of understanding often achieved through study abroad. The nuances of complex societies are evident in the reports of students and professionals who crossed the Atlantic between 1898 and 1939. The young Americans and French people who articulated these cultural differences were penetrating quite deeply into the host society, more so than most tourists and even travel writers who provided much of the information available to the general public about the other country. It was the profound personal transformation of adapting to another culture, confronting preconceptions and stereotypes, and reconstructing individual and national identities that enabled young people to achieve a new level of understanding of their own and another society. This constitutes internationalism in the sense of a lived appreciation for cultural, social, and national differences.

The story of Franco-American educational travel in the early twentieth century also indicates that anti-Americanism and Americanization were not the only manifestations of cultural relations between France and the United States. Curiosity, fascination, and admiration regarding the other country propelled French and American young people to compete for fellowships, take ship across the Atlantic, leave their homes and families for an extended period of time, and immerse themselves in a foreign culture and educational system. The knowledge gained from living and studying in the other country was often integrated into careers as teachers and professionals. A measure of the success of this transatlantic exchange is the persistence of study abroad between France and the United States throughout the twentieth century. At the level of high diplomacy and national leaders, Franco-American relations have hardly been smooth, but they have not hindered educational travel, and indeed, interstate controversies sometimes became the opportunities for mutual understanding during study abroad.[61]

The evidence presented here suggests the compatibility of national interest and internationalism as outcomes of individual fellowships for educational travel. Much recent scholarship on U.S. cultural relations emphasizes the presumption, especially by the U.S. government but also by private individuals, that American values and practices are superior and universal, and that educational travel serves mainly to spread them to the rest of the world.[62] The pervasiveness of this attitude, particularly among U.S. government officials during the Cold War, is indisputable. However, fellows themselves did not necessarily share this position, and living and studying in another country often caused individuals to reassess, or consider for the first time, the meaning of one's national identity.[63] Whatever their fields and professions, fellows rarely abandoned their original national identity, and indeed, they found that living and studying in another country reinforced and also transformed that identity. At the same time, they learned to understand and respect, if not admire, another national culture and become more tolerant of cultural difference generally. As Simone Téry noted, educational travel confronted the individual with universal and commonplace problems of human existence.

Appendix

Statistics on French students in the United States, foreign students in the United States, and Americans in France, from IIE bulletins, 1921–1943

	1919–20	1921–22	1922–23	1923–24	1924–25	1925–26	1926–27	1928–29
French in U.S.	212	127	144	126	128	90	103	122
All foreign in U.S.	6,740	6,488	7,494	6,988	7,518	6,961	7,541	9,685
Americans in France	400	NA	NA	NA	NA	NA	NA	5,584

	1929–30	1930–31	1931–32	1932–33	1933–34	1934–35	1935–36	1936–37
French in U.S.	NA	143	126	104	68	88	82	89
All foreign in U.S.	NA	9,961	8,688	6,850	5,805	5,887	5,608	7,343
Americans in France	NA	NA	NA	NA	2,400	NA	NA	NA

	1937–38	1938–39	1939–40	1940–41	1942–43
French in U.S.	96	102	76	106	186
All foreign in U.S.	7,253	6,004	6,630	7,152	8,056
Americans in France	NA	NA	NA	NA	NA

Total numbers of foreign students in the United States often vary in different tables in different years.

NOTES

1. Archives Nationales (hereafter AN) [French National Archives] AJ 16/7023 Bourses de voyage autour du monde 1898–1930. Dossiers individuels et rapports, L-W. Simone Téry, report 28 May 1928.

2. Christopher Endy, *Cold War Holidays: American Tourism in France* (Chapel Hill: University of North Carolina Press, 2004); Shelley Baranowski and Ellen Furlough, eds., *Being Elsewhere: Tourism, Commercial Leisure and National Identities in 19th and 20th Century Europe and North America* (Ann Arbor: University of Michigan Press, 2000); Eric J. Leed, *The Mind of the Traveler: From Gilgamesh to Global Tourism* (New York: Basic Books, 1991); Harvey Levenstein, *Seductive Journey: American Tourists in France from Jefferson to the Jazz Age* (Chicago: University of Chicago Press, 1998); Harvey Levenstein, *We'll Always Have Paris: American Tourists in France Since 1930* (Chicago: University of Chicago Press, 2004); Rudy Koshar, "Seeing, Traveling, and Consuming: An Introduction," in Rudy Koshar, ed., *Histories of Leisure* (New York: Berg Publishers, 2002), 1–24.

3. Akira Iriye, *Global Community: The Role of International Organizations in the Making of the Contemporary World* (Berkeley: University of California Press, 2002).

4. Christopher Endy, "Travel and World Power: Americans in Europe, 1890–1917," *Diplomatic History* 22 (Fall 1998): 565–94; Frank Costigliola, *Awkward Dominion: American Political, Economic, and Cultural Relations with Europe, 1919–1933* (Ithaca: Cornell University Press, 1984); Emily S. Rosenberg, *Spreading the American Dream: American Economic and Cultural Expansion, 1890–1945* (New York: Hill and Wang, 1982).

5. The following works emphasize the role of educational and transnational travel in promoting American national interests, and suggest that internationalism was not much more than rhetoric: Liping Bu, *Making the World Like Us: Education, Cultural Expansion and the American Century* (Westport, Conn.: Praeger, 2003); Giles Scott-Smith, *Networks of Empire: The U.S. State Department's Foreign Leader Program in the Netherlands, France, and Britain 1950–70* (Brussells: P. I. E. Peter Lang, 2008).

6. Bruce Robbins, "Introduction Part I: Actually Existing Cosmopoli-

tanism," in Pheng Cheah and Bruce Robbins, eds., *Cosmopolitics: Thinking and Feeling Beyond the Nation* (Minneapolis: University of Minnesota Press, 1998), 1–19; Kwame Anthony Appiah, *The Ethics of Identity* (Princeton: Princeton University Press, 2005).

7. Kwame Anthony Appiah, "Cosmopolitan Patriots," in Cheah and Robbins, *Cosmopolitics,* 91–114.

8. Richard F. Kuisel, *Seducing the French: The Dilemma of Americanization* (Berkeley: University of California Press, 1993); Denis Lacorne, Jacques Rupnik, and Marie-France Toinet, eds., *The Rise and Fall of Anti-Americanism: A Century of French Perception,* trans. Gerry Turner (New York: St. Martin's Press, 1990); Philippe Roger, *The American Enemy: A Story of French Anti-Americanism,* trans. Sharon Bowman (Chicago: University of Chicago Press, 2005); Seth D. Armus, *French Anti-Americanism, 1930–1948: Critical Moments in a Complex History* (Lanham, Md.: Rowman & Littlefield Publishers, 2007).

9. Stephen Kern, *The Culture of Time and Space, 1880–1918* (Cambridge, Mass.: Harvard University Press, 1983); F. S. L. Lyons, *Internationalism in Europe 1815–1914* (Leyden: A. W. Sythoff, 1963); Thomas J. Schaeper and Kathleen Schaeper, *Rhodes Scholars, Oxford and the Creation of an American Elite* (New York: Berghahn Books, 2004); Leila J. Rupp, *Worlds of Women: The Making of an International Women's Movement* (Princeton: Princeton University Press, 1998); Sandi E. Cooper, *Patriotic Pacifism: Waging War on War in Europe, 1815–1914* (New York: Oxford University Press, 1991).

10. Schaeper and Schaeper, *Rhodes Scholars,* 1, 13–16; Robert I. Rotberg, *The Founder: Cecil Rhodes and the Pursuit of Power* (New York: Oxford University Press, 1988), 665–69; Eugen Weber, "Pierre de Coubertin and the Introduction of Organised Sport in France," *Journal of Contemporary History* 5 (1970): 3–26; Allen Guttmann, *The Olympics: A History of the Modern Games,* 2nd ed. (Urbana: University of Illinois Press, 2002), 8–19; Iriye, *Global Community,* 9–19. See also Lee Shai Weissbach, "The Nature of Philanthropy in Nineteenth-century France and the *Mentalité* of the Jewish Elite," *Jewish History* 8 (1994): 191–204. The research of F. S. L. Lyons indicates that nongovernmental international organizations in Europe multiplied around the turn of the century, and though they did not prevent World War I, they nonetheless accustomed a small minority of Europeans to international

practices. Lyons, *Internationalism in Europe,* 14–15, 203–45, 366–69. According to Merle Curti, American philanthropy was primarily humanitarian at the turn of the century in the sense of providing disaster relief in troubled areas. A more cosmopolitan and internationalist orientation started with the founding of the Carnegie Endowment for International Peace in 1910. Merle Curti, *American Philanthropy Abroad: A History* (New Brunswick, N.J.: Rutgers University Press, 1963), 178–97.

11. *Albert Kahn, 1860–1940: Réalités d'une utopie* (Boulogne: Musée Albert Kahn, 1995); Sophie Cœuré and Frédéric Worms, eds., *Henri Bergson et Albert Kahn, correspondances* (Strasbourg: Desmaret and Boulogne: Musée départemental Albert-Kahn, 2003), 76; Jay Winter, *Dreams of Peace and Freedom: Utopian Moments in the 20th Century* (New Haven: Yale University Press, 2006), ch. 1.

12. Fondation Albert Kahn, *Autour du Monde,* par les boursiers de voyage de l'Université de Paris (Paris: Félix Alcan, 1904), i.

13. Ibid., ii–iii.

14. Ibid.

15. Ibid., ii.

16. Chart compiled by Nathalie Clet-Bonnet, attachée de conservation, Musée départemental Albert Kahn, Boulogne-Billancourt, France. Among the British fellows was one woman, the medieval historian Eileen Power.

17. AN AJ 16 7004–7007 Bourses de voyage David Weill—Rapports, procès, verbaux, etc.

18. "First Annual Report of the Director," *Institute of International Education* Bulletin no. 1, 1920: 1, 2.

19. Stephen Mark Halpern, *The Institute of International Education: A History,* PhD dissertation, Columbia University, 1969, 45, 188. In Proquest Dissertations & Theses database, http://www.proquest.com (publication number AAT 7123595; accessed August 5, 2009). See also Stephen Duggan, *A Professor at Large* (New York: MacMillan Company, 1943).

20. "First Annual Report of the Director," *Institute of International Education,* Bulletin no. 1, 1920: 3–4.

21. Ibid., 6–7.

22. George Rock, *The History of the American Field Service, 1920–1955* (New York: Platen Press, 1956), http://www.ourstory.info/library/Rock/ROOTC.html.

23. "American Field Service Fellowships for French Universities, Inc.," *Institute of International Education,* 14th series, Bulletin no. 3, April 1, 1933: 1.

24. "Observations on Higher Education in Europe," *Institute of International Education,* Bulletin no. 3, 1920: 385–86. The IIE tracked numbers and origins of foreign students in the United States, and though it admitted to the limitations of its statistics (depending on the number of institutions reporting to them, whether or not summer sessions were included, etc.), their figures are, to my knowledge, the only ones available. It is important to note that the majority of foreign students in the United States in the 1920s came from Latin America and Asia, and the country with the most students in the United States was China, a pattern started with the use of the Boxer Rebellion Indemnity Scholarship Program to fund study in the United States for Chinese students. See Appendix 1.

Total numbers of foreign students in the United States often vary in different tables in different years. The IIE bulletins indicate that the number of American institutions reporting to the IIE increased over time. Consistently throughout the years, the highest numbers of foreign students were from China: 959 in 1919–1920, 1,240 in 1921–1922. Other nations represented in high numbers of foreign students in the United States include Canada, Japan, Mexico, Philippines, and Russia. Numbers from England and Germany rose throughout 1930s; numbers from Russia declined; numbers from Japan dropped from 1,419 in 1937–1938 to 306 in 1938–1939.

The numbers of American students and scholars in France peaked at 5,584 in 1928–1929, then declined during Depression. Figures are from Horatio S. Krans, "The American University Union in Europe," *Institute of International Education,* 17th series, Bulletin No. 4, October 1, 1936: 11.

25. Theodosia Hewlett, "A Decade of International Fellowships: A Survey of the Impressions of American and Foreign Ex-fellows," *Institute of International Education,* 11th series, Bulletin no. 2, June 1, 1930: 6 [foreword by Stephen P. Duggan].

26. "Seventh Annual Report of the Director," *Institute of International Education,* 7th series, Bulletin no. 2, December 31, 1926: 13–14.

27. "The Problem of Fellowships for Foreign Students in American Universities and Fellowships for American Students in Foreign Universities," *Institute of International Education,* 5th series, Bulletin no. 1, March 1, 1924: 1.

28. Ibid., 3.

29. Joan W. Scott, "The Evidence of Experience," *Critical Enquiry* 17 (Summer 1991): 773–97.

30. G. Weulersse, "L'Education publique aux Etats-Unis, impressions et réflexions," *Autour du Monde,* 385–418.

31. Madeleine Mignon, draft report, Albert Kahn Museum archives, Carton: Boursiers français M-W.

32. AN AJ 16/7021, Bourses de voyage autour du monde, suite. Dossiers individuels de boursiers, A-C. Folder: Allard-Bourgogne

33. Ivan M. Linforth, "Report to the Trustees," *Albert Kahn Foundation for the Travel of American Teachers: Reports,* vol. 2, no. 1 (New York: Printed by the Trustees, 1913), 25–26. This report was translated into French: Ch-M Garnier, "Le Rapport de M. Ivan M. Linforth," *Bulletin de la Société Autour du Monde* 3 (July 1914): 238–40.

34. Emile Hovelaque, "L'Opinion américaine et la guerre," *Bulletin de la Société Autour du Monde* 3 (January–April 1916): 48–68.

35. Anne Main, "De la neutralité à la guerre: notes d'un séjour à New York, 1916–1917," *Bulletin de la Société Autour du Monde* (November 1918): 37–56. Located in Albert Kahn Museum, Carton: Boursiers français M-W, folder: Main, Anne. Lauréate 1914.

36. "Allocation de M. Félicien Challaye, au nom de la fondation française," *Bulletin de la Société Autour du Monde,* 17th year (1930), only number (June 14, 1931) : xvi.

37. Ivan M. Linforth, "Nouvelle expérience d'entente internationale," *Bulletin de la Société Autour du Monde* 17 (June 14, 1931): 37–42.

38. Anna Amieux, a *boursière* in 1905, became director of the Ecole Normale Supérieure de Sèvres after 1919; Félicien Challaye (1900–1901) became an anticolonialist writer and activist. *Albert Kahn, 1860–1940,* 1, 146, 150–51, 157–67, 181–85.

39. Quoted in *Albert Kahn,* 238.

40. Quoted in *Albert Kahn,* 163.

41. André Siegfried, *Les Etats-Unis d'aujourd'hui* (Paris: Armand Colin, 1927); Georges Duhamel, *Scènes de la vie future* (1930). According to Pascal Ory, Duhamel's book was first published in April 1930. Pascal Ory, "From Baudelaire to Duhamel: An Unlikely Antipathy," in *The Rise and Fall of Anti-Americanism,* 42–54.

42. Edmée Hitzel, "Deuxième partie: Etats-Unis," *Bulletin de la Société Autour du Monde* (1929–1930): 48.

43. The IIE confidential archives are not available to the public according to an e-mail of June 30, 2008, from Becky Yi at the IIE, so this section relies on published bulletins and pamphlets.

44. "The Problem of Fellowships for Foreign Students in American Universities and Fellowships for American Students in Foreign Universities," *Institute of International Education,* 5th series, Bulletin no. 1 (March 1, 1924): 4–5, 11.

45. Theodosia Hewlett, "A Decade of International Fellowships: A Survey of the Impressions of American and Foreign Ex-fellows," *Institute of International Education,* 11th series, Bulletin No. 2, June 1, 1930: 10, 13–18.

46. Ibid., 19.

47. Ibid., 25–33.

48. "Impressions of American Field Service Fellows," *Institute of International Education,* 14th series, Bulletin no. 3 (April 1, 1933): 42.

49. Ibid., 40–41, 43–44, 48.

50. Ibid., 46, 42, 43, 45.

51. Maurice Caullery, "Les Clubs universitaires; la vie intellectuelle aux Etats-Unis," *Revue de Paris* 24, pt. 4 (1917): 333–48; Louis Vigouroux, "Les Universités américaines et la réforme de l'éducation en France," *La Revue scientifique* 56 (1918): 164–67; Ch. Guignebert, "Les Universités américaines et les notres," *Revue politique et littéraire* 56 (March 16, 1918): 171–73.

52. Gary N. Calkins, "France and Modern Science," *Institute of International Education,* 8th series, Bulletin no. 3 (November 1, 1927): 20–25.

53. AN AJ 16 7006 and 7007 Rapports des boursiers David Weill A-M, 1910–1939, N-W 1910–1939.

54. "Seventeenth annual report of the director," *Institute of International Education,* 17th series, Bulletin No. 5, October 15, 1936: 3–5.

55. "Fifteenth Annual Report of the Director," *Institute of International Education,* 15th series, Bulletin no. 3, October 1, 1934: 9

56. Nancy L. Green, "The Comparative Gaze: Travelers in France before the Era of Mass Tourism," *French Historical Studies* 25 (Summer 2002): 423–40.

57. "Seventeenth annual report of the director," *Institute of International Education,* 17th series, Bulletin No. 5, October 15, 1936: 10.

58. Etienne Dennery, "A French Economist's Visit to Western Colleges," *Institute of International Education,* Pamphlet series no. 1, April 15, 1936: 1–17.

59. Frank A. Ninkovich, *The Diplomacy of Ideas: U.S. Foreign Policy and Cultural Relations, 1938–1950* (Cambridge: Cambridge University Press, 1981); Halpern, *The Institute of International Education,* ch. 6.

60. "The Institute of International Education 1919–1944: Its Aims and Achievements during Twenty-Five Years," *Institute of International Education,* Pamphlet series no. 9, September 1, 1944: 8, 18.

61. Whitney Walton, *Internationalism, National Identities, and Study Abroad: France and the United States, 1890–1970* (Stanford: Stanford University Press, 2010). Small portions of this essay also appear in chapter 2 of my book.

62. Scott-Smith, *Networks of Empire;* Bu, *Making the World Like Us;* Halpern, *The Institute of International Education.*

63. See Whitney Walton, "Internationalism and the Junior Year Abroad: American Students in France in the 1920s and 1930s," *Diplomatic History* 29 (April 2005): 255–78; Whitney Walton, "American Girls and French *Jeunes Filles:* Negotiating National Identities in Interwar France," *Gender & History* 17 (August 2005): 325–53.

PART 2

German Travelers in the United States

Social Crossings: German Leftists View "Amerika" and Reflect Themselves, 1870–1914

Dieter K. Buse

After five weeks, I thought I knew everything about England.
After five years, I knew that I had to start to get to know it.
—*Wilhelm Liebknecht, 1887*

In early studies of the great migration river that swept millions of people from Europe to the Americas, some undercurrents were not given much attention. One was return migration, which has been charted in the last decades and in some years found to be as high as 30 percent.[1] Returnees reraise the question of what repelled as well as what drew migrants. Another, smaller but important undercurrent was the Atlantic crossing of entrepreneurs, who were learning commercial systems and exchanging goods.[2] Entrepreneurial travels reraise the question of the common elements within the production and commercial systems on both sides of the Atlantic.

Less defined by historical studies is the mass of laborers who constituted a large portion of the migrants, especially those from German-speaking countries. Some brought hopes of finding social equality in America, others intended to create new social landscapes. German migrants brought organizational concepts such as social clubs across the Atlantic. Endless choral societies, workingmen's clubs, theater groups, and poetry societies illustrated the first generation's transport of home culture.[3] However, the lower-class German migrants' establishment of unions, a labor press, socialist organizations, and anarchist societies has received little attention, mostly because World War I buried many of them.[4] Having a German past became suspect and even organizations dedicated to entertainment or heritage declined until post–World War II revivals.[5]

Many concepts have been employed in studies seeking to understand the interplay between Germans and Americans: encounters, transfers, interaction, common space, transnational institutions, feminist dialogue, and cultural borrowing, among others.[6] "Social crossings" can be added because some leftist travelers highlighted social issues, conditions, and reform, and even revolutionary transformation as they viewed America.

One set of nineteen-century travelers from Germany belonged to the union and socialist movements that were strong both in Europe and North America before World War I. They came to observe the progress of related movements that fought for social justice and democracy. Often forgotten is that the modern concept and practice of "democracy," meaning universal suffrage regardless of race, gender, religious affiliation, or registration restrictions, is a very recent development. Mostly the political left advocated and advanced that cause.[7] All the travelers examined in this chapter were astute observers and they described more than the American working-class movements at whose invitation they mostly traveled. They commented on landscapes, social customs, and styles of life. They too shaped the *Amerikabild* of Germans, their view of Americans, though they are infrequently acknowledged in studies of travel literature.[8] Well-educated, they wrote books, long letters, and newspaper articles about their observations. In addition, they sent children and friends notes and postcards about their American adventures, sights seen, and oddities observed, which included sharing stereotypes of their era. Their *Amerikabild* offered a novel perspective since, in addition to tourist meccas, they visited work and living spaces, and mostly were in contact with lower-class persons or their representatives. Though the views they held shifted during their travels, to a large extent their findings reflected themselves. That reflection will be explored to show the contrasting views of leftist German travelers.

The Travelers and the American Situation

By the middle of the nineteenth century a variety of images of America had been established and discussed among Europeans. Slogan-like, vague assertions predominated. "Land of freedom," "land of liberty," land of revolution," "land without history," and "land without aristocracy and status": the United States was called all of these. "Corrupted republicanism" and "democracy" were frequently cited.[9] Nearly all views served the political purposes of some group advocating or opposing what the American Revolution had instituted. But until mid-century, emigration remained limited, the mail very slow, and travelers' accounts sporadic. By the 1880s, with extensive migration, telegraph, mail packets, and steamboats, the exchange became regular and the reports much more frequent and lengthy.[10]

From among those increasing numbers of travelers, emphasis here will be on four male leftist internationalists and their travel companions, including an astute woman. Their writings were chosen—there are few from which to select—because of the fullness of their accounts and the similarity of places visited. Further, they represent a wide strand of ideological stances, and their accounts span two generations of observations. Wilhelm Liebknecht, a moderate German Social Democratic leader who tried to explain European social and political trends to Americans in the early 1870s, visited in 1886. His three-month tour took him through northeastern cities together with Eleanor Marx, Karl Marx's daughter, and her husband Edward Aveling, who were not German but published in Germany. Liebknecht's son Karl Liebknecht, who represented radical antimilitarists among the second generation of German socialists, came in 1910 for five weeks, going across the northeast, then to California and New Orleans. Friedrich Engels, Karl Marx's partner and administrator of his publications, took a short tour, mostly of the northeastern states and into southern Canada in 1888. He came to improve his health, see friends, and partly to supervise translation of his and Marx's writings. He too traveled with Eleanor Marx and Aveling. By contrast, a moderate and one of Germany's leading trade unionists, Carl Legien, spent four months during 1912 in the United States after much preparation, including reading guides such as *Baedeker.* The purposes of these trips varied, but all the travelers had connections to emigrants and American socialist or union organizations.

Sometimes the extent of labor and socialist organizations in America before World War I is forgotten. Or current prejudices are projected backward to avoid considering workers who were eking out a living under horrendous conditions. Those conditions of early industrialization received attention, even in semi-fictional form, by Americans of the day such as Rebecca Davis in *Life in the Iron-Mills,* serialized in the *Atlantic Monthly* during 1861. They were confirmed, especially during the 1890s, by many American social reformers of the time and by a thorough commission of industrial relations just before World War I. Those accounts found hovels instead of housing, and reported on dangerous work and lack of sanitation. Social historians have detailed the extent of child labor, rotating bed usage at boarding houses, violent repression of efforts to improve working conditions, unwillingness to institute an eight-hour working day, unemployment during bust times, electoral manipulation, racism, and segregation of late-nineteenth-century America.[11] Like their European reformist counterparts, Americans created movements of protest in response to such conditions. Much of what those movements advocated on both sides of the Atlantic was maintaining basic human dignity with respect to work, education, and civil rights. Most of their proposals now do not seem very radical, except in some cases seeking to go beyond regulation toward imposing social equality. Given the shared views of the guides from the American labor movement and the leftist German travelers, how did the latter see "Amerika"?

Wilhelm Liebknecht's Amerikabild *of Exceptionalism*

Wilhelm Liebknecht was originally planning to visit the United States with the other main leader of German Social Democracy, August Bebel.[12] They wanted to raise money for their social reform cause, which had been partly driven underground by Otto von Bismarck's repressive Anti-Socialist Law of 1878. As the two main founders and unifiers of the German Social Democrats, Liebknecht and Bebel influenced the development of social reform movements in a number of countries, including the United States, and especially among migrant Germans. Before World War I, the German Social Democratic Party (SPD) would come to be seen as the model mass party in the international movement for social reform.[13]

After theological studies Liebknecht participated in the Revolution of 1848, which sought to implement such basic civil rights as freedom of speech and freedom of assembly.[14] During its repression he went into exile in England from 1850 to 1862. There he met Karl Marx and Friedrich Engels and accepted much of their understanding of class, history, and politics. During 1870–1871 he had opposed the Franco-Prussian War and spent two years in jail for "treason"; later he would again be exiled, to Switzerland and England. All observers, even the Prussian secret police, noted that Liebknecht spoke clearly and to the point.[15] He had a pragmatic, open-minded outlook. Liebknecht's famous phrase "knowledge is power" (*Wissen ist Macht*) was more repeated than understood. It had a double meaning: "*Bildung*" (self-development) meant empowerment for the individual, while workers' awareness of their class situation, interests, and rights meant understanding the possibility of achieving change. Learning thus formed one of Liebknecht's basic principles, and he could put his skills of observation as a former journalist, including fluency in English, to use during the trip. By his commitment, popular phrases, and informed writings on history and contemporary problems, as well as his adroit tactics, he became known to social activists around the world. It was in that capacity the American socialists invited him to visit.

By the 1870s Liebknecht had an idealized image of the United States: "Composed of free citizens belonging to every nationality and race, you are no nation, but the greatest people of the world."[16] After outlining the Social Democratic demands in Germany for universal suffrage, free education, separation of church and state, free press and assembly, and limited working hours (especially for women and children), he argued that these unaccomplished goals showed how "backward" Europeans were. They did not have "the blessings of the political liberty" that Americans enjoyed.[17] In Germany by comparison he found political and press corruption under "military despotism."[18] For one German industrial area he cited a doctor who found "[t]he men stunted, weak, the women sickly, the children growing up into men still more stunted and weak," eating mostly potatoes to survive.[19] He concluded "that in the American union the people are all, and that in the German mock-confederacy they are nothing."[20] This idealized image of America Liebknecht took on his voyage.

Liebknecht visited the United States for three months during 1886. He spoke in German and English to huge crowds of both German and English audiences, some twenty-five thousand in New York according to the New Haven *Workmen's Advocate* of September 26, 1886. New Haven (in Germania Hall), Detroit, and Milwaukee witnessed massive receptions accompanied by the playing of the French "Marseillaise," symbolizing liberty, fraternity, and equality. In Chicago, where the Haymarket massacre had placed the city in a state of siege, he challenged the anarchists' violent approach to social change. At the end of his trip, when the Socialist Singing Society presented Heinrich Heine's poem "Weavers" at the Cooper Union in New York, Liebknecht commented (as reported in the *Workmen's Advocate* of December 5), that in the United States he had found "a large, intelligent audience of Socialists." He noted that bourgeois journalists had "at first misrepresented the movement; they confounded us with Anarchists, dynamiters, and goodness knows what. Toward the end of my visit I have noticed a marked improvement."[21]

Liebknecht's visit, starting September 13, 1886, was billed as an agitation tour, seeking monies to support the repressed movement in Germany. Under Bismarck's Anti-Socialist Law, the Social Democrats were allowed to participate in elections for parliament but not allowed to maintain their organization or agitate on behalf of their cause. Some eight hundred persons went into exile, and the movement operated with an underground organization until 1890 when the law and others that had followed it were terminated. Liebknecht returned to Europe in December 1886, while his companions stayed until January 1887. The trip was carefully observed by the German state representatives in Washington, who hired a Pinkerton agent to follow them around the country to report their speeches and meetings.[22] Liebknecht traveled some three thousand miles and covered primarily the industrializing strip between Boston and St. Louis, Missouri.[23]

Within a year Liebknecht published a substantial book, *Ein Blick in die Neue Welt* (Views of the New World), about his American experiences. Composed mainly of his letters and journals, this work generally offered a very positive view of the United States. However, Liebknecht could be critical, saying that he was shocked that "in this free land that people could be condemned to death with no evidence."[24] In general, Liebknecht's book helped many German workers see the New World as a land of opportunities. In workingmen's lending libraries in Germany it was among the most popular of the circulated travel literature.[25]

Putting his observations in context, and offering an insight on travel writing, Liebknecht later modestly acknowledged how little knowledge outsiders could acquire about other societies.[26] That applies also to Liebknecht's 300-page book which reinforced the idea of American exceptionalism. Though most countries have a tradition of seeing themselves as special and different, this tendency has been particularly strong among Americans. However, in the last decades the concept has been much challenged.[27]

In Liebknecht's book descriptive observations predominate. New York did not meet his expectations. It lacked the noise and the bustle he anticipated, being outstripped by Berlin. Broadway, about which he had read so much, seemed less pretty than Regent Street in London: "The dirt in the streets and the poor quality of paving are immediately noticeable . . . one almost sank in them . . . garbage lay everywhere."[28] He complained about custom controls, lack of beer gardens, and oppressive heat, but appreciated the elevated railways, abundance and variety of fruit, and the high quality of California wines—predicting that American wine production would outpace that of Europe. Some of the street observations are amusing: well-behaved horses, dogs, and cats, but rowdy children, especially the boys. Some descriptions appear outlandish from our perspective. For instance, he asserted, "The real American wears wool underwear throughout the entire year, while the German immigrant does not follow this example and wears his customary linen shirts thus becoming a victim of rheumatism."[29] He commented on social and cultural differences such as a huge advertisement revealing a number of women whose lower parts were as "décolleté as their upper." He claimed to have seen more women's legs in advertising in New York during eight days than in his whole life, yet among Americans the use of the word "leg" was considered impolite, and in the presence of ladies even "shocking."[30] Many such references to past practices in American life—from the opulence of its railways, to the good service in its hotels without tipping, the poor quality of singing (perhaps due to the climate)—can be seen as a charming collection of superficialities, though revealing of social attitudes.[31]

Liebknecht found the children well fed, asserting that many ate more meat per day than some Germans consumed in three months. But that did not mean hunger did not exist. He thought that the limits of laissez-faire had been reached, as Americans saw that it led to anarchy.[32] Liebknecht maintained that Americans would eventually advance to the forefront of civilization because they were so unencumbered by any past, hence repeating the "land without history" theme. Speaking with an acquaintance who had gone to the United States as a laborer and become a well-off factory owner employing five hundred workers, he heard that the German workers had to adjust to the faster pace of American production. However, he added that within a year of arrival they adapted, and he thought it laudable that assimilation was so thorough in America.[33]

Distances and remarks about distance figure large in all such travelers' accounts. Liebknecht noted that a place five hours distant by express train was considered "nearby."[34] Comparisons of the passing landscapes and forests to those in eastern Germany dotted his text, and he found many parks grander and strikingly different.[35] Regarding urban attributes, in Philadelphia he had reservations about claims to its being the "most American" of American cities, since he later found just as much of the "go-ahead" spirit in Chicago and Milwaukee. Though few Philadelphia streets were found to be impressive, he listed the many imposing buildings, including the railway stations, which could match those of Europe. He extolled the new marble-covered city hall and Independence Hall.

He also lauded American railways and the gentlemanly behavior of Americans, who he claimed had "no lower class"–a surprising claim for a socialist witnessing segregation.[36] This was offered on the way to New Haven, about which he pointed to the size of the city, so spread out compared to European ones. There he stayed in what he considered his "first pure American hotel," referring to its exemplary service.[37] Since Liebknecht, Eleanor

Marx, and Edward Aveling had meetings in a different city nearly every day, these travelers became experts on train travel, hotels, hotel food, and bars, including the hypocrisy surrounding prohibition of alcohol. After Maine enacted prohibition in 1851 a few states tried to follow, but the constitutionality of such laws was successfully challenged. In the 1890s only six states had prohibition, but by 1917 eighteen states were dry. In addition, many local communities restricted saloons and drinking establishments. But the travelers' image of America also included more substantial issues, such as the state of education, Americans' self-image, the nation's cultural level compared to Europe, and the status of women, Native Americans, and African Americans.

Education deeply interested Liebknecht and he sought to inform himself directly. He observed teaching in New York schools, spoke with German émigrés about their children's development, and gathered information about the state of public education and its financing. His findings were highly positive. For instance, he reported that an innkeeper of German background "could not praise the schools enough. All instruction is free, all school books and supplies are free and every boy and girl can choose their educational path."[38] After discussions with people who knew both the German and the American system, Liebknecht concluded: "the American public school achieves more than the German."[39] American children read, wrote, and calculated better, he claimed after examining children's exercise books. Furthermore, in geographic and historical understanding the Germans could "in no way measure up." He participated in a history examination of twelve-year-olds in New York and found "the fostering of independent thinking runs as a red thread through the whole curriculum."[40] He applauded that religious instruction remained private.

Some surprising assertions appear about his visit to a school in which only fifty of twelve hundred children were not German. He stated: "One must remember that the Jews here, as nearly everywhere in foreign countries, are considered to be German. In some classes all the children without exception speak German."[41] Many of the children, though, did not want to be considered German. Along the same vein, he made much of the need to have clean and tidy schoolbooks, as he thought it helped learning. His own concepts of culture and education are revealed by his statements on the need for good quality paper and sturdy notebooks as found in America. He maintained that the "American way" was as it should be among all people, adding that by this he meant "of course cultivated people [*Kulturvölker*]."[42] In such claims Liebknecht revealed much about how he saw cultural others, and that he was prepared to criticize Germany's comparative shortcomings.

Liebknecht found that he had to relinquish some preconceptions as he traveled. However, he knew before he came that the United States was "a new world" of gigantic proportions and that Americans were convinced "that America was the biggest, most beautiful, richest, best governed and best administered country in the world."[43] Nowhere else had he found such striving to be the first and such energy to be foremost. He opined, "Such a people must become the leading people of the earth—if they are not already,"[44] because of their liberal outlook. He found that these beliefs came combined with knowledge, though primarily limited to American heroes of the revolutionary era. A more skeptical immigrant told Liebknecht that he overestimated Americans, who were really "very narrow-minded and conservative," in response to which Liebknecht argued that democratic societies were always conservative as they had much to defend.[45] That included the high social status of women, because equality was no mere concept in America but, in his idealistic overestimate, a "living principle: The rights of man have evolved into the rights of humanity."[46] Here he placed America on a "higher cultural level" than his own country. He argued the case, as he did in his speeches in Germany and the United States, for women's right to vote. In support he cited the case of a woman who had studied medicine and now had her own practice. She was for him "A lady *comme il faut*—a real American woman."[47]

Native Americans interested most travelers to the United States. Liebknecht gained some of his ideas about them through a visit to Bill Cody's Wild West Show on Staten Island where he saw "representatives of various tribes and Texas Vaqueros and cowboys." On what basis he decided that these "examples of the populace of the wild west" all appeared to be "real" is left unclear. Certainly it made an impression: "The riding skills, the shooting displays, the buffalo chase (real buffalos!), the fight between cowboys and Indians. . . . I lived for a few hours in the wild west."[48] Liebknecht generally had sympathy with natives, as illustrated by his comments about historic sites in Pennsylvania when he underscored that William Penn was the only leader to have kept a treaty with them. However, like many contemporaries, he assumed that they would disappear, overrun by the march of "civilization." He posed the question as to whether it had to happen, then accepted it as fate. "From among the Indians, as with the buffalo, bears, and elks, examples remain, they are even carefully preserved and here and there displayed before a curious audience, but these sad remains are only living monuments—under them a race has been buried."[49]

The "peculiar institution" of slavery and its portentous aftermath were commented upon by almost all travelers to the United States. Some observers merely repeated the racial and negative stereotypes about "the Negro" common to Western civilization in the nineteenth century. Liebknecht too posed naive questions about the diligence and the learning abilities of African Americans, to which he received the reply that their learning faculties were the same in the young but declined rapidly in puberty.[50] While he applauded the "cleansing of the blot of slavery,"[51] he astutely noted that emancipation had not altered the separation of races: "Paradoxical as it may seem, the abolition of slavery has not reduced the distance between Negroes and whites, but rather increased it."[52] Yet, earlier he proved to be colorblind when he claimed that "the republic of the star-spangled banner has no second-class citizens."[53]

Liebknecht saw a state and society that generally fostered human rights. However, that same state tolerated the use of crude security guards, namely the Pinkertons. That security agency was especially infamous for its violent attacks upon strikers and protesters. Liebknecht asked how a "modern state could tolerate medieval *condottieri*," namely Italian warlords.[54] Similarly, he strongly criticized the extensive use of child and female labor with few laws and little protection.

Liebknecht judged countries according to their development on the way to "civilization." Hence he much applauded the United States because he found that Europe "with its 1500 years of cultural development. . . . is two-thirds, if not three-quarters, living in semi-barbarism."[55] He added that undoubtedly much was unfinished in America, especially in the West, but asserted that "in the middle of the wilderness oases of highest culture spring forth." By contrast, civilization was moving at a snail's pace in eastern and southern Europe. Noting the negative comments about North America by English people, he attributed their enmity to jealousy and contrasted American advances to the disunity of Germans who could not move beyond their petty state differences. Anticipating that some might think that he painted a very rosy picture of American conditions, Liebknecht countered that he simply reported what he found. What filled him with "amazement" was "that the cultural differences there are much less than in the European, so-called civilized states."[56] In Europe he still found places mired in the eighteenth, seventeenth, and even the sixteenth centuries, because if examined thoroughly "our much reputed culture is only the possession, or monopoly, of a tiny group of selected persons." This praise of America was circumscribed by reservations about the need to overcome the excesses of individualism. However, what became clear to him through his voyage was "how superficial our old-world culture, as well as how few the crumbs which fell off the rich table of civilization" for the majority.[57]

Comparative Aside: Eleanor Marx and Edward Aveling

Liebknecht's associates, Eleanor Marx and Edward Aveling, wrote a lengthy study, *The Working-Class Movement in America* (1886), the second edition appearing in 1891 (reprinted in 2000). Who would have thought that European leftists would write a chapter on cowboys? In "The Cowboy," Marx and Aveling present cowhands as "proletarians" instead of fostering the prevalent stereotype of a "'bold, bad man,' as reckless of the lives of others as of his own, with vague ideas as to morals, and especially as to the rights of property; generally full of whiskey, and always handy with a revolver."[58] Marx and Aveling recount how they met their first cowboys in Cincinnati on a visit to a dime museum, where one spoke: "To our great astonishment he plunged at once into a denunciation of capitalists in general and of the ranch owners in particular."[59] This chance encounter they followed up with a private meeting at which they heard the cowboys' complaints, which the western newspapers allegedly refused to print. Marx and Aveling then outlined the number working as cowhands (over ten thousand), their lack of representation, poor pay, long hours, solitary existence, bad "grub," and repression by the cattlemen. The cowboys hoped for some league, which Marx and Aveling prophesied would soon be created, especially to fight "repleving" of cattle, namely owners taking away unbranded individual cattle mostly owned by cowboys. The prediction would prove wrong.

Marx and Aveling's book had a different purpose than Liebknecht's. They sought to influence both the American and European protest movements. Hence, they stated immediately: "The working-class question is the same in America as in Europe."[60] They outlined their credentials, including having worked on similar issues in Britain, having toured the United States for fifteen weeks, and having read much of its extensive labor press, listing titles that run for over two pages. Like Liebknecht they were assailed by the upper-class press, such as the *New York Times,* but thought that they had received a fair hearing from workers. They gathered facts and generalizations which they wanted to put before a broad public. Hence, their work offered the following categories as the organizing themes of their book (quite different from Liebknecht's chronological approach): general impressions, general conditions of workers, the conduct of employers, wages, work and methods of living, woman and child labor, organizations, Knights of Labor, unions, socialist parties, cowboys, anarchists, and labor leaders, followed by a statistical appendix. They painted a negative portrait of the United States, finding that "in this country of extremes, those of poverty and wealth, of exploitation . . . are more marked than in Europe."[61] The parallels they found were with the England of the 1830s when child labor, slum housing, and factory inspections shocked many contemporaries. Their account is full of statistics. They reported that in New York the number of children of school age was 1.6 million, with just over 1 million registered, but that daily attendance was 583,000. In Michigan, they wrote, inspectors found in seventy-one establishments in forty-six towns some 292 boys and 62 girls aged eight to fourteen employed; in Detroit it was ninety-two establishments with 287 boys and 85 girls between ten and fifteen working.[62] Regarding working women they reported that factory inspectors could not understand how women survived on their low wages, with prostitution often filling the gap.[63] Marx and Aveling's analytical study combined systematic research with their experiences, thus going beyond the personal reporting of most travel writing.[64]

More in keeping with traditional accounts of personal sojourns, in 1887 Aveling separately published *An American Journey,* a lengthy account based on his notes and letters. He hardly acknowledged his wife or Liebknecht as companions during his fifteen-month stay. He prefaced his book by claiming to have encountered "Americans of all grades of society, and all shades of opinion." Most of the book consists of reprints from pieces published in American and English newspapers and journals. Much more descriptive than the book coauthored with his wife, Aveling's travelogue allows comparisons with how Liebknecht simultaneously observed the United States as well as with Legien's later experiences, in particular his descriptions of traveling, hotels and people's habits.

Aveling insisted that he provided an "unprejudiced record, made at the time and on the spot . . . of first impressions."[65] Sometimes travel accounts amount to one first impression piled upon another, and only a small part of Aveling's 250 pages need be drawn upon to contrast with or confirm Liebknecht's observations. Aveling too went to Buffalo Bill's Wild West show, despite his reservations about its hideous billboards everywhere in New York. He admitted to being "excited" during the performance, and wrote that he saw "the most interesting show in the most interesting country. The Wild West is an attempt to bring home to the mind of the town dweller, life and death in the Rocky Mountains, where the wave of savage life is beating itself out against the rock of an implacably advancing civilization. Over a large open space, partly surrounded by raised seats, Indians, Mexicans, cowboys, mustangs, elks and buffalo process [parade?], race, shoot, dance, jump, throw lariats, carry imaginary mails by pony express, rope and ride Texas steers, attack stage coaches and settlers' cabins, kill one another, and generally carry on after the wild, free and not very easy fashion of the West."[66] Like Liebknecht, he found it entrancing: "This fascination is in part due to coming face to face with conditions that in some sense represent our own ancestral ones. Those dusky Indians, with their unearthly streaks of color on their faces and with their weird, monotonous and hollow cries, as they ride past, fine as many of the faces are, yet remind us of the earlier forms of savage man whence we have evolved, not by any manner of means always in the right direction." Evidence of Europeans not evolving in the right manner could be found in Aveling's own linguistic lapse when he described an angered servant as going into a "true nigger dance."[67]

In addition to assumptions shared with Liebknecht about "advancing civilization," Aveling offered views on train travel, hotel and bar life, personal habits, and hypocrisy about drinking (such as "blind pigs"—a system where buyers and sellers could not see each other), and often witty comments appear in his chapters on American travel, habits, journalism, and theatre. For him, Kansas City and Washington represented America's extremes of roughness and refinement. Like Liebknecht he experienced New York as ugly, muddy, "over-eager to get rich,"[68] even ill-mannered. A blizzard in Minneapolis he found intriguing, as he did the journey of ten miles in five hours from St. Paul: "strangest sight of snow-veiled land."[69]

Aveling did not offer much on women, though he was impressed by female teachers. For him the problem was that almost all the women, as chewers of gum and takers of snuff with little spoons, shared the bad habits of the men. He castigated as immoral the men's foul habits of spitting everywhere, not using handkerchiefs, rarely bathing, cleaning their nails in public, and spewing lewd language. He decried the endless spitting into and beside the spittoons, on sidewalks, and all over bars. In general Americans were found to be "very, very dirty people" at all levels of society.[70] Everywhere the hotels lacked baths; if available they were only infrequently useable. As an example among many, he recounted his experience at the German-American Hotel in New York where he had discovered a bathing place in the evening. Next morning he went for a bath but since there was no lock on the door a boy entered—while Aveling was scrubbing himself—and wanted to know what he was doing. Aveling was in the vat in which they washed the vegetables.[71] Aveling cemented his argument about dirty people by outlining the difficulties caused for one head of a library: he was heavily criticized for having removed the spittoons and forcing people to spit outside. That librarian had even closed the washroom "because people were so dirty."[72] Though the "hotels of America compare most favorably with those of Europe,"[73] Aveling could not understand the few baths and limited food times. What most disturbed him were the "indecent" pictures in the bars.[74]

Like Liebknecht, Aveling was very impressed by American education, its facilities, its training of staff, and especially that it was all free. In Boston he found "magnificent buildings" with many meeting and play rooms.[75] Though some of the Latin recitations were dull, the language instruction was of the "best." In one class he found "true teaching," as questions were employed to force thinking. He summarized, "The stay in America did much to disabuse my mind of the idea, on the whole, they manage things better than over on the other side of the Atlantic. . . . But on one matter America is assuredly . . . more happily circumstanced . . . that is in respect to education."[76] Like Liebknecht he went into schools as well as colleges, noting the student-to-teacher ratio: 56 to 1 in the lowest and 38 to 1 in the higher. However, of Boston's twenty-four thousand school-age children, about eight thousand were totally absent. Truant officers found over two thousand of them, some as young as twelve, working. Aveling looked a bit more closely at the social situation of education than Liebknecht, and again child labor appeared as an American failing to visitors.

Friedrich Engels's Ambiguities

Friedrich Engels, the entrepreneur and social analyst, was also often in exile after participating in the Revolution of 1848. Well before his trip to the United States, in January 1887, Engels wrote to an American reformer, Florence Kelley, who had offered to translate his writings, that some "Americans think their country exempt from the consequences of fully expanded capitalist production."[77] He pointed to the labor bureaus created in Massachusetts, New Jersey, Pennsylvania, and Ohio to illustrate that these states had needed to undertake measures to improve working conditions. By mid-year Engels recorded that the American Knights of Labor had increased from 104,000 to 720,000 members during 1886–1887; thus American workers were moving in the right direction. In particular, he maintained that the "delusion" that "America stood above class antagonisms and struggles,"[78] was being broken. His American correspondent, however, argued that U.S. labor leaders mostly continued to preach harmony between capital and labor, and so workers were in a state of confusion. Partly to see for himself and partly to recuperate his health, Engels went to the United States, which he had in 1886 termed "the most progressive land in the world."[79]

Engels had been a careful observer of the American scene for decades and thought that the American pattern of economic and social developments might be similar to the European. For the preface of the 1887 U.S. edition of his classic study *The Condition of the English Working Class,* Engels noted the current upswing in massive strikes and worker organizations. The sources of the conflict between labor and capital he found were "the same in America as in Europe." Yet he concluded that the situation proved to be a "true American contradictory puzzle."[80] That phrase summarizes the ambiguities that Engels observed and reported.

Engels toured from August 8 to September 27, 1887.[81] He visited fourteen cities, many in upstate New York. He went to ports and industrial centers such as Boston, New York, Buffalo, and Albany, smaller centers such as Hoboken, Concord (Massachusetts), Cambridge, and Roxbury, and tourist places such as Niagara Falls, Plattsburgh, and Lake Placid. He also crossed over into Canada where he traveled from Toronto to Montreal via Port Hope and Kingston. He had contacts, such as Friedrich Sorge, one of the exiled Germans who led American socialist groups, and could thus gather information and obtain entry to factories. He was positively impressed by a prison, the "reformatory" in Concord, where "prisoners could read novels and non-fiction, create clubs,"[82] and had pictures and running water in all cells. On the return voyage he wrote of being rejuvenated by upstate New York where hotels were excellent, the wine passable, and German-style beer available.[83]

Engels's extensive correspondence revealed his assumptions regarding "how essential the Americans' feverish spirit of speculation is to the rapid development of a new country."[84] However, he never made use of the notes of his travels to create a real travelogue. Those notes suggest his continued ambivalence: "Country of unexpected contrasts: more railways than roads and the latter appalling . . . elevated railways above and dreadful pavement below—log cabins but carpets and pianos inside. . . . Go-ahead nation—

pushing past, not being able to see anyone walking or standing in front of them . . . women too. Spitting—privies—hypocrisy about drink not only in prohibition states . . . All aesthetics trampled underfoot as soon as monetary profit comes in view. . . . Americans no nation. 5–6 different types. . . . and the feeling that they have in them the making *of the greatest nation of the 20th century.*"[85]

After Engels's return to Europe he continued to share his views, as on October 8, 1888: "I found America most interesting. It is a place one really must have seen with one's own eyes, this country whose history goes back no further than commodity production and which is the promised land of capitalist production. People's usual conceptions of it are as false as those a German schoolboy has of France."[86] He specified some of those misconceptions, including the idea of a classless society. Generally, he distinguished between the built environment and nature, stating that with the exception of the Statue of Liberty most of what was created by humans was "horrid," repeating the "land without culture" slogan. By contrast, at Niagara he found parks "without police and with safe stairs . . . a thing you do not find anywhere in such places in Europe." Further, the state of New York had a "wonderful setting" and "much natural beauty to be enjoyed at Niagara, on the St. Lawrence, in the Adirondacks."[87]

Engels perceived the United States differently than Liebknecht, while reiterating some of Aveling's findings on Americans' bad habits, despite traveling nearly at the same time and covering some of the same places, sometimes with the same companions. In the 1880s no one leftist view of America existed, any more than there was one middle-class reformist or conservative or aristocratic view of the changing land.

Karl Liebknecht: Idealism Tested and Stereotypes Confirmed

Since Georg Forster wrote his bestselling "philosophic travel report" about his round-the-world expedition with James Cook at the end of the eighteenth century, many have seen travel writing as "*Wahrnehmung der Fremde*" [acknowledgment of the foreign], sometimes termed "experiencing the Other." Forster himself spoke of the "nice appearance of diversity," while another famous German traveler, Alexander von Humboldt, sought to find "the unity within diversity." Perhaps critical leftist travelers, in keeping with Humboldt, suggest another approach to transoceanic reconnaissance, namely noting and exposing the similar. Certainly, after the great burst of industrialization at the end of the nineteenth century, the United States provided opportunities to witness many social similarities with Europe. That is precisely what Karl Liebknecht observed during and after his agitation tour.

By 1910 Liebknecht was well known in Germany and in left-wing circles abroad. He had made a reputation advocating the end of military conscription in a society where that institution had very high status.[88] Like his father, he ended in jail on numerous occasions for his beliefs and because he supposedly had insulted the emperor and imperial institutions. He remained a strident and assertive radical socialist all his life.

Karl Liebknecht's *Amerikabild* of 1910 is not pretty. In Newark on October 10 he asserted: "Today's America is no longer America. It is no longer the land of Columbus or Washington, the land of freedom. America has to be rediscovered. It again needs to be freed. . . . And its liberator can be none other than the working populace . . . They must become the discoverers and liberators of America."[89]

From October 14 to November 7 Liebknecht held speeches in almost the same industrial rectangle—St. Paul, Minnesota, to St. Louis, Missouri, to Wilmington, Delaware, to Manchester, Massachusetts—that his father had traversed. He added a sightseeing tour to California and New Orleans before leaving New York on November 30 and returning to Germany on December 7.[90] Liebknecht spoke as an ideological agitator, but he had also informed himself about conditions and attitudes in America. He placed his information within a pattern he thought applied to the whole industrial world of capitalism and imperialism. Among American socialists he received a very positive reception.[91]

American socialism, during the time of his father's and Engels's visits, had been a movement primarily of emigrant Germans, but by the turn of the twentieth century, it was a mass movement growing among all laboring groups, especially in industrializing centers. By 1912, the "Socialist party had elected some twelve hundred local officials and thirty-three state legislators, and controlled municipal governments in such cities as Schenectady, Milwaukee and Berkeley," and Eugene V. Debs obtained nine hundred thousand votes in the presidential election that year.[92] Simultaneously in the textile industry, Jewish socialists and unions had strong representation in the northeastern cities, especially New York, as well as Chicago and Cleveland. The socialists had some influence in the American Federation of Labor (AFL), though by 1910 loyalties were divided between two major factions, namely the left radical Industrial Workers of the World (the Wobblies) versus the moderates and business unionism under Samuel Gompers in the AFL.

This labor and political movement, together with middle-class reformers and suffragists, challenged America's elite during the era of trusts, repressed strikes such as at Pullman in 1894, and horrendous working conditions, including the extensive use of unregulated female and child labor. One example: "By 1911, more than two million American children under the age of 16 were working—many of them 12 hours or more, six days a week. Often they toiled in unhealthful and hazardous conditions; always for minuscule wages."[93] Further, Florence Kelley, who worked with orphans and homeless people in Chicago's slums, became the first female factory inspector in Illinois. She unearthed horrid working and living conditions, but lacked support to enforce the meager laws. In her memoirs she related what she experienced during the 1890s: "Hull-House was surrounded in every direction by homework carried on under the sweating system. From the age of eighteen months few children able to sit in high chairs at tables were safe from being required to pull basting threads. . . . the [kindergarten-age ones] used coarse sharp needles for sewing buttons on garments . . . [often] the children fell asleep at their work in their homes."[94] She pointed to the "smoke, soot, crude [and] uncoordinated building," and spread of diseases such as smallpox by contaminated cloth and lack of vaccination."[95] That was the America at which Liebknecht pointed an accusing finger and which he wanted changed.

Liebknecht thought he saw in the United States similarities with the political and economic rule in Germany and he hoped for a similar outcome—namely a socialist transformation of both. Though acknowledging that a wider suffrage existed in America, he noted that the ruling class employed the military against strikers just as in Germany. He asserted on October 12, 1910, "There is no great difference between the United States and Germany. There is no great difference between a monarchical form of government and a republic, if both monarchy and republic are ruled by the same golden god of Mammon ... We have a class of Junkers [rural aristocrats] which rules over the populace. Here you have a band of pirates, financial pirates who rule over you. No great differences exist, in regards to how the working class is impacted."[96]

Skeptics might dismiss Liebknecht's assertions as simple propaganda, but American reformers from middle-class backgrounds also witnessed child labor, hovels, and dangerous working conditions, and demanded an end to them. They too wondered why the United States was engaging in the militarism of fleet building. The German antimilitarist pointedly asked, after watching Columbus Day celebrations, "Why do people put their children in military uniforms? The whole celebration had an atmosphere which had little in common with freedom. A warlike tone filled the streets." [97] He concluded, "In reality your world is no longer new. I see here the same repression and slavery—yes, slavery to an extreme degree—as one finds in Germany. In fact your slavery is worse than what we have. You use up your energies faster. You are done in more quickly than our workers. You are more quickly thrown on the refuse heap than workers in Germany, because you find yourself in the heart of capitalism."[98] The intensity of work and child labor evidently struck all the leftist travelers. Liebknecht's condemnation ended, "I found, that in America the rule of the dollar is so strong, that even electors are bought and paid—something which is unknown in Germany."[99]

In his departing speech, Liebknecht repeated his litany of complaints about industrial life in America. Speaking to an overfilled hall in Brooklyn, he compared the United States to Russia in its waste of people and disregard for human rights. Though not denying the great potential, wonderful open spaces, and technological progress of the land, he decried the social scene. The era of free fertile land was over, the trusts controlled railways, mining and machinery; industrial workers' treatment was the equivalent of the Russian disregard for life and limb. He invited everyone to visit, as he had, the factories in Pittsburgh where twelve-hour shifts ran seven days a week until a successful strike altered the situation. He based his claims on visits to steelworks, textile factories, and sweatshops. Further, Liebknecht asked, "Where else in the world is child labor as immorally widespread as in the United States? In what other civilized land on earth does one find so many private police forces to repress strikers?"[100] He cited court cases to illustrate a system of class justice and asked "where is your freedom?" He insisted that this freedom primarily lay in the opportunity to rob and exploit. "Not the dream of paradise, rather the nightmare of hell, is dreamt here."[101] In regard to what socialism offered, he had been questioned by an American woman whether it did not destroy the family. In response he pointed out that he had observed the American family and thought "nothing worse could exist," because extensive prostitution was part of the American economic system. Many young women were forced to the streets out of economic necessity. He added, "I walked down Washington Street in San Francisco and I saw what one cannot see elsewhere. There women offered their bodies crudely and openly. And not only women but children, young girls of twelve and thirteen, led an unacceptable life. Where was your police [force], I wondered. My guide pointed out that the police collaborated with the owners [pimps] in the area."[102] They were part of the system of "degeneration and immorality."

Liebknecht also saw a lighter side, the renewal and awakening of America. Of course it was the emerging and growing labor movement and socialist parties that embodied the potential for change.[103] He encouraged workers to organize, to read the labor press, to support their candidates. A banquet in Liebknecht's honor had the usual rituals of a furniture workers' choir opening, a poetry reading, and a speech by the founder of the socialist Sunday school before Liebknecht concluded about America: ready for a social transformation.

How to evaluate Liebknecht's ideological outlook? By going abroad he had come to appreciate aspects of Germany. The surprise is his high regard for German society in comparison with the American: Germany's system of justice, its labor regulation (which had limited child labor and regulated work conditions), and its police control of prostitution, all of which differed positively from the American situation. Liebknecht had come across the Atlantic as a relentless critic of Germany, especially its militarism. But, unlike his father, Karl Liebknecht ended disillusioned with America. Yet, his beliefs that labor organizations were the hope for the future in a crass industrial world were reaffirmed. One must remember that by 1910 the social faults of the United States and the industrial world in general were well known, and many liberal reformers of the Progressive Era reacted similarly to the slums and trusts. Certainly Liebknecht overestimated the ability of Germany's labor movement to achieve change, and he underestimated the substandard housing and extensive industrial accidents of his homeland. He may have been harsh, yet by 1910 even middle-class Germans, in such magazines as *Simplicismus,* made fun of the multitude of trusts enveloping American liberties.[104]

An underlying side of Liebknecht may also have motivated his writing. He was a loving family man, who wanted everyone to receive the benefits of an education. Hence he was concerned about how child labor robbed youth of their rights of personal development. This side of Liebknecht is revealed through the postcards by which he chronicled his American trip for his children, nephews, and nieces.[105] The feisty agitator gives way to the father as educator who tells of his "adventures," of seeing Native Americans, alligators, and superb scenery. His son Helmut's notes indicate that Liebknecht recounted his "adventures" in America, evidently providing a very different image than he offered to adults as agitator. For example, a journal entry of November 23, 1910, relates that three cards had arrived: "Vera [received an] Indian baby, Bobbi [an] Indian in an automobile. I [an] Indian chief. During [the] afternoon read Jules Verne's study on the discovery of the earth. Evening played Zeppelin, then dice."[106] On December 7, he recorded three more postcards from his father, one of an alligator farm in California, one of an alligator in front of a cart, another of tomato plantings. After his father returned home he listed the gifts of more cards, one showing logbooks of the ships used to cross the Atlantic, others depicting gold mining and cotton picking, another showing sugar cane fields, and one labeled "Got a Dollar?" Later that day the son of the strident antimilitarist bought a model U-boat and torpedo boat. "Papa often talks about his experiences," Helmut said. On one of the cards Karl Liebknecht had written, "That is how the

Karte an die Nichte Charlotte, 25. November 1910

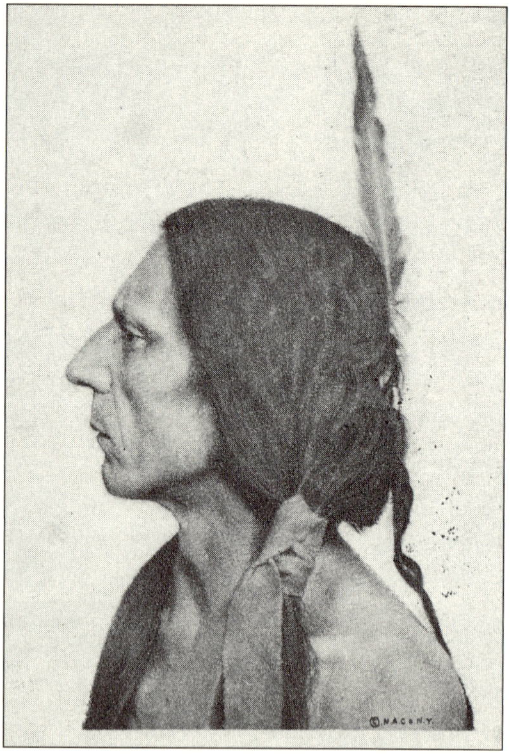

Postcards from Karl Liebknecht to his to niece Charlotte. Reproduced from the Collection International Institute of Social History (Amsterdam).

young girls go for a drive. And the bad crocodiles are very well behaved." On another he had penned, "That is how the Indian mamas appear."[107]

The bourgeois lifestyle of many German radicals and reformers has been noted by scholars.[108] Certainly all these travelers left photographs of themselves attired in suits, vests, ties, and pocket watches with chains.[109] Or has the designation "bourgeois" been misapplied, since most people desire—and therein these leftists were no different—the best opportunities for their children and want to participate in the material benefits of industrial society? They definitely believed in the motto of "knowledge is power," in which educational development of themselves and their children was highly valued, as was the belief that all persons should work to their highest potential to improve society. Decency is not restricted to any class and Karl Liebknecht has been shown to have been a very ethical person.[110] To his children and relatives he offered some of the stereotypical images of America gathered by any tourist. A double irony is that the antimilitarist allowed his children to purchase military models as toys.

Carl Legien: Labor, Society, and Rituals

"House [of Representatives] hears Karl Legien: Leader of Socialists in Reichstag Speaks in German," the *New York Times* announced on April 21, 1912. To Congress Legien presented greetings from the German unions and stated that "organized workers do not only stand for progress but also are the strongest advocates of peace among nations." Two years later the Bolshevik leader Vladimir Iljitsch Lenin wrote about Legien's tour, under the title "What Should Not Be Copied from the German Labor Movement," and pointed to Legien's recently published book about his U.S. visit, *Aus Amerikas Arbeiterbeweung.*[111] Lenin objected to Legien's moderate evaluation of the United States. Ironically, Legien's generally positive account of his lengthy trip included reports of his having witnessed a startling amount of corruption, regarding police, politics, and prohibition. The other theme that is strongly and sometimes delightfully portrayed is drinking and hotel customs. Despite Legien's participation in the frequent imbibing, he provided a rational and full accounting of his tour.

Legien covered much of the country, some eleven thousand miles. He began as the others did in Manhattan and Brooklyn, which he viewed by car. In New York City, he was struck by the many billboards. In descriptions of his train travels, Legien employed terms common to his era, for instance, about going to Boston on the night train, he did not write of the porter but simply "the Negro."[112] After Washington he continued by train to Buffalo and Niagara Falls, then to Toronto, where he found slums as elsewhere.[113] About Canada he noted many immigrants returning to the United States because of failing soils. From there he went to meetings in Cleveland, then Pittsburgh and Homestead (famous for its 1892 strike). About all these places he repeatedly wrote that he had witnessed atrocious housing, such as could not be seen in Germany.[114] From McKeesport he journeyed on to Cincinnati, finding many who spoke German there, especially the brewery workers. At Indianapolis he observed the easy surmounting of prohibition—beer served in coffee cups.[115] After Chicago, especially in Milwaukee, he thought that Germans predominated at the meetings. Both Germans and black peoople gained his attention on the train trip to Minneapolis and St. Paul, followed by St. Louis where he recorded 700,000 people, of whom 100,000 were Germans and 35,000 "Neger."[116] Next was Kansas City, then via St. Louis back to Indianapolis to reach to Denver and Colorado Springs. On the way to Los Angeles, Legien stopped in Salt Lake City and Yosemite Valley. Speeches at Sacramento and Merced preceded San Francisco and Fresno. Santa Cruz and Monterey allowed fishing and viewing the redwoods, coming back via the Santa Clara valley. Oakland was his last California stop before a train trip to Portland and Seattle. Legien maintained that one "cannot know the United States without going to the West,"[117] ignoring another part of the country: he did not get anywhere near the Deep South or Southeast. His return across the continent went via Davenport in Iowa (with more workers' choral groups), and Dayton, Ohio; then to the Republican Convention in Chicago, before Detroit, Toledo, and Altoona; and finally Erie, Rochester, Schenectady, Philadelphia, Providence (via New York City), and back to New York. There the local entertainment of throwing baseballs at a "Neger" whose head poked through a hole in a wall, disgusted him.[118] Speaking and sightseeing, which meant viewing tourist spots plus touring workers' housing and getting inside factories, were combined in Legien's travels.

Legien viewed the United States through the lens of his own successful trade union and socialist party work. He had worked his way up the organizations while helping to build them. By 1912 more than two million workers were members of the central association of German trade unions and many of them were part of the nearly million-member Social Democratic Party. Legien, by then the leader of the general union federation and also head of the international union secretariat, was a moderate and pragmatic leftist.[119] He had devoted his life to improving laborers' working conditions and political rights. He had put off visiting the United States in 1910 with Karl Liebknecht, partly because he did not want to be associated with the latter's radicalism, especially since Liebknecht advocated mass strikes, which Legien strongly opposed. Partly he wanted to have more than a quick tour so he could really learn about the United States. Indeed he had harsh words for those who only spent a few weeks in a place where they did not know the language, and then pontificated about it.[120] Thus, like Wilhelm Liebknecht, he reflected on problems inherent in travel accounts. By the time Legien undertook his four-month trip he had informed himself and had many contacts in both the U.S. Socialist Party as well as in the American Federation of Labor that had invited him. On his way west he toured on behalf of the AFL, and, on his return east, for the American Socialist Party. His colleague Adolf Baumeister, another moderate union reformer, accompanied him as translator.

Legien's book appeared in two hundred pages of fine print supplemented by a dozen illustrations. The work received a wide hearing and was reprinted three times, with an English excerpt appearing in 1913. Legien separated out the tour, namely his extensive travel report, from accounts of the meetings he attended or at which he spoke. The last half of his study offered his analysis of the American workers' associations, subdivided into unions, the American Federation of Labor, boycott tactics, the Knights of Labor and Industrial Workers of the World, and the Socialist Party. Unlike Edward Aveling, Eleanor Marx, or Karl Liebknecht, his criticisms were modest.

Legien repeated the difficulties of understanding such a large land. The fast train from New York to San Francisco took seven days or 188 continuous hours, of which he did one long stretch of 72 hours on his return from the west. He stated that Americans pretend to only have one class of railway travel, whereas Germans have four. But he insisted that if one considers price and types of carriages, the Americans really had eight. However, life on trains was different than the rowdy and joking scene in Germany: "The American . . . retains his serenity in such situations and agitation seems foreign to him. He neither makes jokes nor swears. During my three-month stay, I only once heard, aside from new immigrants, that an American swore and he was not of Anglo-American descent."[121] Though he thought some German trains were better, he concluded that travel by train was "quite good." However, connections were difficult and the names confusing, with, for instance, fourteen places named St. Louis and twenty-eight called Berlin. About the new train station of the Pennsylvania Railroad, he thought it "the greatest building of that type that he had seen," though he poked fun at the tendency of Americans to describe something as "the biggest" or "most important," or even, near San Francisco, "the most twisted" ("the most twisted train track in the world").[122] Legien saw that the big U.S. rail companies put magnificent stations at the ends of their lines though in between left "mostly miserable" ones.

Unlike during the era of Edward Aveling and Eleanor Marx's visit, he found that the hotels had baths and on the whole were better than the European ones. He liked the fact that few hands reached out for tips, though he found that the meal times were restrictive. In his experience Americans undercooked their food, and as someone who had not drunk water since he had contacted typhus in Hamburg during 1892, he worried about the water offered everywhere, with few drinking containers. Indeed, he could not adjust to the style of drinking in the bars. It was copious and fast, with emphasis upon paying. Whereas Germans drank, Americans guzzled. However, he complimented Americans on the tradition of eating a full breakfast: grapefruit with sugar, cutlets with baked potatoes, "the latter a specialty of the United States," then cheese, radishes, and finally coffee or tea with pastry.[123] Like the other travelers he observed how easily prohibition was circumvented in supposedly dry states. Another aspect struck him as odd in Milwaukee when he wanted to continue a conversation with colleagues in a bar: "We were informed, that the wife of an accompanying unionist . . . was not allowed to enter the bar."[124] When Legien and his colleagues asked what would happen if she did enter, they were told that then the men would have to leave. Legien commented, "Bizarre, in a city with a majority of Germans and a strong socialist movement to have such prudery."[125]

In Boston, Legien met the mayor, John F. Fitzgerald, and the governor of Massachusetts, Eugene Foss. Both had been to Germany, a reflection of the increased travel possibilities as well as the willingness to learn from across the Atlantic. With them a discussion ensued about the cost of living and how to calculate comparisons. Legien defended his country: "It is unjust, when Americans visiting Germany convert German wages with dollars equal to marks," because that did not reflect prices.[126] Direct comparisons also appeared when he described spread-out Washington to compact Berlin. The grandeur of the capital contrasted with the slums in which ninety-two thousand blacks lived in segregated areas. Legien did not hide his dislike of the lack of real equality of rights, and, as he said, the privileges of money that ruled "everywhere in the world."[127]

About U.S. politics and race relations, he recounted that "a Texas cotton plantation owner calmly stated. . . . that whites there could in no way imagine blacks, who only 50 years ago had been slaves, as their equal. Blacks officially had the right to vote but it was understood that whites would prevent their actual participation, by electoral fraud if necessary. The tradition continued that blacks rode in separate compartments on trams and trains."[128] Legien added that he did not know the truth of a story about blacks, including a bishop, being thrown out of moving trains when they tried to sit with whites, but he saw everywhere the blatant "segregation and disrespect for blacks." He tried to explain the situation by reference to the "cultural level which resulted from a race having been kept in slavery for hundreds of years."[129]

By contrast, on his invitation to speak to Congress as well as the warm reception there, he commented: "It would be unthinkable, that a foreigner, a

Social Democrat, would be allowed to speak to the German parliament."[130] Similarly, he remarked positively about the possibilities of rising socially in America through education. Indeed, he met a number of lawyers who previously had been skilled workers and who had taken evening classes. Another specifically American institution that impressed him was the land-grant college. Like Engels he found that "[w]ork, whatever type it may be, is respected and every waiter or busboy, the streetcar conductor or train worker, sees themselves as a free citizen, and whoever tried to put down these people at their work or look down upon them, as is often the case in Germany by individuals whose only work is in trimming their nails and who do nothing useful for society, would encounter difficulties."[131] However, Legien did not want anyone to conclude that class did not matter in the United States, because possessions continued to create exclusivity.

Another problem that Legien encountered in the United States, especially in Chicago, Pittsburgh, Kansas City, and Los Angeles, was substandard "workers' housing, which could not be found in Germany."[132] Even when he crossed into Canada at Niagara and took a side trip to Toronto he found the same problem of wonderful parks and buildings but also slums with "horrid barracks," similar to Kansas City. He witnessed the same situation in the steel-producing region, made worse "by the many cripples . . . victims of this industry."[133] His guides informed him about the strikes put down by Pinkertons at Homestead, a place he saw more workers' housing: "these are huts, as do not exist in any industrial region of Germany."[134] He acknowledged Carnegie's worker libraries, but thought much more would be achieved if better wages, working conditions, and living conditions existed. Workers who toiled for $1.50 per fourteen-hour day had no time for such important institutions as libraries. The intensity of work struck him as it had Karl Liebknecht. After observing the lack of protective scaffolding used in the building of skyscrapers, Legien added that animals were treated better than workers.[135] During a visit to a flour mill he again noted the lack of protection in a "gigantic factory in which the worker becomes part of the machinery."[136] By contrast, at a hosiery plant, after the owner had been convinced that the visitors were not out to steal production secrets, he found "a model concern."

Among traits he ascribed to Americans, especially the trade unionists, were "friendliness" and "accommodation." Another was honesty in small matters such as leaving money after taking a newspaper from a pile, yet if someone pulled a fast one, that was not cheating but being "smart."[137] The wild landscapes west of Colorado, especially the redwoods, impressed Legien but at Wawona, in California, where he finally saw Indians, "they did not compare with the figures [James Fenimore] Cooper delineated in his *Leatherstocking.* It is a deeply degenerated race, which slinks about in worn-out European clothing. A woman with a child in her arms was embarrassed that we looked at her intently."[138] By such remarks as well as the comments about a "land without owners," [139] Legien revealed that leftists too could see with imperial eyes.

Legien's account offers insight into organized labor's customs and rituals. The endless handshaking, the specific order of speaking, the rules and posts such as sergeant at arms, the solemn approach to union business and the role of each executive member are recounted as a contrast to less-structured German meetings. Again some of his commentary focuses on drinking style—in offices, at any hours—but also on the use of boycotts and advertising as negotiating tools. He had found Broadway the "biggest billboard street of the world,"[140] but later came to appreciate the union movement's use of advertising, for instance handbills in opposition to nonunionized shops.

In the United States Legien found a labor movement that had impressive buildings and prepared well for contract negotiations. He applauded the reformist, evolutionary approach in attempting to defend worker interests as well as in seeking to moderate America's shortcomings. However, aside from housing, he did not see conditions as extreme and appreciated the country's civil rights and political institutions. Unlike Karl Liebknecht, he did not advocate socialist revolution, but suggested moderate reforms similar to the pragmatic improvements being implemented in Germany. His speeches outlined the struggle for reduced hours and work regulations that unionists and Social Democrats fought for in Germany without much embellishment to audiences that to him were disappointingly small. Legien's is a traditional travel account, extended to labor and its institutions. America was neither better, nor worse than Germany.

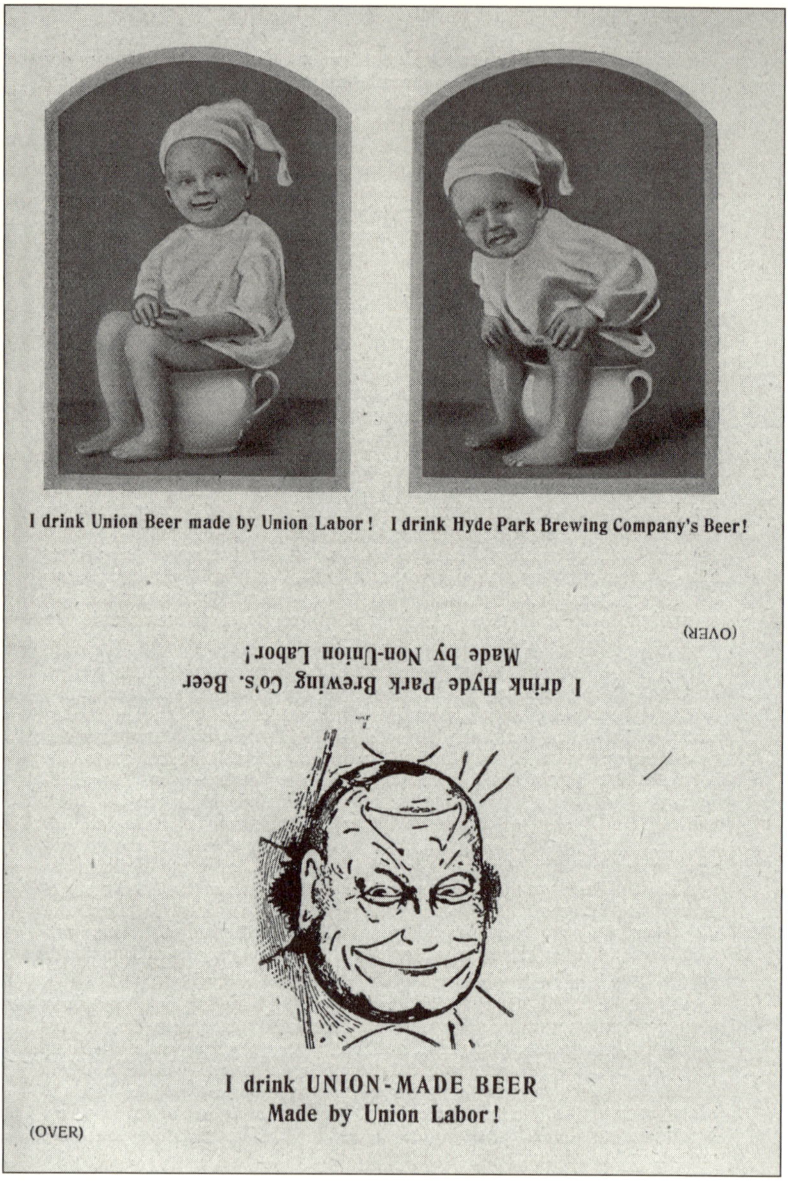

Reproduced from C. Legien, Aus Amerikas Arbeiterbewegung *(Berlin: Generalkommission, 1914), 159.*

Conclusion: Reviewing "Amerika" from the German Left

One might expect critical perspectives from leftist travel writers. Yet, the mini selection offered here provides a mix, including familiar stereotypes. For the German left, the United States sometimes served as a model even for those who had not been there. For instance, during 1902, Friedrich Ebert, local head of the Bremen Social Democrats and later national leader, argued in favor of introducing social statistical offices which a few U.S. states already had.[141] Similarly, the existence of women's voting rights in some states was used to buttress arguments for attaining them in Germany. Of course, American leftists did the reverse: looking to European labor laws regarding children and women, and requesting such regulations.[142] Many social crossings slowly traversed the Atlantic.

Three results emerge from the German leftists' accounts. First, there was no one leftist stance on America. Their diverse but informed observations about living conditions, Native Americans and other minorities, social patterns, and political institutions indicate that travel writing on the United States remains incomplete without including their views. Second, the first phase of industrialization resulted in similar social problems on both sides of the Atlantic and hence many comparisons were made to how the problems were addressed. Third, the travelers examined here can hardly be accused of anti-Americanism.[143] They reported in credible fashion with much evidence on the positive as well as negative aspects of the United States. Freedom of the individual as well as education receive high marks while child and female labor, racial segregation, and slum housing were noticeable to Europeans coming from a much more regulated world.

One element all the travelers had in common was hope for the American future in which they foresaw a strong working-class movement. That view reflected their ideological preferences. The most radical, Karl Liebknecht, proved the most critical, but still saw potential in American ideals. The concept of reflection has been employed in some analyses of travel literature to argue that America represented modernity and the Germans of the imperial era who traveled there mostly embraced technology and liberalism as reflected in their reports.[144] The leftists fit within that position.

Like other travelers the German leftists appreciated American landscapes, found some habits odd, and rejected the intensity and pace of working conditions, especially combined with private armies and ruthless employers. None of this was very different than what was found by contemporary American critics and later historians examining the social and political situation. Certainly, the leftist views of Native Americans and of black people—at least in their terminology about civilization and race—reflected standard European linguistic terms.

Can one detect assumptions of superiority among German Social Democrats who looked for American laborers to build a movement as strong as their own? Or were they just offering comparisons, noting differences and similarities? Certainly, they wanted a common, better future on both sides of the Atlantic. If Wilhelm Liebknecht thought he found in America the country that was "foremost" and highly developed as a civilization, the others had valid reservations. In general, their experiences and observations fit with the trend to finding the United States less exceptional by the beginning of the twentieth century.[145] Repeatedly they pulled the yardstick of social conditions out of their German backpack to measure America against its own ideals.

Travel and travel writing from the left is as valid as any other perspective because it adds to the known, and it offers a fuller account of another society. The authors presented here should be read in conjunction with the many middle-class and aristocratic travelers, as well as later social historians, the historians of gender, ethnic groups, and manners. Then two elements of their travel writing would stand out. First, their observations about American customs and conditions, especially hotels and railways, overlapped with other travel reports, so they could be seen as typical bourgeois German travelers. However, their ideological outlook taught them to look beyond the railway stations and saloons to search out factories, workers' residences, and comparative costs of living. German leftist travelers found significant social and democratic deficits. Second, they had a predilection, given their social beliefs and politicized travel agendas, to judge according to the criteria of what human dignity existed for the ordinary person, as opposed to the elite. No matter how moderate or reformist in their party, political, and tactical stances, all these travelers employed the language of class as a fundamental category by which to judge societies. Hence, leftist travel writing offers an entry into the working-class world, even if the world they described mirrors many of the ideological concerns of a visitor or viewer empathetic with the lowest class.

America, then and now, is hard to understand: it is so vast, so varied, and so changing. Extremists such as Adolf Hitler perceived it as a model of racism, expansionism, and technology. By contrast German leftists have almost always looked at what America might be, hoping its original idealism would manifest itself in a socially just and democratic society. Some were disillusioned and demanded immediate alterations; others were prepared to wait for the fulfillment of their hope.

Acknowledgments

Judith and Lisa Buse, Glenn Penny, and Thomas Adam provided editorial advice for this work; Laurentian University contributed research funds.

Appendix A: Excerpt from Wilhelm Liebknecht, Ein Blick in die Neue Welt[146]

The American is always conscious of saving work time, because work here is expensive. I mean: he seeks to save human work. He removes superfluous endeavors, simplifies the necessary work, and wherever possible uses machines or mechanical systems. The railroad personnel here is about one-half, perhaps two-thirds less than in Germany—and everything functions well, with more order and much less noise than in Germany. Further, the result is achieved with half the population to serve. Every man, every woman, every child has here understood the principle of self-help. The American does not need to have someone direct him to a place—he finds it himself; he needs no warnings, rules and commands—he does from himself what he has to do and keeps his eyes open. And since he respects the rights and comforts of his co-travelers in ways unknown to a patronizing police-state person, everything runs smoothly and without friction. One turns up one's nose so frequently in Germany at the American "equality-boor" and his rough manners. I noticed none of these rough manners. It is true, if he wants to be comfortable, the American puts his feet on the table, but is that disrespectful? It is strange to us—that's it. . . .

. . . The Americans are especially proud of the "magical fall colors of the leaves." And they are very beautiful, as I can attest from various excursions into the forested areas. However, if it is claimed that we have nothing similar in Europe, that is a patriotic exaggeration. Our German forests are just as attractive in the fall as those on the Hudson. The Hudson, the "American Rhine," deserves its fame—indeed, it surpassed all expectations; and the New Yorkers proclaim that it exceeds the Ohio that also carries the title of "American Rhine." And I believe, there are other "American Rhine" rivers, since the German, wherever he ends, brings his fatherland along and what is more natural than to give strange rivers the favorite name from the homeland. . . .

15 October. Around 12, when the factories close for lunch, I happened to find myself in front of one of the great mills and I saw the "hands" going by me. First came men in dense groups, only a few women and children among them; then ever more women and girls and—children [*sic*], and then nothing but women, girls and—children. The United States has no laws to limit women and child work; and from the individual states only Connecticut and Massachusetts have protective laws. Here in New Hampshire women's work is completely unregulated and the same with child labor, provided that the child is 12 years—I repeat has completed his 12th year. . . . As this army of women and girls and children passed by me, and I looked at the faces of the women and girls with their deep furrows from worry and lack of sleep, as well as seeing the faces of the children already marked by the tragic struggle for survival—then my fascination with America moved a step backward and the star-spangled banner which flew in the fall wind, no longer seemed so pristine to me.

. . . The American woman is socially completely equal to the male, and she is on the path to attain political equality as well. In order to achieve this she has not had to sacrifice her femininity, rather she gained her high status precisely due to her strong and finely developed femininity. Another trait supports it: the masculinity of the men. Under masculinity I understand what one wrongly often designates as "knightly." This falsely named knightliness, is however, despite all prejudiced claims, real masculinity, and it is to be found most highly developed among the Anglo-Saxons, namely among the Americans. . . . The cultural level of countries should be measured according to the status of women. Seen from this standpoint, I cannot but conclude that Americans are on a higher cultural level than we are.

Appendix B: Excerpt from Carl Legien, Aus Amerikas Arbeiterbewegung[147]

Not only the enormous spread of the land makes it hardly possible, even with a lengthy stay, to comprehend the situation and to come to a comprehensive judgment [about America]. Additionally there is the spread of the cities. Even though the transport means are very good in all the big cities, . . . it is not possible by a visit of a day or sometimes only hours to tour all parts of a place. . . . A notion of the spread of American cites can be gained in the numbers offered by the Baedeker travel guide. It reports that Chicago, with 1.8 million inhabitants in 1903 covered 495 square kilometers; while [a similar population in] Berlin covers only 63. However, one cannot compare the cities of Germany to those of the United States. In the latter the business section is separated from the living areas. In the business area are huge buildings, often 18 to 26 stories high with stores, warehouses, and offices, while in the living areas the one-family house predominates and is separated from other buildings. In nearly every city there are large open grassy spaces which do not have signs [as in Germany] that say "keep off the grass," rather they can be used by everyone as play and camp ground. In all American cities one finds such spaces, though Chicago may be in first place for the number and extent of them. Yet despite the spread of the cities we were able to gain an overview . . . As transport means we used the car which was placed at our disposal in most centers. Even though it may only be a quick view one does gain a general impression and one could not avoid the contrasts of American cities especially between the basic existence of the possessing classes and the proletariat.

A certain uniformity marks all American cities. Aside from Washington and the older parts of New York and Boston, they are rectangular. . . . The cities did not grow slowly but were created from the beginning by a general squared pattern. Many aspects in the west as in the east are from a notable similarity. Most items for sale have the same price. The constitution for the whole country is also unitary. It is a great work, created in 1789, which still today unifies all parts of the large land and which in a short time takes those coming from the old world, from nations which see each other as enemies, and lets them see themselves as citizens of one land. The written law is also uniform, even if as in other countries, capitalists know how to turn it more to their advantage than those without possessions. The legal system in the individual states is similarly uniform. . . . The possibility, not only to participate in the law making, but to attain decisive influence, is open to the working class in the cities, in the individual states, and in the federation. Electoral rights exist for all American citizens without distinction for all institutions and in some states such as California and Iowa even for women to vote for the legislature. . . . What is missing is the unity of the proletariat, which is evident in older countries, especially in Germany. To create this unity is difficult, but not impossible . . . the belief in quickly attaining riches has not yet disappeared though capitalism is demonstrating thoroughly that here too the world is divided and the proletariat only works to attain basic subsistence. . . .

I was surprised by the much greater influence of the churches among the working class than I had anticipated. It may have been the only disappointment which I experienced in the United States, since my initial impression of the extent of the land, of its cities, its powerful transport system, its industry, its public infrastructure, and the rights of its citizens was far surpassed by what I found. . . . Hence despite the many descriptive travel accounts of America I believe I can offer the German worker many worthwhile insights. . . . The whole system of having public meetings as well as their procedure is quite different than the German. Even the publicity has something American about it. Placards or handbills, on which the meeting is announced, usually have a picture of the speaker. The newspapers, including the bourgeois ones, include in addition to the picture of the speaker, a summary of his activities or biography. In one case, Pittsburg[h], the placards were hung on the side of a streetcar, in another, Minneapolis, attached to the side of a wagon containing a music group to gain attention of the passerby through noise. . . . The low attendance at the meeting stood in sharp contrast to the publicity . . .

At the beginning and the end of a meeting a musical presentation of some kind is normal. . . . In the meeting of the Jewish unions of New York there was not only singing between each speaker but a young violin virtuoso played to practice for his European tour. . . . The organizer of the meeting went on stage with the speakers. After opening the session he presented the chairperson for the meeting and this person gave each of the persons on the podium a turn to speak. . . . Discussion and debate on the presented theme did not exist in the meetings.

NOTES

The quote in the epigraph is from Wilhelm Liebknecht, *Ein Blick in die Neue Welt* (Stuttgart: J. H. W. Dietz, 1887), 41.

1. Max Paul Friedman, "Beyond 'Voting with their Feet': Toward a Conceptual History of 'America' in European Migrant Sending Communities, 1860s to 1914," *Journal of Social History* 40 (2007), 557–75, places migration to the United States in the larger context of European migration within and outside Europe, including return migration (page 558), with relevant literature; and Günther Moltmann, "American-German Return Migration in the Nineteenth and Early Twentieth Centuries," *Central European History* 13 (1980), 378–92.

2. Pioneering studies by Rolf Engelsing, for example, "England und die USA in der bremischen Sicht des 19. Jahrhunderts," in *Jahrbuch der Wittheit zu Bremen* I (1957), 33–65, have been complemented by Sam Mustafa, *Merchants and Migrations: Germans and Amercans in Connection, 1776–1835* (Aldershot: Ashgate, 2001) and Lars Maischak, "A Cosmopolitan Community: Hanseatic Merchants in the German-American Atlantic of the 19th Century," PhD diss., Johns Hopkins University, 2005.

3. Numerous examples are cited in Thomas Adam, ed., *Germany and the Americas: Culture, Politics, History,* volumes 1–3 (Santa Barbara: ABC-Clio, 2005),

see list under topic finder "Organizations," vol. I, xxv; Hartmut Keil, "Lebensweise und Kultur deutscher Arbeiter in Amerikas Industriezentren," in Frank Trommler, ed., *Amerika und die Deutschen* (Opladen: Westdeutscher, 1986), 204ff., and Carol Poore, "Wessen Feier? Die Hundertjahrfeier von 1876 und die deutschamerikanische sozialistische Kultur," in ibid., 192–203.

4. A solid account is Stan Nadel, "The German Immigrant Left in the United States," in Paul Buhle and Dan Georgakas, eds., *The Immigrant Left in the United States* (New York: SUNY Press, 1996), 45–76.

5. Frank Trommler and Joseph McVeigh, eds., *America and the Germans: An Assessment of a Three-hundred-Year History* (Philadelphia: University of Philadelphia Press, 1985), 2 vols., introduction.

6. For examples of the concepts, see Thomas Adam and Ruth Gross, eds., *Traveling Between Worlds: German-American Encounters* (Arlington: Texas A&M University Press, 2006), 7–19; Kathryn Kish Sklar, et al., eds., *Social Justice Feminists in the United States and Germany: A Dialogue in Documents, 1885–1933* (Ithaca: Cornell University Press, 1998); and the astute review essay by Glenn Penny, "Atlantic Transfers: Recent Work on the German-American Exchange," *German History* 16 (2008), 563–75.

7. See Geoff Eley, *Forging Democracy: The History of the Left in Europe, 1850–2000* (Oxford: Oxford University Press, 2000), including comparisons with other areas; also Anne Lopes, *Men's Feminism: August Bebel and the German Socialist Movement* (Amherst: Humanity, 2000), which places Bebel's influential book on women in the wider context of feminist movements.

8. Two accounts provide the exceptions, R. Laurence Moore, *European Socialists and the American Promised Land* (New York: Oxford University Press, 1970), using an undifferentiated "Marxists," and Werner Kremp, *In Deutschland liegt unser Amerika: Der sozialdemokratische Amerikabild von den Anfangen der SPD bis zur Weimarer Republik* (Münster: Lit, 1993); more typical: Viktor Otto, *Deutsche Amerika-Bilder: zu den intellektuellen Diskurs um die Moderne* (Paderborn: Wilhelm Fink, 2006) presents American "workers" only as Ernst Jünger imagined them. A standard work, Peter J. Brenner, *Reisen in die Neue Welt. Die Erfahrung Nordamerikas in deutschen Reise-und Auswandererberichten des 19. Jahrhunderts* (Tübingen: Niemeyer, 1991), cites Wilhelm Liebknecht but omits Engels, Karl Liebknecht, and Legien. Kremp provides the most thorough historio-

graphic overview and analyzes the Social Democratic press in depth, though sometimes too schematically.

9. Volker Depkat, *Amerikabilder in politischen Diskursen: deutsche Zeitschriften von 1789 bis 1830* (Stuttgart: Klett-Cotta, 1998) and Horst Dippel, *America Germanica 1770–1800* (Stuttgart: J. B. Metzler, 1976) illustrate the early establishment of persistent images.

10. An informed overview but including no Germans or leftists is Marc Pachter, ed., *Travelers to the New Nation 1776–1914* (Washington: Smithsonian Institution, 1976); an important example is the African Liberian, Edward Blyden, who in 1895 noticed an "almost entire absence of the ideal and spiritual, owing to the overwhelming influence of the material" (104) among both blacks and whites.

11. A sample: Gwendolyn Mink and Alice O'Connor, eds. *Poverty in the United States: An Encyclopedia of History, Politics and Policy* (Santa Barbara: ABC-Clio, 2004); the so-called muckrakers tried to expose the social situation via journalism (*How the Other Half Lives,* 1890) or novels on slums, child labor, and gerrymandering and machine politics, while the suffragists sought change through the ballot box, and others through settlement houses and charity.

12. Karl Obermann, "Die Amerikareise Wilhelm Liebknechts im Jahre 1886," *Zeitschrift für Geschichteswissenschaft* 14 (1966), 612.

13. See Peter Nettl, "The German Social Democratic Party 1890–1914 as a Model Political Party," *Past and Present* 30 (1965), 65–95; for a specific case, see Robert Mikkelsen, "Immigrants in Politics: Poles, Germans and the Social Democratic Party of Milwaukee," in Dirk Hoerder, ed., *Labor Migration in the Atlantic Economies* (Westport: Greenwood, 1985), 283.

14. For biographical information, see William A. Pelz, *Wilhelm Liebknecht and German Social Democracy: A Documentary History* (Westport: Greenwood, 1994), 397–404 (here are reprinted news reports of his American speeches); and Raymond Dominick, *Wilhelm Liebknecht and the Founding of German Social Democracy* (Chapel Hill: University of North Carolina Press, 1982).

15. See summary police report on the "success" of Liebknecht's trip, sent to the German Minister of the Interior, in Gerhard Becker, "Die Agitationsreise Wilhelm Liebknechts durch die USA 1886: Ergänzendes zu einer

Dokumentation von Karl Obermann," *Zeitschrift für Geschichtswissenschaft* 15 (1967), 855.

16. Philip S. Foner, ed., *Wilhelm Liebknecht: Letters to the "Chicago Workingman's Advocate," November 26, 1870–December 2, 1871* (New York: Holmes & Meier, 1982), 37.

17. Ibid., 47.

18. Ibid., 66, 72 (quotation), 90.

19. Ibid., 83 (quotation), 93.

20. Ibid., 89.

21. Cited in Pelz, *Wilhelm Liebknecht,* 404; compare *New York Times,* September 11, 1886, September 20, 1886, and November 26, 1886: "Liebknecht talks wildly: he says that Socialism is to be the Ruling Power in America."

22. The reports have been printed in Obermann, "Die Amerikareise Wilhelm Liebknechts," 614–17, and Becker, "Die Agitationsreise Wilhelm Liebknechts," 847–62.

23. After two weeks in New York and Brooklyn, he went to Philadelphia on October 1, then to Bridgeport, New Haven, Meriden, Middleton, Hartford, Springfield, Boston, Clinton (Massachusetts), Providence, Albany, Syracuse, Rochester, Buffalo, Cleveland, Sandusky, Toledo, Detroit, Chicago, Milwaukee, Davenport, Quincy, St. Louis, Indianapolis, Cincinnati, Pittsburgh, Altoona, Williamsport, Baltimore, Washington, Baltimore, Wilmington, and back to New York. For a different analysis of Liebknecht's travel report, compare Kremp, *In Deutschland,* 466ff.

24. Becker, "Die Agitationsreise Wihlehlm Liebknechts," 86; he was commenting on the Haymarket affair.

25. August Bebel's international bestseller *Die Frau* was the most popular, being lent twenty-four times in 1894, while Liebknecht's had six, per Hans-Josef Steinberg, "Workers' Libraries in Germany Before 1914," *History Workshop Journal* 1 (Spring 1976), 177; travel literature amounted to approximately one quarter of the borrowing.

26. Daniel T. Rodgers, "American Exceptionalism Revisited," *Raritan* 24 (2004), 41.

27. See Rodgers, "American Exceptionalism Revisited," 21–47.

28. Ibid., 42.

29. Liebknecht, *Ein Blick*, 73. Some German immigrants tried to retain an air of superiority and chauvinistically declared to Liebknecht that the Americans needed German culture, an idea which Liebknecht dismissed. However, he ascribed much importance to national character, for instance asserting that the English were more individualistic than Germans, but lacking their "steeled energy" (5, 56 for quotation).

30. Ibid., 110.

31. Ibid., 75, 115, 122, 131.

32. Ibid., 52.

33. He said "they were more decisive, less loud, and have a proud bearing" (ibid., 59–60). The cited employer also offered no opposition to the eight-hour workday, then being fought for by the Knights of Labor, and he thought that American industry had continued to progress as working hours became shorter.

34. Ibid., 63.

35. Ibid., 82.

36. Ibid., 94.

37. Ibid., 115. Liebknecht offers enjoyable tales, for instance of a "secret bar" in a state with prohibition, due to which he ended locked out of his hotel, because the hotel clerk was next door in the bar and could not hear his knocking.

38. Ibid., 65.

39. Ibid., 78.

40. Ibid., 79–80.

41. Ibid., 90.

42. Ibid., 93.

43. Ibid., 82.

44. Ibid., 83.

45. Ibid., 87–88. Dan Diner, *America in the Eyes of Germans: An Essay on Anti-Americanism* (Princeton: Markus Wiener, 1996), 47–48. Despite a penchant for finding anti-Americanism everywhere, Diner acknowledges Liebknecht's defense of conservatism in democracy, but muddles the context since Liebknecht's piece came from his journals (perhaps because Diner cited from an anthology).

46. Ibid., 215.

47. Ibid., 217.

48. Ibid., 69; the fascination with "Wild West" shows is summarized in by Gregory Shealy, "Buffalo Bill," in Adam, *Germany and the Americas,* 190–92.

49. Liebknecht, *Ein Blick,* 121.

50. Ibid., 211.

51. Ibid., 126.

52. Ibid., 259.

53. Ibid., 78.

54. Ibid., 242.

55. Ibid., 248.

56. Ibid., 280–81, also for the following quotation.

57. Ibid., 284.

58. Eleanor Marx and Edward Aveling,. *The Working Class Movement in America,* ed. by Paul Le Blanc (New York: Humanity Books, 2000), 153; parts had been printed as a series "Die Lage der Arbeiterklasse in Amerika," *Die Neue Zeit* (1887), 241–46, 307–13, 355–62.

59. Marx and Aveling, *The Working Class Movement in America,* 155.

60. Ibid., 69.

61. Ibid., 75.

62. Ibid., 126–27.

63. Ibid., 193; generally on child and women labor, 115–32; and appendix to 1888 reprinting.

64. During the nineteenth century some travel writers tried to get beyond what could be seen on the surface and to delve thoroughly into the insides of society. For instance, the bestselling author Johann Georg Kohl of Bremen would research a country, then live and travel for some months in it. After traveling in the northeastern United States and Canada he lived among the Ojibwe south of Lake Superior for six months before penning his ethnographic accounts, including *Kitchi-Gami* (1859); for details and references, see Dieter K. Buse, "Kohl, Johann Georg," in Adam, *Germany and the Americas,* 620–21.

65. Eward Aveling, *An American Journey* (New York: Lowell, 1887), preface.

66. Ibid., 144–45, also for following quotation.

67. Ibid., 102. The relative contributions of the authors is not clear; on Marx and Aveling's cooperation and their agitation style, see Lisa Frank, "On the Uses of Eleanor Marx," in Le Blanc, *Working Class Movement,* 37–66, especially 41–43, who suggests that their book is a "reworking of the bourgeois travelogue" (50).

68. Ibid., 27; some of Aveling's outlook may have been influenced by he and his wife having been evicted from a New York club to which they had been invited by a member: "What impressed me most was the excessive ill-breeding of the whole affair. We belong to the cultured classes. . . . of England and Germany. . . . the [Manhattan Club's] spirits were bad but their manners were a great deal worse. " *New York Times* October 2, 1885, 5.

69. Ibid., 92.

70. Ibid., 101.

71. Ibid., 102.

72. Ibid., 103.

73. Ibid., 161.

74. Ibid., 166.

75. Ibid., 239.

76. Ibid., 226.

77. Dorothy Blumber, "'Dear Mr. Engels': Unpublished Letters, 1884–1894, of Florence Kelley (-Wischnewetzky) to Friedrich Engels," *Labor History* 5 (1964), 107. On Kelley's dedication to social causes, see Kathryn Kish Sklar, *Florence Kelley and the Nation's Work: The Rise of Women's Political Culture, 1830–1900* (New Haven: Yale University Press, 1995).

78. Ibid., 109. Because Kelley proved indiscrete and compromised Engels's relations with the Socialist Party of America, he admonished her. Despite reconciliation he avoided her and her husband during his American trip. Kelley continued to work on the issue of child labor laws and enforcement of factory inspectors' reports, and eventually Engels's translated works appeared.

79. Letter to August Bebel, August 31, 1888, Karl Marx and Friedrich Engels, *Collected Works,* vol. 48 (New York: International Publishers, 2001), 391.

80. Karl Marx and Friedrich Engels, *Werke,* vol. 23 (Berlin: Dietz, 1975), 337, 339.

81. Two documentary accounts are Thomas Pohle, "Die Reise von Friedrich Engels nach den USA und Kanada im Sommer 1888," *Beiträge zur Geschichte der Arbeiterbewegung* 30 (1988), 72–80, and Dirk J. Struik, "Frederich Engels in New England," *New England Quarterly* 22 (1949), 240–43, while Malcolm Sylvers, "Marx, Engels und die USA—ein Forschungsprojekt über ein wenig beachtetes Thema," *Marx-Engels Jahrbuch,* 2004, 31–54, provides a very terse but informed analysis on Engels's trip (48–50). A short, biased account is *Frederick Engels: A Biography* (Berlin: Zeit, 1972), 445–47.

82. Marx and Engels, *Werke,* vol. 23 (Berlin: Dietz, 1975), 207.

83. Engels to his brother Herman, September 27–28, 1888: "The tour isn't at all fatiguing; everywhere, in the better hotels, the food is first-rate and the German beer, i.e. brewed after the German fashion, quite excellent, . . . nor is American wine at all bad." Marx and Engels, *Collected Works,* vol. 48 (1975), 219.

84. Ibid., 213.

85. Marx and Engels, *Collected Works,* vol. 26, 581–83.

86 Marx and Engels, *Collected Works,* vol. 48, 221.

87. Ibid., 211, 221.

88. Karl Liebknecht, *Militarism and Anti-militarism,* trans. by Alexander Sirnis, intro. by Philip S. Foner (New York: Dover Publications, 1972); for the context in which Liebknecht was seen in 1908 as the coming party leader but undercut by 1910, see Dieter K. Buse, "Party Leadership and Mechanisms of Unity: The Crisis of German Social Democracy Reconsidered, 1910–1914," *Journal of Modern History* 62 (1990), 477–503.

89. Cited in Philip S. Foner, "Karl Liebknecht und die Vereinigten Staaten von Amerika: Eine dokumentarische Studie," Jahrbuch für Wirtschaftsgeschichte 3 (1968), 19.

90. A precise listing of places which he visited and at which he spoke appears in Karl Liebknecht, *Gesammelte Reden und Schriften,* vol. 3 (Berlin: Dietz, 1960), appendix.

91. See examples in ibid., 504ff.; compare *New York Times,* October 16, 1910.

92. Eric Foner, "Why Is There No Socialism in the United States?" *History Workshop* no. 17 (1984), 71.

93. "Child Labor Reform Exhibits," United States Department of Labor, http://www.dol.gov/oasam/library/special/child/childlabor.htm (accessed June 20, 2010).

94. Florence Kelley, "I Go to Work," *Survey,* June 1, 1927, 272.

95. Ibid., 274.

96. Foner, "Karl Liebknecht und die Vereinigten Staaten von Amerika," 36.

97. Ibid., 38.

98. Ibid, 38–39.

99. Ibid., 42.

100. Ibid., 44.

101. Quoted in Heinz Wohlgemuth, *Karl Liebknecht: Eine Biographie* (Berlin: Dietz, 1975), 188.

102. Foner, "Karl Liebknecht," 47.

103. See especially speech of December 2, 1910, reprinted in Karl Liebknecht *Gesammelte Reden und Schriften,* vol. 3, 510–15. Franz Mehring, another radical Social Democrat who took a trip in 1906, appreciated the liberal atmosphere of the United States; see Moore, *European Socialists,* 50.

104. Examples in Diner, *America,* 78ff.

105. On postcards as a historical source for travel writing, see Christiane Harzig, "Gender, Transatlantic Space, and the Presence of German-Speaking People in North America," in Adam and Gross, *Traveling between Worlds,* 146–82.

106. Karl Liebknecht, *Lebt wohl, Ihr lieben Kerlchen. Briefe an seine Kinder* (Berlin: Aufbau, 1992), 70–71.

107. Ibid., 68. Nearly a year later Liebknecht wrote to his sons, who were going to relatives on their own, telling them not to be afraid as there would be nice people with them, but saying "[you will] have to be nice and well behaved, as you can be, even if sometimes you are not. So: it is not a dangerous but a good experience for you. And you must be steady and not undercut my honor, you must be courageous (ibid., 71).

108. Robert Michels, *Political Parties: A Sociological Study of Oligarchic Ten-*

dencies of Modern Democracy (New York: Free Press, 1966; original German 1911), tries to provide an explanation based on group behavior; by contrast a charming positive example is August Bebel as reflected in his companionate marriage: Ursula Hermann, ed., *Briefe einer Ehe, August und Julie Bebel* (Berlin: Dietz, 1997).

109. Google image searches confirm the bourgeois dress norms.

110. Helmut Trotnow, *Karl Liebknecht: A Political Biography (1871–1919)* (Hamden: Archon Books, 1984), 10–13; the American trip is not mentioned. Compare Wohlgemuth, *Karl Liebknecht,* 185–88.

111. Vladimir Lenin, *Collected Works,* vol. 20 (Moscow: Progress Publishers, 1972), 254–58, V. I. Lenin Internet Library, http://www.marxists.org/archive/lenin/works/1914/apr/00.htm (accessed June 19, 2010); Lenin criticized Legien for not seeing through "the American bourgeois method of killing unsteady socialists with kindness" and for being an opportunist.

112. C. Legien, *Aus Amerikas Arbeiterbewegung* (Berlin: Generalkommission, 1914), 26, 57, for examples.

113. Ibid., 39.

114. Ibid., 44.

115. Ibid., 54.

116. Ibid., 63. Legien reported on the many Germans working in the breweries and on the multitude of German societies, with their reading rooms, meeting halls, and gymnastic halls. He noted, and others confirmed, the assimilation tendencies among the second generation (49). As he traveled farther west he encountered many more German societies, especially singing groups in St. Louis and Kansas City (65).

117. Ibid., 83.

118. Ibid., 94.

119. No full biography exists; for an overview and basic literature, see John A. Moses, "Carl Legien," in Dieter K. Buse and Juergen C. Doerr, eds., *Modern Germany: An Encyclopedia of History, People and Culture, 1871–1990* (New York: Garland, 1998), 591–92.

120. Legien, *Amerikas Arbeiterbewegung,* 5.

121. Ibid., 7.

122. Ibid., 29. An earlier French traveler had noted the same but placed

it in context: "Thus in Europe each nation arrogates to itself the first rank. I do not see why the Americans should be more modest than people on the other side of the Atlantic." Michael Chevalier, *Society, Manners and Politics in the United States* (Gloucester: Peter Smith, 1967), 94.

123. Legien, *Amerikas Arbeiterbewegung,* 25–27, regarding food and drink. Further examples: on false labeling and kegs of beer in adjoining rooms (36); or beer in coffee cups and the police taking a cut, "bribery system according to size of locale" (54).

124. Ibid., 56.

125. Ibid.

126. Ibid., 27. The theme was much discussed by social scientists as well as labor leaders since it was crucial to judging social mobility; see Wolfgang Helbich, "Different, But Not Out of This World: German Images of the United States between Two Wars, 1871–1914," in David Barclay and E. Glaser-Schmidt, eds., *Transatlantic Images and Perceptions: Germany and America since 1776* (Cambridge: Cambridge University Press, 1997), 118. A check of Governor Eugene Foss's records at the Massachusetts Archives produced nothing on his German trip.

127. Legien, *Amerikas Arbeiterbewegung,* 7.

128. Ibid., 30, also for following quotations.

129. Ibid.

130. Ibid., 32.

131. Ibid., 33.

132. Ibid. 37.

133. Ibid., 41.

134. Ibid., 44.

135. Ibid., 54.

136. Ibid., 60–61.

137. Ibid., 73; Engels had found the same, with the latter being termed "greenhorns."

138. Ibid., 73.

139. Ibid., 75.

140. Ibid., 25.

141. For example, Friedrich Ebert, *Kampfe und Ziele* (Dresden: Carl Reiss-

ner, 1926), 123, regarding Americans gathering social statistics for employment purposes. See also Alice Salomon for the example of settlement houses in Sklar, *Social Justice Feminists,* 160–67.

142. Numerous examples in Sklar, *Social Justice Feminists,* esp. 79ff.; compare middle-class American travel writers who "used Europe for both social and personal purposes," in William W. Stowe, *Going Abroad: European Travel in Nineteenth-Century American Culture* (Princeton: Princeton University Press, 1994), vii.

143. More important in the long run has been the assumption that criticism of the United States is equivalent to anti-Americanism, a viewpoint that repeatedly has been in the public realm since the anti–Vietnam War protests by Europeans. Further, after the French and German refusal to participate in the Iraq War, some neoconservative Americans began to formulate views to the effect that a European left-wing conspiracy against the United States existed. Just like the left-wing German travelers of the late nineteenth century, those neoconservatives took some of their own social assumptions and transposed them on others. At least the German leftists took lengthy tours to see and hear from people in the United States, sought out precise data, and looked at social context.

144. Alexander Schmidt, *Reisen in die Moderne. Der Amerika-Diskurs des deutschen Bürgertum vor dem Ersten Weltkrieg* (Berlin: Akademie, 1997). Otto, *Deutsche Amerika-Bilder,* 267, argues similarly about some German authors reflecting their own antimodern views.

145. Helbich, "Different, but Not," 129; see also Hoerder, *Labor Migration,* 8–13, on the myths of exceptionalism.

146. Liebknecht, *Ein Blick in die Neue Welt,* 68–69, 74, 123–24, 213–15.

147. Legien, *Aus Amerikas Arbeiterbewegung,* 10–14, 99–101.

Mapping Modernity: Jews and Other German Travelers

Nils H. Roemer

In the nineteenth century, in exchange for their religious, cultural, and political transformation, Jews in German lands received civic liberties. With the granting of equal rights, the political status of Jews radically changed, their religious practice modernized, and their culture was transformed. Identifying themselves to a large extent with the emerging German middle class and its culture, Jews in Germany became in many ways Germans with one difference: they remained Jewish.

As travelers to America, Jews did not markedly differ from other Germans. Indeed, Jews, like other Germans, became increasingly mobile. Not "only the privileged few had ventured abroad," as Stefan Zweig observed in his memoirs.[1] Moreover, the celebrated Jewish writers, journalists, novelists, and artists from central Europe partook in the debate over America's virtues and vices, published their travelogues for a wide and diverse audience, and intensely reflected on Jewish life in the larger American urban centers. Yet their curiosity, literacy, and intellectual mobility strike a familiar chord with Yuri Slezkine's characterization of Jews as "Mercurians," whom he views as moderns par excellence.[2] To many Jewish travelers, visiting the United States offered an opportunity to compare and contrast it with Europe, the Soviet Union, and Palestine. Whereas the United States commonly stood for capitalism, liberalism, equality, and the ideology of the melting pot, the Soviet Union promised to solve and overcome class, ethnic, and religious differences by promoting a new, radically secular Yiddish Jewish culture during the 1920s, in contrast to Zionists' aspirations in Palestine, who labored to forge a new Hebrew national Jewish community.[3] Surveying these different locations, Arthur Holitscher, Egon Erwin Kisch, Joseph Roth, Stefan Zweig, and Hermann Struck became highly mobile itinerant writers, who explored for themselves and their readers these new worlds.

Unlike many other German travelers to the United States—who in their own way do not form a cohesive group, but are differentiated by gender, class, and politics—most of the more famous Jewish travel writers of the early twentieth century never fully committed themselves to any of the competing ideologies of liberalism, communism, and nationalism. Kisch remained critical of the United States, and Holitscher's enthusiasm about America quickly waned. Their endorsement of the Soviet Union had its limits too and their political leftist orientation remained eclectic and unorthodox. Roth combined his celebration of Europe and his infatuation with Paris with his nostalgia for the Austro-Hungarian Empire, and his dismissal of America with his ambivalent hopes for the Soviet Union. Roth never endorsed Zionism, while Holitscher's hopes for Palestine diminished. The famous illustrator Struck discovered the grandeur of New York's skyscrapers, but found solace in images of eastern European men and also in Palestine's landscapes. Even in Stefan Zweig's writings, defenses and celebrations of Europe grated against a romantic approach to America. A marginal and global perspective shaped the Jewish travelers' intellectual and political uncertainty and distinguished them from other German tourists in America. Like many other Jewish intellectuals of the Weimar Republic, their liminality resists classification and describes them at the same time.[4]

Indeed, travel formed a cultural practice that involved transcending cultural, political, and national boundaries. The travelers' cosmopolitan competencies—the arts of crossing, translation, and hybridity—situated them and their readers in a global context.[5] To survey foreign places became a way to experience, situate, and think about the self and the community. The German Jewish journalist, satirist, and writer Kurt Tucholsky instructed travelers to let go and open themselves to new experiences, and the perceptive sociologist Siegfried Kracauer observed that travel "granted access to the Beyond."[6]

Crossing the Atlantic brought Jews and other Germans into contact with a decisively different society that encapsulated other concepts and models of modernity, Jewish cultures, and identities.[7] Yet, travelers' descriptions often combined confidence with a sense of crisis, and enchantment with critical distance. They traversed freely and often ambivalently over the conflicting American terrain of modernity. Moreover, America during the 1920s significantly lost its appeal for many travel writers. Traveling therefore became more often a search than an experience of homecoming, a search that testified not only to a great deal of curiosity but betrayed a profound sense of not feeling at home at home. In his path-breaking essay, the sociologist Georg Simmel noted that "wandering is the liberation from every given point in space," and thus the opposite to any fixation.[8] What Simmel describes here—the key elements of the stranger who does not belong—became also often a key feature of the traveler. This is particularly true for travel writers from the Austro-Hungarian Empire like Holitscher, Zweig, Roth, and Kisch, who had all moved to Berlin. To many, the German capital appeared as an urban center without tradition, that was destined to reinvent itself constantly, destroy its own history, and leave its inhabitants alienated and in isolation.[9] Holitscher, who had been born into an upper-middle class Jewish family in Budapest in 1869, felt that already the size of the German capital made any sense of community impossible, and was probably extrapolating from his own experience when he observed that modern humans do not have a home.[10] Struck's etchings of the turn of the century chronicle the rapid industrialization of the capital. He juxtaposed images of untainted natural landscape with intrusion on the outskirts of Berlin of factories and new buildings with chimneys.[11] Within the modernizing and industrializing urban setting that gave rise to a sense of anonymity and disenchantment, longing and belonging took on varied forms and emerged as interrelated categories, and not necessarily in opposition. Nevertheless, the fleeting curiosity, encounter, and enchantment with America allowed travelers to think about themselves, culture, and politics in a more global context, and to engage the conflicting forms of Jewish identity and culture.

America's Modernity and the Jews

Travel and travel writing situated Jews at the borders of various overlapping interests, and balanced national context with a global orientation. Already during the nineteenth century, many Germans read travel books about America, like the *Report on a Journey to the Western States of North America* (1829) by Gottfried Duden, in addition to letters of emigrant friends and family members. Enticed by Duden's celebration of America, many Jews and other Germans could also recite Goethe's famous utopian lines from 1827: "America, you've got it better."[12] The promise of a new life, equality, and economic advancement lured in particular many German Jews across the Atlantic who were denied legal rights at home. Beginning in the 1820s, a process of continuous German Jewish, family-oriented chain migration to America began, that constituted what is called the "German period" in American-Jewish history, spanning roughly from 1825 to 1870.[13]

During those decades, reports about the United States in the German Jewish press fluctuated, reflecting the constant changing conditions in Germany. To some German Jewish writers, America symbolized liberty and the promise of the new era, as was the case with Ludwig Boerne, and even with Heinrich Heine during the 1820s.[14] During the Revolution of 1848 the Bohemian Jewish writer Leopold Kompert penned his famous "Off to America," in which he despaired about the Old World and flagellated those who wanted to remain in Europe. He compared them to the Israelites who had succumbed to the fleshpots of Egypt. In contrast, emigration to Kompert represented the opportunity to be "free at once."[15]

The widely traveled German Jew Israel Joseph Benjamin explored the new Jewish communities in his published *Drei Jahre in Amerika, 1859–1862* (1862). With a number of impressive letters of introduction by Alexander von Humboldt and others, he traveled all over the country and detailed the lives of the various Jewish communities and their social and religious institutions. To him, America represented the realm in which the common bond between all people was manifesting itself and where Jews were playing an important role in the making of the new civilization.[16]

Yet, the United States remained for most Jews less important than European countries. Newspaper articles on the United States were few and often presented the country as exotic, as did descriptions about Jews in Argentina, North Africa, or New Zealand.[17] Moreover, despite the promises of equality, some Jewish commentators were less infatuated and pointed to slavery and the extermination of American Indians.[18] Others warned in their articles of the threat that materialism and the total voluntarism of religious life posed for the Jewish community in America.[19]

When Jews in Germany finally achieved full legal equality with the creation of the Wilhelmine Reich in 1871, America initially became less appealing. German Jews, as George Mosse observed, "had been emancipated simultaneously into the age of *Bildung* and middle-class respectability."[20] Yet the nation-state that Bismarck created was little more than a federation of largely sovereign states, and even under Wilhelm II, Prussia's political dominance did not dampen the strength of regional cultures and identities. For many Jews, Germany's religious, social, and regional diversity provided ample justification for their self-assertion as a distinct ethnic group in the fin de siècle.[21]

Moreover, uncertainties and the growing discontent of the fin de siècle gave rise to a revival of Jewish cultures. The later Zionist Max Nordau in his famous *Degeneration* (1892) declared that all values and norms had become dislodged from their previous places of common acceptance, giving way to an almost apocalyptic sense of the end of civilization. The resurgence of anti-Semitism and the perceived threat of wide-scale assimilation only intensified the sense of unease amongst many Jews. Searching for alternative paths, the "renaissance of Jewish culture," a concept coined in 1901 by Martin Buber, who was both a western and eastern European Jew, was partly spurred by a new enchantment with eastern European Jewry, which took hold of a generation that was rebelling against the Jewish culture inherited from their fathers and mothers.[22] The initial glorification of the *Ostjuden* reflected the searching generation, which placed the notion of an authentic and thriving eastern European Jewry in opposition to allegedly faltering western European Jewish communities.

The location of eastern European immigrants in western European and American urban centers therefore captured the curiosity of many urban Jews. Beth Wenger underscored how uptown Jews temporarily visited the East Side during the first decades of the twentieth century. Indeed, New York's Lower East Side formed a formidable space of exotic curiosity for uptown Jews, but its place was not limited to the Jewish imagination of America.[23] Eastern

European quarters in larger metropolitan centers, and their initial association with the dangerous, mysterious, unknown, and impenetrable, produced a wealth of literature by Jewish and non-Jewish social investigators, journalists, and travelers. Sociological studies conducted in New York quickly became available and made German Jewish readers familiar with the degradation and squalor of New York's East Side.[24] Yiddish poems translated in the German Jewish press captured New York awakening in the morning "in grey fog," where the citizens emerge in "sorrow" and "rotten."[25] Articles from the correspondent of the *Berliner Lokalanzeiger* reprinted in the Zionist *Die Welt* portrayed the Lower East Side as a realm of squalor, where immigrants lived in poverty without access to education, destined to be exploited in the city's sweatshops.[26]

The emerging curiosity about American cities and the frontier amongst German Jews therefore initially did not entail the Jewish neighborhoods in larger metropolitan centers. Kafka's famous letter to his father encapsulated the generational rift and his quest for a new source of Jewish authenticity, while his well-known lecture on Yiddish, delivered in 1912, testifies to his infatuation with eastern European Jews.[27] Yet Kafka, the devout traveler and an even more enthusiastic reader of travel literature, never merged his interest in the United States with his searching enthusiasm for eastern European Jews.

To be sure, Kafka never visited America, but several of his relatives had emigrated there and sent back accounts of their lives to Europe. The bohemian Jewish writer also attended in June 1912 a lecture by Frantisek Soukup, a Czech sociologist who had visited the United States to study its political and social structures. Kafka's most important source was Arthur Holitscher's 1911 travel diary, which gave him a geographical and architectural sense of America. Despite these many sources, however, the United States appears in his *Amerika (The Man Who Disappeared)*, published posthumously in 1927, as both recognizable and disfigured in contrast to his sources, and without any mention of the eastern European Jewish immigrants.[28]

Holitscher was in this respect very different. Initially, he made his name with a novel exploring the early modern Jewish legend of the Golem, which he published in 1908 in Berlin, testifying thereby to the search amongst his generation for an alternative Jewish past. Yet this was a passing curiosity to Holitscher, who became one of the most prolific travel writers of this period. He crossed the Atlantic in 1911 and in 1912 and subsequently published the impression of his journeys.[29] Attracted to America as the land of modernity and rapid technological change, Holitscher recommended surveying New York initially from a skyscraper.[30] Despite the distant and yet all-encompassing view this provided, his enthusiasm became dimmed as he surveyed the country from a socialist perspective, attacking social values, the commodification of culture, racism, and anti-Semitism.[31]

His experience of eastern European Jews also remained ambiguous, marked and marred both by paternalistic views and initial envy. En route to America, Holitscher decided to learn more about eastern European Jews, but instead of an idealized appreciation, Holitscher viewed the immigrants from a critical distance. To him, these eastern European Jews remained isolated from others and formed their own ghetto even while traveling. With dismay he assumed that they were not intending to conquer the West, and would remain impoverished in New York.[32] Meeting eastern European Jews gave Holitscher a sense of cultural and social superiority at a time when his future collaborator Herman Struck, the widely traveled artist, religious Zionist, and native of Berlin, began to promote a very different perspective of New York and of eastern European Jews in his paintings.

Struck, author of the standard text *The Art of Etching* (1908), captured in New York not only famous Liberty Island and the Statue of Liberty, Central Park, Brooklyn Bridge, and New York's skyline, but also various New Yorkers—newspaper boys, shoe cleaners, smokers of opium, factory workers, African Americans, and several notables of the established German Jewish community.[33] In response to the exhibition of some of his drawings in New York, the *New York Times* published an article entitled "German Etcher Finds Our Skyscrapers Beautiful." To the journalist of the *New York Times,* Struck's praise indicated that what hitherto had often been seen "as gawk and grotesque architectural freaks" had found "their first enthusiastic champion abroad in one of the leading German artists of the day."[34]

America and Its Weimar Critics

Struck's admiration of New York's skyline reflected an early fascination with New York as the emblem of modernity. With the collapse of political and social order in Germany at the end of the First World War, America came even more to symbolize everything modern, whether it was admired or feared. Some intellectuals became steadily scandalized at how efficiency, conformity, and capitalism reigned, while jazz, American movies, and modern forms of mass-produced goods for the consumer society radically altered Germany's culture. To others, America served as a promising alternative offering potential redemption for those disenchanted with Germany's own path.[35]

The varied perceptions reflect that the new German republic was simultaneously giving rise to a sense of confidence and crisis. The new progressive government under the socialist Friedrich Ebert and the political and economic weakness created a culture marked by violent political clashes and hopes for renewal and regeneration. The more clearly politicized travel accounts of this period therefore bespoke a measure of hope, as well as a profound dissatisfaction and weariness with present-day Germany and the state of Jewish communities. Heightened expectations and pessimism increasingly grated against each other in these accounts and testify to the upending of previously existing convictions and certainties.

Jews and other Germans investigated these options as travelers. The famous German Jewish author Alfred Kerr, who was one of the most widely read theater critics of the Weimar Republic, sought to reacquaint readers with the United States and criticized the dichotomy of viewing America as the embodiment of civilization and Europe as the bulwark of culture. To him Germany was "lacerated," but New York was genius.[36] Not all Jewish travelers shared this enthusiasm for the United States. El Lissitzky viewed America critically with his *Boat Ticket* in 1922, which the Russian Jewish artist had produced in Berlin. The painting that illustrated a story about an old man waiting for a boat ticket from his son in the United States sardonically contrasts the symbols of hope—the ticket and an advertisement of an American liner—with the Hebrew inscription "Here lies buried."[37]

In Holitscher's prewar *America: Today and Tomorrow*, a photograph of the Statue of Liberty welcomed and introduced the continent to his readers.[38] Kafka, in his *Amerika (The Man who Disappeared)*, dramatically changed this iconographic entry when he replaced the statue's torch with a sword, thereby replacing the notion of liberty with an icon of dreadful power.[39] Echoing his even further diminished enthusiasm for America, Holitscher too now felt that in the face of skyscrapers, all existing concepts of humanity, beauty, and harmony had been shattered.[40]

Walking around the Lower East Side with his illustrator was therefore for Holitscher no experience of homecoming. Turning to the Bowery, they found eastern European Jews, who had always been wandering, lost on their way to the Promised Land enveloped in longing. The immigrants' transition from Europe to America embodied not just their liberation from hostility but resulted in the creation of a new ghetto.[41] Moreover, what had hitherto been a symbol of New York's modernity appeared now as an emblem of Jewish degradation. To Holitscher it seemed that as much as the iron chains that secured the Brooklyn Bridge and tied the upward-fleeing construction to the ground, the East Side was wedded to squalor and depravity.[42] In view of the impoverished Jewish population, Holitscher no longer saw the "Babylonian stronghold" (*Zwingburg*) on the Hudson as a home for Jews; rather, he saw Palestine as the old and new home.[43]

The Austrian journalist and novelist Joseph Roth equally derided America. Roth, who was born in a small Jewish community on the eastern border of the Habsburg monarchy, surveyed eastern European Jews in the East and in the West. *The Wandering Jews* essentially narrates Roth's encounters with eastern European Jews, composed of several articles he had previously published in major German newspapers. In describing various eastern European quarters, Roth retraced his own biography. He depicted Vienna (the city that had welcomed him at the age of nineteen), Berlin (where he had worked as a journalist), and Paris, his destination as a foreign correspondent for the *Frankfurter Zeitung* in 1925.[44] To Roth, eastern European Jews were no longer an embarrassment or an embodiment of authenticity. Chronicling the life of eastern European Jews promoted his preference for transnationality. His identification with eastern European Jews led him to dismiss Zionism as a form of hyper-assimilation and the desire for a homeland as an anachronistic return to nationalism.[45]

Roth also dismissed the land of promises as a false hope for Eastern European immigrants. His exploration of eastern European Jews in Europe therefore stood in sharp contrast to his discussion of New York; in a telling fashion, those who crossed the Atlantic were quickly quarantined in sight of the Statue of Liberty and only dreamed about New York, reflecting the restrictive immigration laws passed in 1921 and 1924.[46] Yet even their hopes and dreams Roth viewed as false. Like Kafka and Holitscher before him, Roth derided the Statue of Liberty as a symbol of liberty tainted by racism: "To some extent, the reality does correspond to the symbol. Not because they really are all that serious about liberty in the new country, but because they have people who are more Jewish than Jews, which is to say the Negroes.... For the first time a Jew's race is actually to his advantage."[47] Moreover, life on New York's Lower East Side would mean living "among twelve-story buildings, surrounded by Chinese, Hungarians, and other Jews. Once more he will be a peddler, once more fear the police, once more be bullied."[48] Equally, Roth portrayed Jewish life in America in similar negative fashion in *Job: The Story of a Simple Man* (1930), which captured the miserable life of Mendel Singer. An east European Jew, Mendel, a poor Bible teacher from a small village, leaves Berlin and immigrates with his family to America. The journey to America appears as a process of assimilation and corruption.[49]

Like Holitscher and Roth, Egon Erwin Kisch was critical of America, and he opened his report with a satirical description of the difficulties a reporter faced in entering "God's own country." His portrait amounted to an indictment of America's culture and what appeared as an excessive capitalist system that produced social injustice.[50] Growing disenchantment with the United States in light of restrictive immigration policy also informed Holitscher's renewed discussion. At the end of the 1920s, he had given up hope that the American melting pot could overcome ethnic differences, noticing existing social and racial segregation, and was fully aware of the fate of the homeless and weak.[51] Holitscher left the United States dismayed at a time when his infatuation with the Soviet Union and Palestine had also faded.

However, the more critical explorations of America during the Weimar Republic also reflected the perceived threat posed by the popularity of American culture in Europe. During the beginning of the 1920s Roth captured the growing presence of this culture in the German capital.[52] He became increasingly critical of this trend and saw the United States as the nemesis of Paris. In an article on the celebration of the fourteenth of July in Paris in 1925, he described "America over Paris" in the shape of large advertisement balloon. The balloon became a haunting presence of America in Paris and made him feel a "sense of darkness."[53]

In the same year, horrified, Stefan Zweig published a feuilleton in the *Neue Freie Presse* describing an American cultural invasion sweeping Europe. Differences in nationality, heritage, race, and class were systematically eliminated by this intrusion that obliterated traditional European modes of thought, conversation, and inquiry, the novelist believed.[54] Zweig rejected Helene Scheu-Riesz's call to Europeans to look beyond their parochial church tower toward the energy generated between large skyscrapers, a call she made in the *Neue Freie Presse* in her review of Alice Salomon's *Culture in Transition: Travel Impressions of America (1924)*.[55]

Salomon, a prominent advocate in the German and international women's movement, had indeed much more positively reviewed the United States in her travelogue after she had published numerous travel letters in German newspapers, magazines, and scientific periodicals. She believed that women were better off in America.[56] A convert from Judaism to Protestantism, she approached the immigrant quarters not from the perspective of Jewish culture, but seeing overall the intermingling of various immigrant groups as the space where America was in the making. Keenly aware of the raging racism,[57] it was in the immigrant quarters that she saw the new American race was being born. Apparently informed by Israel Zangwill's play *The Melting Pot* (1908) and Mary Antin's account of her migration, the Lower East Side became a blueprint of the future. Change manifested itself here early in the women, as Salomon believed that Jewish girls already appeared slimmer and that they had lost other visible markers of their ethnicity.[58]

Notwithstanding Zweig's indictment of American culture and society, his own view of America hinged almost entirely on his perception of Europe. One of the most popular writers of the period, he had visited America for the first time in 1911. In the years prior to the First World War, Walter Rathenau suggested that Zweig explore either India or America to gain a better perspective on Europe.[59] Zweig first visited America when he was no longer a frequent traveler but a refugee. In his memoir *Die Welt von Gestern,* which Zweig started to write in 1939 in exile in the United States, he gave a very different sense of America. Contrary to his vehement criticism during the 1920s of the United States, he recalled in exile that he had approached America in a romantic fashion: "America was Walt Whitman, the land of the new rhythm and the coming world brotherhood."[60] In this spirit, he entered New York with "fraternal feeling instead of the usual arrogance of the European."[61] Slightly bored after a few days, he nevertheless found pleasure in imagining the city from the eyes of a European immigrant. After leaving his hotel, he experienced a virtual immigration, looking for work and housing: "I invented a game for myself. I pretended that I was friendless and alone, a jobless emigrant with my last seven dollars in my pocket." Less dismayed by the fate of immigrants, this diversion convinced him of the "divine freedom of the country. No one had asked me about my nationality, my religion, my origin."[62]

Conclusion

Many central European travelers came out of the war disillusioned and hoping for a new beginning. Visiting the United States not only testified to vicarious interest but underlined the constant search for alternative models of Jewish culture and self-understanding. Yet already during the 1920s a much more critical perspective was emerging. For Jewish travelers, worries about the pace of modernity and the intrusion of American culture faded into the background, and restrictive U.S. immigration policies and racism became the prism through which they made sense of their American experience. This realization further complicated the already highly idiosyncratic political orientation of Jewish travelers, who often combined what otherwise seem contradictory orientations in their outlook. Thinking about culture, modernity, and identity in the highly charged political climate of the Weimar Republic and within a global context intensified the sense of dislocation, alienation, and isolation, which otherwise had often been associated with the urban culture of the German capital. In the end, most of the published travel reports about America, while revealing cosmopolitan competence, document not a process of homecoming but only an ongoing search, a process of disappointment and loss.

NOTES

1. Stefan Zweig, *The World of Yesterday: An Autobiography by Stefan Zweig* (Lincoln: University of Nebraska Press, 1964), 194.

2. Yuri Slezkine, *The Jewish Century* (Princeton: Princeton University Press, 2004).

3. Nils Roemer, "Jewish Traveling Cultures and the Competing Visions of Modernity," *Central European History* 42, no. 2 (2009): 1–21.

4. Steven E. Aschheim, *Beyond the Border: The German-Jewish Legacy Abroad* (Princeton: Princeton University Press, 2007), 101.

5. James Clifford, "Mixed Feelings," *Cosmopolitics: Thinking and Feeling Beyond the Nation,* ed. Pheng Cheah and Bruce Robbins (Minneapolis: University of Minnesota Press, 1998), 368.

6. Kurt Tucholsky, "Die Kunst, falsch zu reisen," in *Kurt Tucholsky: Gesammelte Werke (1929–1932),* ed. Mary Gerold-Tucholsky and Fritz J. Raddatz (Reinbek: Rowohlt, 1961), 115–18, and Siegfried Kracauer, "Travel and Dance," in *The Mass Ornament: Weimar Essays,* ed. and trans. Thomas Y. Levin (Cambridge, Mass.: Harvard University Press, 1995), 71.

7. Anselm Doering-Manteuffel, "Dimensionen von Amerikanisierung in der deutschen Gesellschaft," *Archiv für Sozialgeschichte* 35 (1995): 1–34. For a survey of German travel writing about America, see Theresa Mayer Hammond, *American Paradise: German Travel Literature from Duden to Kisch* (Heidelberg:

Winter, 1980) and Alexander Schmidt, *Reisen in die Moderne: Der Amerika-Diskurs des deutschen Bürgertums vor dem Ersten Weltkrieg im europäischen Vergleich* (Berlin: Akademie, 1997).

8. Georg Simmel, "Stranger," in *The Sociology of Georg Simmel,* ed. and trans. Kurt H. Wolf (London: Collier-Macmillan, 1950), 402.

9. Steven M. Lowenstein, "Was Urbanization Harmful to Jewish Tradition and Identity in Germany?" *Studies in Contemporary Jewry* 15 (1999): 80–106.

10. Arthur Holitscher, *Mein Leben in dieser Zeit. Der 'Lebensgeschichte eines Rebellen': Zweiter Band (1907–1925)* (Potsdam: Gustav Kiepenhauer Verlag, 1928), 75, 224.

11. *Hermann Struck, 1876–1944,* ed. Ruthi Ofek und Chana Schütz (Berlin: Open Museum, Stiftung Neue Synagoge, 2007), 66–68, 72–73, 228.

12. Victor Lange, "Goethes Amerikabild: Wirklichkeit und Vision," *Amerika in der deutschen Literatur,* ed. Sigrid Bauschinger, Horst Denkler, and Wilfried Malsch (Stuttgart: Reclam, 1975), 63–74.

13. On the German Jewish immigration to America in the nineteenth century, see Avraham Barkai, *Branching Out: German Jewish Immigration to the United States, 1820–1914* (New York: Holmes & Meier, 1994).

14. Steven M. Lowenstein, "The View from the Old World: German-Jewish Perspectives," in *The Americanization of the Jews,* ed. Robert M. Seltzer and Norman J. Cohen (New York: New York University Press, 1995), 26–27.

15. Leopold Kompert, "Off to America" (1848), in *The Jew in the Modern World: A Documentary History,* ed. Paul Mendes-Flohr and Jehuda Reinharz (Oxford: Oxford University Press, 1995), 463–65.

16. Israel Joseph Benjamin, *Drei Jahre in America, 1859–1862* (Hannover, 1862), xii.

17. Lowenstein, "The View from the Old World," 20.

18. Lothar Kahn, "Early German-Jewish Writers and the Image of America (1820–1840)," *Leo Baeck Institute Yearbook* 31(1986): 413–16.

19. Lowenstein, "The View from the Old World," 26–27.

20. George L. Mosse, *German Jews Beyond Judaism* (Bloomington: Indiana University Press 1985), 18.

21. Neil Gregor, Nils Roemer, and Mark Roseman, ed., *German History from the Margins* (Bloomington: Indiana University Press, 2006).

22. Martin Buber, "Jüdische Wissenschaft," *Die Welt* 5, no. 41 (1901): 1–2, and 5, no. 43 (1901): 1–2. In general, see Aschheim, *Brothers and Strangers*, 121–84; Jack Wertheimer, *Unwelcome Strangers, East European Jews in Imperial Germany* (New York: Oxford University Press, 1987); Shulamit Volkov, "The Dynamics of Dissimulation: Ostjuden and German Jews," in *The Jewish Response to German Culture*, ed. Jehuda Reinharz and Walter Schatzberg (Hanover, N.H.: Published for Clark University by University Press of New England, 1985), 195–211; Paul Mendes-Flohr, "Fin de Siècle Orientalism: The Ostjuden and the Aesthetics of Jewish Self-Affirmation," *Divided Passions: Jewish Intellectuals and the Experience of Modernity* (Detroit : Wayne State University Press, 1991), 77–132; David A. Brenner, *Marketing Identities: The Invention of Jewish Ethnicity in "Ost und West"* (Detroit : Wayne State University Press, 1998).

23. Beth S. Wenger, "Memory as Identity: The Invention of the Lower East Side," *American Jewish History* 85 (1997): 3–27. See also Hasia R. Diner, Jeffrey Shandler, and Beth S. Wenger, ed., *Remembering the Lower East Side* (Bloomington: Indiana University Press, 2000).

24. A. C., "Review of 'The Spirit of the Ghetto': Studies of the Jewish Quarter in New-York," *Die Welt* 7, no. 5 (1903): 9; Manfred Georg, "Das Newyorker Ghetto," *Ost und West* 9, no. 7 (1909): 461–66. See also "Vom Ghetto in New-York," *Die Welt* 6, no. 27 (1902): 9–10; "Die Juden in New-York," *Die Welt* 6, no. 37 (1902): 5–6. See also the description based on Jacob A. Riis, *How the Other Half Lives*, in Alfred Weissberger, "Das amerikanische Eldorado!" *Die Welt* 6, no. 50 (1902): 13–14; Maurice Fishberg, "Die Armut unter den Juden in New-York," *Zeitschrift für Demographie und Statistik der Juden* 4, no. 8 (1908): 113–18; and "Health and Sanitation of the Immigrant Jewish Population of New York: Physical Anthropology of the Jews," *Die Welt* 7, no. 10 (1903): 15.

25. A. Walt, "Ein Morgen in New-York," *Die Freistatt* 1, no. 9 (1913): 538.

26. "El Dorado," *Die Welt* 6, no. 34 (1902): 10–11.

27. Franz Kafka, "Letter to His Father" and "An Introductory Talk on the Yiddish Language," in *Franz Kafka: Dearest Father: Stories and Other Writings,* trans. Ernst Kaiser and Eithne Wilkens (New York: Schocken, 1954), 138–96, 381–86. See also *The Cambridge Companion to Kafka,* ed. Julian Preece (Cambridge: Cambridge University Press, 2002), 6.

28. Franz Kafka, *Amerika (The Man Who Disappeared),* trans. Michael Hofmann (New York: New Directions, 2002). On this, see Mark Anderson, *Kafka's Clothes: Ornament and Aestheticism in the Habsburg Fin de Siècle* (Oxford: Oxford University Press, 1995), 104.

29. The book was first published in *Neue Rundschau* in 1911 and 1912.

30. Arthur Holitscher, *Amerika: Heute und Morgen: Reiseerlebnisse,* 2nd ed. (Berlin: S. Fischer, 1912), 57–58.

31. Ibid., 365. There is much that Holitscher admires about America but he remains ambivalent, as his description of Chicago and one of its slaughterhouses makes evident. Influenced by Upton Sinclair's *The Jungle* (1905), Holitscher believes that reforms have only superficially implemented improvements. See Holitscher, *Amerika: Heute und Morgen,* 294–96, 303–4.

32. Ibid., 20–21.

33. *Hermann Struck, 1876–1944,* ed. Ofek und Schütz, 216–21, 236–37, and Jane Rusel, *Hermann Struck: Das Leben und das graphische Werk eines jüdischen Künstlers* (Frankfurt am Main: P. Lang, 1997), 131–42.

34. "German Etcher Finds Our Skyscrapers Beautiful," *New York Times,* January 26, 1913.

35. Dan Diner, *America in the Eyes of the Germans: An Essay on Anti-Americanism* (Princeton, N.J.: Markus Wiener Publishers, 1996), 70. See also, Adelheid von Saldern, "Überfremdungsängste: Gegen die Amerikanisierung der deutschen Kultur in den zwanziger Jahren," in *Amerikanisierung: Traum und Alptraum im Deutschland des 20. Jahrhunderts,* ed. Alf Lüdtke, Inge Marssolek, and Adelheid von Saldern (Stuttgart: Steiner, 1997), 213–44; Mary Nolan, *Visions of Modernity: American Business and the Modernization of Germany* (New York: Oxford University Press, 1994); and Beeke Sell Tower, "'Ultramodern and Ultraprimitive': Shifting Meanings in the Imagery of Americanism in the Art of Weimar Germany," in *Dancing on the Volcano: Essays on the Culture of the*

Weimar Republic, ed. Thomas Kniesche and Stephen Brockmann (Columbia, S.C.: Camden House, 1994), 85. On the contemporary debate, see *Weimar Republic Sourcebook,* ed. Anton Kaes, Martin Jay, and Edward Dimendberg (Berkeley: University of California Press, 1994), 393–411.

36. Alfred Kerr, *New York and London. Stätten des Geschicks. Zwanzig Kapitel nach dem Weltkrieg* (Berlin: S. Fischer, 1923), prologue without pagination, vii, 88. See also Alfred Kerr, *Yankee-land. Eine Reise* (Berlin: R. Mosse, 1925) and Hans Goslar, *Amerika 1922 mit 10 Bildern von Hermann Struck* (Berlin-Wilmersdorf: Hermann Paetel Verlag, 1922).

37. Grace Cohen Grossman, *Jewish Art* (New York: Hugh Lauter Levin Associates, 1995), 287.

38. Holitscher, *Amerika: Heute und Morgen,* 11.

39. Kafka, *Amerika,* 3.

40. Arthur Holitscher, *Amerika, Heute und Morgen: Reiseerlebnisse* (Berlin: S. Fischer Verlag, 1919), 6–7.

41. Arthur Holitscher, *Amerika. Zwanzig Radierungen von Hermann Struck* (Berlin: Hans Heinrich Tilgner Verlag, 1922), 14.

42. Ibid., 17–18.

43. Ibid., 23–24.

44. Joseph Roth, *The Wandering Jews,* trans. Michael Hofmann (London: Granta Books, 2001); Joseph Roth, *What I Saw: Reports from Berlin, 1920–1923,* trans. Michael Hofmann (London: Granta Books, 2003), 31–50. See also David Horrocks, "The Representation of Jews and of Anti-Semitism in Joseph Roth's Early Journalism," German Life and Letters 58, no. 2 (2005): 141–54.

45. Roth, *What I Saw,* 49.

46. Roth, *The Wandering Jews,* 102. See also the reprint in Josef Roth, "Ein Jude geht nach Amerika," *Menorah* 5, no. 9 (1927): 517–21.

47. Roth, *The Wandering Jews,* 102.

48. Ibid., 103.

49. Peter W. Jansen, "Der autofiktive Erzähler. Roman und Existenz bei Joseph Roth," *Joseph Roth und die Tradition: Aufsatz- und Materialiensammlung,* ed. David Bronsen (Darmstadt: Agora, 1975), 364–73.

50. Egon Erwin Kisch, *Paradies Amerika. Landung in Australien,* Gesammelte Werke 4, ed. Bodo Uhse and Gisela Kirsch (Berlin: Aufbau-Verlag, 1983), 248.

51. Arthur Holitscher, *Wiedersehen mit Amerika. Die Verwandlung der U. S. A.* (Berlin: S. Fischer, 1930), 24–26.

52. Roth, *What I Saw.*

53. Joseph Roth, *Report from a Parisian Paradise: Essays from France, 1925–1939,* trans. Michael Hofmann (New York: W.W. Norton, 2004), 27.

54. Stefan Zweig, "The Monotonization of the World," in *Weimar Republic Sourcebook,* ed. Kaes, Jay, and Dimendberg, 397–400. Zweig's "Die Monotonisierung der Welt" was first published in the *Berliner Börsen-Courier,* February 1, 1925.

55. Helene Scheu-Riesz, "Kultur im Werden," *Neue Freie Presse,* January 24, 1925, 11.

56. Alice Salomon, *Kultur im Werden. Amerikanischen Reiseeindrücke* (Berlin: Ullstein, 1924), 23–30.

57. Robert B. McFarland, "Migration as Mediation: Neue Freie Presse American Correspondent Ann Tizia Leitich and Stefan Zweig's 'Die Monotonisierung der Welt,'" *Seminar: A Journal of Germanic Studies* 42, no. 3 (2006): 242–60.

58. Salomon, *Kultur im Werden,* 32.

59. Zweig, *The World of Yesterday,* 182.

60. Ibid., 188.

61. Ibid.

62. Ibid., 189.

Between Modernity and Antimodernity

From Enthusiasm to Hostility in German Perceptions of Big Cities in America, 1870s–1930s

Andrew Lees

This essay considers two discourses (or topics) in German thought and some of the ways in which they intersected and overlapped as they found expression in a large outpouring of observation and commentary by writers in German between the 1870s and the 1930s. Drawing on a broad base of investigations by others as well as research of my own, I begin with summary accounts both of German views of America and of German views of big cities, to which I shall add at various points in my later remarks. This discussion will provide background for the empirical core of what concerns me in the greater part of what follows: the variety of ways and changes in ways in which numerous Germans viewed, reported on, and evaluated urban environments and urban life in the United States—not only in New York and Chicago but in a host of other places as well. Commentary on built environments will come in for particular attention. Attitudes toward streets, houses, and other structures of a physical sort will, however, be situated in relation to responses to additional aspects of the urban scene. This approach will illuminate not only relations between Germany and America, and German thinking about big cities, but also German encounters with modernity more generally, inasmuch as both the United States, often referred to as *das land der Zukunft* (the land of the future), and the *Großstädt* (big city) were widely regarded as central sites of modernizing developments.

Introduction

The essay focuses on three periods: the early years of the Second Empire (the 1870s and 1880s, when Otto von Bismarck, the empire's architect, still served as imperial chancellor); the second half of the Wilhelmine period (overall, 1888–1918); and the interwar years (1919–1939), beginning with the era of the Weimar Republic and concluding with the first half of the Third Reich. I shall concentrate on half a dozen of the hundreds of writers in German whose writings about urban life in the United States appeared during the period treated here, two from each of these periods: Friedrich Ratzel and Ernst von Hesse-Wartegg; Ludwig Fulda and Arthur Holitscher; and Adolf Halfeld and Colin Ross.[1]

During a somewhat longer period than the one focused on here—between the late 1840s and the early 1940s—and in the writings of many other commentators, German views both of the United States in general and of big cities in general went from affirmation through ambivalence to growing hostility. Many other writers participated in this intellectual and emotional transformation, which was part and parcel of a larger crisis of confidence with regard to modernization. The specific views discussed here are thus put forward not simply because of their inherent interest but also because of the larger developments and trends they represent.

Two Themes in German Thought

For close to half a century, scholars of German history and of German literature have been publishing works that pertain to German perceptions of the United States. Beginning with the period of the American Revolution, they have traced a multifaceted process of reporting about and reflection on a country that drew the attention of central Europeans for a host of reasons. The United States, they have shown, fascinated Germans as well as other Europeans in part because, as an increasingly democratic republic, its political system differed so sharply from the ones that prevailed in their own country well into the twentieth century. Although the natural beauty of a relatively unspoiled and idyllic landscape long attracted many visitors, Germans focused increasingly, starting around 1850, more on what was human-made than on what was "natural," evincing a sense of America as the land of the future not only politically but also economically, socially, and culturally—whether for good, or, as some argued, for ill. Commentators who displayed a negative outlook became increasingly vociferous in expressing their dislikes and their hostility after the United States entered the First World War on the side of the Entente Powers. Criticism of America became still more pronounced during the next quarter-century. It shifted in a positive direction only after the onset of the Cold War. To be sure, anti-Americanism resurfaced, especially on the left, during the Vietnam War and the second Iraq War. Although criticism of the United States emanated particularly from the left, those who voiced it often drew on traditional stereotypes. Their animosities, however, never reached the level of intensity that had been so readily apparent in earlier years.[2]

What about the *Großstadt?* Although there is a large and growing literature of modern *Städtegeschichte* (the history of cities), works that deal with the narrower subject of how Germans thought and felt about urban centers are understandably much less numerous. Scholars have, however, devoted enough attention to this subject so that one can piece together an overall narrative that coincides chronologically with much of the period referred to in the brief account of views of America sketched above. Starting roughly in the 1840s, as the economic, social, and political tensions that contributed to the revolutions of 1848 became increasingly intense, big cities–Berlin in particular–began to emerge as subjects of careful scrutiny and often vigorous debate. Critics of the urban milieu pointed to overcrowding, poor housing, defective sanitation, high death rates, and low birthrates. They also emphasized the decline of religious observance, the putative prevalence of crime and other forms of immorality, and the threats posed to conservative values by politically radical troublemakers. Men and women who defended the big cities did so by emphasizing not only their centrality to the process of economic development but also ways in which they helped to promote cultural institutions and also cultural activity outside institutional frameworks. They pointed, moreover, to further ways in which big cities contributed to progress by serving as laboratories of communal action, where efforts were constantly being undertaken to find urban solutions to urban problems. The conflicting outlooks of critics and defenders remained in an uneasy balance from the mid-nineteenth through the early twentieth century, with a shift in favor of the big city's ideological opponents–like the shift in favor of America's opponents—setting in only after the traumatic experience of the First World War. But unlike ideas about America, ideas about the big city in general (as opposed to the problems and possibilities inherent in particular big cities) have not featured very prominently since the Second World War. The *Großstädte* had largely been accepted as essential features of German society–well worth being rebuilt after the end of a war launched by men whose professed hatred of modern civilization had led to particularly destructive consequences in their country's own cities.[3]

The Ascendancy of Hope

In the nineteenth century, interest in America—in particular, interest in the United States as an increasingly modern, urban society—became widely apparent in German consciousness. Although German travelers, many of whom reported as emigrants back to readers in their native land, had written as early as the 1820s about their experiences in urban settings,[4] the American city came into sharp focus only after German unification. Increasingly after 1871, accounts by Germans of their transatlantic voyages paid just as much attention to urban as to nonurban parts of the country. Indeed, they focused more and more on particular cities in which their authors spent time during their stays, beginning usually with New York, their port of arrival, and going on to discuss at least several others, one of which was generally Chicago. Analytic works—among which (to jump briefly into a slightly later period) the classic two-volume study by the German émigré Hugo Münsterberg stood out[5]—also demonstrated growing interest in developments that pertained to social and economic modernization, whether or not they identified the city as such as a separate variable.

A few statistics that pertain to particular places in America and in Germany will help to clarify some of the reasons for rising interest among Germans in the process of urbanization on the other side of the Atlantic. Both

New York and Chicago clearly qualified already in 1890 not just as *Großstädte* but also as *Weltstädte* (world cities), the first boasting a population of a little over 2.5 million, the other a population of almost 1.1 million, with Philadelphia coming in a close third, at almost 1.05 million. At this time in Germany only Berlin exceeded the million mark, and its size amounted to only about 60 percent of New York's. Germany was itself urbanizing rapidly—more so than any other country in Europe. Its urban sector's overall share of the country's inhabitants, having risen between 1871 and 1890 from 36.1 to 47 percent, was to reach 60 percent in 1910. But both the rate of urban growth and its results were more spectacular in the United States than they were in the German empire.[6] These discrepancies greatly stimulated the belief that Germans could gain needed insight into their own future by contemplating what was taking place in urban centers across the Atlantic. Rapid urbanization in the United States during the late nineteenth century meant that the American example could serve during that period in ways that resembled the functions served by the British example half a century earlier.[7]

Within less than a decade after the German empire's birth, two works appeared in Germany as a result of travels to America by men who had concentrated their attention on the urban scene. Written at a time when urban development still seemed to many observers in central Europe, as elsewhere, to represent a largely unalloyed good, these volumes evinced an unmistakable view of cities as places where progress was proceeding at a swift pace.[8] As an urban country, America was catching up with and in many respects surpassing the continent from which it had sprung—socially, economically, architecturally, and in other ways as well, many of them readily visible to the traveler's eye. Consequently, in this view, it was leading the way toward not only new but also improved models of city living.

The author of the first of these works was a young journalist, Friedrich Ratzel (1844–1904), who later became Germany's most distinguished geographer. Midway in his preparation to become an academic, he published articles in the leading newspaper in the city of Cologne, the *Kölnische Zeitung*, several of which dealt with his travels to various parts of Europe. Based in a city that lay near Germany's industrial heartland, the Ruhr Valley, the newspaper's editors soon commissioned Ratzel to travel in and report about the United States as well. Developments here, they felt, were bound to be of great interest to their readers, owing to the fact that Germany and America were facing many of the same problems. Ratzel spent the period between August of 1873 and October of 1874 in the United States, journeying from the Northeast to the Southeast and thence to the West before embarking in San Francisco on a return voyage to Europe. Following publication of the articles he wrote about his travels, which comprised accounts of advances, conditions, and structures in more than two dozen localities, he selected and revised some of them for a book which was published in 1876.[9]

In a general introduction that preceded his specific reports about individual settlements, Ratzel offered a brief but wide-ranging view of urbanization as a process that both expressed and facilitated social progress. "The life of a people," he argued, "is blended, compressed, and accelerated in cities, with the result that it not only becomes richer and more productive but also that its characteristics become clearer and present a lasting testimony to posterity. Urban areas bring out the greatest, best, and most typical aspects of a people." This had been so in ancient times, and it remained the rule. To be sure, advances in the area of transportation were breaking down earlier barriers between cities and the countryside that surrounded them. People did not need to live as closely together as had formerly been the case in order to engage in fruitful interaction, whether economically or intellectually, and the lifestyles of rural dwellers were themselves becoming increasingly urbanized as a result of industrial mechanization. On balance, however, enhanced transportation continued to favor the growth of an urban civilization, which was springing up in much of North America "in fresh, unspoiled, virgin soil as luxuriantly as corn or wheat in the black soil of the prairies." The agricultural metaphor here functioned as a further means of highlighting the vitality and the health of urban life, in America as well as elsewhere.[10]

American cities not only bore witness to the economic and the geographic factors that had stimulated their growth but also made manifest various "accomplishments of a higher intellectual order." What Ratzel had in mind in this respect involved not only support for "the arts and sciences" but also schools, libraries, and inexpensive books and newspapers.

Mention of achievements in these areas helped to provide a context for largely favorable references to American initiatives in the area of city planning, which had greatly enhanced the human-made environments in which city dwellers lived. While noting that Boston, New York, and New Orleans contained old sections that, "with narrow, winding little streets," somewhat resembled European cities, he emphasized that such places were unusual, and he pointed with approval to the tendency to design cities "spaciously, airily, and regularly." Among the other features that Ratzel ascribed to most American cities, several clearly counted as evidence of qualities he found attractive. Single-family houses, which testified to "a healthy preference for private family dwellings," separation of residential areas from commercial ones, well-developed systems of horse-drawn trolleys and of water mains (both of which were facilitated by straight streets), beautiful parks, public gardens, and cemeteries (all of which indicated close links between culture and nature), and magnificent bridges all heightened the appeal of the urban scene.[11]

Ratzel readily admitted that not all was well. Houses for individual families were steadily receding in big cities such as New York in favor of tenement houses, which used land and capital more effectively, and they would inevitably continue to do so. Such buildings had become increasingly prevalent and increasingly crowded in New York, and as a result the poorer quarters of the city were more densely inhabited than those of London. Still, he observed, the problems experienced by some German cities in the area of housing were worse even than New York's. And yet, effective attention to these problems by his compatriots fell well below the level displayed by the standards set in America. Widespread concern in the United States about matters pertaining to public health—not only in New York but also in Boston and Philadelphia—reflected purposeful and effective desires among American activists to find urban solutions to urban problems.[12]

Ratzel reported enthusiastically about educational and cultural developments in many of the places he visited. He wrote a great deal early in his work about schools, colleges, and other evidence of intellectual life not only in New York and in the Boston area (reporting at length about Harvard University), which he regarded as the mental center of North America, but also in cities to their south and west. Philadelphia had its Franklin Institute, which fostered knowledge about progress in the areas of chemistry and physics, the University of Pennsylvania, with its magnificent building for the faculty of arts and sciences, and Girard College, which provided free education at the secondary level for over five hundred orphans. It could also boast of 396 public elementary schools, two major libraries, a library for books in German (containing about 10,000 volumes), and fourteen daily newspapers. St. Louis had fifty-eight municipal schoolhouses, which were "by no means the worst looking of the city's buildings," many private schools, two public libraries, and eight newspapers, four published in English and four published in German. San Francisco too had grown rapidly in culture as well as in wealth. The rise of schools and libraries was supplemented by the work of authors and painters. "It would be a wonder," Ratzel remarked, "if the magnificent scenery, which California has in its Sierras, its coastal range, and its ocean, did not awaken and foster a feeling for the beautiful and the grandiose."[13]

Figuratively if not literally following in many of Ratzel's footsteps, another writer from central Europe, by the name of Ernst von Hesse-Wartegg (1854–1918), published an account that in many ways resembled his predecessor's. A native of Austria, Hesse-Wartegg served at one point as a consular official of Venezuela for Switzerland. He combined governmental work abroad with much foreign travel. His voyages resulted in a large output of descriptive literature that was intended for popular audiences—among them, as in Ratzel's case, newspaper readers in Cologne. His writings depicted many parts of the world outside Europe and earned him a position as a corresponding member of numerous geographical societies.

Much longer and—with its numerous illustrations—more imposing visually than Ratzel's book, Hesse-Wartegg's four-volume study *Nord-Amerika, seine Städte und Naturwunder, sein Land und seine Leute* (North America, its cities and its natural wonders, its land and its people)[14] similarly guided its readers from New England to California. It too made numerous stops along the way in the South and the Midwest. How much of his work rested on personal observations and how much of it resulted from his reading in works by others remains somewhat obscure. Like Ratzel, however (whose *Sketches* he cited in his acknowledgements as an important source, albeit without mentioning Ratzel himself as the work's author), Hesse-Wartegg articulated a view of urban America according to which American cities deserved just as much attention and praise as did the countryside.

Making no effort to offer an introductory overview, Hesse-Wartegg escorted his readers directly into the city of New York, which he described as the most impressive of all of the "wonders of the modern world . . . in every respect: in magnificence, in significance, in grandeur, and in beauty." Asserting the superiority of its charms even to those of Constantinople, Naples, and Rio de Janeiro, he compared the excitement travelers to New York from Europe felt as they glimpsed its skyline on the horizon to the excitement Columbus had experienced when he first spied the New World. People who came to New York other than as visitors did so in the hope of bettering themselves economically through hard work, and most succeeded in this regard. Indeed, perhaps half of the owners of the splendid mansions on Fifth Avenue had risen from lowly status as immigrants who had passed through Castle Garden (a forerunner of Ellis Island). Marks of bustling prosperity and urban vigor more generally were discernible throughout New York, not only on Fifth Avenue but also and even more clearly on Broadway, which no other street in the world could rival when it came both to lively variety and to aesthetic attractiveness. The combination of dense traffic in the street and magnificent buildings (designed in historic styles that recalled contemporary architecture in Europe), such as the main post office, various banks, and other centers of commerce that lay along Broadway, clearly made an overwhelmingly favorable impression. "Everywhere," Hesse-Wartegg wrote lyrically, there was "the same greatness, the same splendor, the same liveliness," with gas and water lines leading to each building and elevators within them.[15] Like Ratzel, Hesse-Wartegg also mentioned urban poverty and overcrowded tenements, but he firmly believed that on the whole New York's vibrant commerce and industry were contributing to the well-being of its citizens and of humankind more broadly. They did so, moreover, in ways that by no means marginalized structures and activities not devoted

Der Broadway.

A German illustrator looks down Broadway in Manhattan, conveying a vivid image of prosperous city dwellers who were frequenting the most famous street in the United States, both for pleasure and for profit. Source: Ernst von Hesse-Wartegg, Nord-Amerika, seine Städte und Naturwunder, sein Land und seine Leute, vol. 1, 2nd ed. (Leipzig: Weigel, 1888), 9.

to making money, as was made clear by large numbers of fine neo-Gothic churches, such as Trinity Church and St. Patrick's Cathedral, and by the vast expanse of Central Park.[16]

Although New York's charms were in many respects peculiar to it alone, New York was by no means the only city in America that Hesse-Wartegg regarded with awe and admiration. Philadelphia, with its harbor that rivaled New York's and its industry that surpassed that of New York, deserved recognition as "the archetype of American creativity and American energy." Less distinguished overall than New York for individually noteworthy sights, it boasted nonetheless a splendid new city hall (built in the neo-Renaissance, or Second Empire style) and many other public buildings worthy of note.[17] Hesse-Wartegg was impressed too by the regular layout of Philadelphia's streets, which in his view typified the layouts of American cities more generally. To be sure, he found them rather monotonous. He also criticized the way they were paved. But his disapproval in these respects did little to diminish the generally favorable tone of his comments.[18] Chicago elicited still greater enthusiasm. Apparently forgetting the accolades he had bestowed on New York, he described the windy city as "the greatest wonder in either the New or the Old World." Benefiting legitimately in the court of world opinion from the zeal its inhabitants had displayed in rebuilding it after the devastating fire of 1871, Chicago deserved as much esteem as any city anywhere. Splendid hotels and four thousand factories as well as grisly slaughterhouses testified to the vital energies of the people who lived there. Commercial and industrial advances were accompanied in equal measure by urban beautification, the city being wreathed by boulevards and public parks on three sides. Moreover, an "aristocratic quarter that consisted of palatial dwellings for members of the upper classes, which looked out toward Lake Michigan, stood comparison in every respect with New York's Fifth Avenue.[19]

Shifting his attention to San Francisco, Hesse-Wartegg reprinted an essay on that city by a German-American, Theodor Kirchhoff, according to whom it too had experienced a period of extraordinary development. In the 1840s, the area it now occupied had been nothing more than an impoverished village. But following the discovery of gold in California the number of people who resided in San Francisco had grown to more than

Philadelphia: Broad-Street und das neue Stadthaus.

Like New York, Philadelphia attracted favorable attention on account of its busy street life and the buildings that lined its main thoroughfares. In this picture, a new city hall, constructed at the intersection of Broad Street and Market Street in the neo-Renaissance style that had gained currency in France during the period of the Second Empire, is framed by churches to the left and the right, with a new Masonic Temple also being shown to the left. Source: Ernst von Hesse-Wartegg, Nord-Amerika, seine Städte und Naturwunder, sein Land und seine Leute, vol. 1, 2nd ed. (Leipzig: Weigel, 1888), 144.

three hundred thousand inhabitants. Broad streets were lined by impressive structures, and as a result the city fully equaled the main cities on the east coast and in fact surpassed many of them in "elegance and big-city appearance." Social and cultural life was also marked by pronounced vitality. Theaters and concert halls played regularly to full houses. Moreover, each of the city's different ethnic groups—among which Germans as well as Chinese stood out—had its own clubs and meeting places, but all of these groups lived peacefully with one another. In the author's view, the fear of urban diversity that was to mark later writing by Germans about American cities was nowhere in evidence.[20]

The Rise of Ambivalence around the Turn of the Century

The Wilhelmine era (1888–1918), named after Emperor Wilhelm II, witnessed a sharpening of the debates that surrounded both the United States and the big city. As Alexander Schmidt-Gernig has demonstrated convincingly in his exemplary study of what he calls "voyages into modernity," the "America discourse" of late nineteenth- and early twentieth-century travelers who ventured from German-speaking lands across the Atlantic was increasingly fraught with disagreement, ambiguity, and controversy. It evinced a steadily intensifying debate about the nature and the relative weights of America's virtues and its vices, or at least its shortcomings. These debates were in part stimulated by a growing perception that, even as the empire was challenging and eventually surpassing Great Britain as the industrial leader in Europe, it faced comparable competition that was arising overseas. Conflicting views of America were articulated alongside an intensifying debate with regard to the *Großstadt,* which had emerged with full force as the putative laboratory within which modernity in Germany itself—for better or worse—was being invented and produced.[21] In this situation, American cities, like their counterparts in the German empire, elicited a broad range of commentary, the characteristic themes of which were ambiguity and ambivalence, as individual authors often veered back and forth between divergent views.[22] It is to two of the many exponents of such uncertainty that I now turn.

Consider, for example, Ludwig Fulda (1862–1939). After gaining a doctorate in philosophy, he became a prolific poet, dramatist, and essayist, who maintained close ties to modernist authors in Munich and Berlin. Fulda produced a widely read book, *Amerikanische Eindrücke* (American impressions),[23] which first appeared in 1906 and was reprinted twice thereafter. Having been invited earlier by the German Society of America to spend several months in the United States lecturing on German literature and other facets of German culture, he reported back to readers in Germany on the basis of observations and conversations in two dozen cities. His commentary comprised reflections on a broad spectrum of American practices and institutions. Providing early chapters both on New York and on American cities more generally, Fulda went on to consider "travel culture" (trains, hotels, etc.), Germans in America, education, art, women, and "climate and nature," before concluding with more general remarks on American "character traits" as exemplified in social and political relationships. In his work overall, he clearly focused on what was new and modern, which found expression most notably in urban settings. He did so, however, in a way that combined sympathy for his hosts and their fellow citizens with a growing—albeit by no means rampant—sense of unease over what America symbolized and portended.[24]

As Fulda, tracing the customary route, arrived in the United States via a ship bound for New York's harbor, he was mightily impressed by the surrounding scenery, both natural and human-made. "A worthier and more striking entry way into this country of world importance," he asserted, "would be inconceivable." A broad bay that narrowed to become a river—lined by more and more buildings and by tracks for electric trains, traversed by multistory ferry boats, and ornamented by the Statue of Liberty—served as a splendid introduction to the island of Manhattan and the "urban giant" (*Riesenstadt*) that covered it. The buildings he observed there symbolized "the titanic strength and the domineering energy of Americanism." The dominant element of the Manhattan skyline, the skyscrapers (*Himmelkratzer*) that had arisen during the quarter century since Hesse-Wartegg's trip, were, he observed, "sinister giants . . . towers of Babel, more huge than they were beautiful," looking like "the dull molars in the lower jaw of a leviathan."[25]

Language of this sort indicated obvious unease and apprehension. Such sentiments found further expression elsewhere, in passages in which Fulda wrote about the absence of the "unified beauty of the cultural centers of the Old World," the city's lack of "historic appeal," and the combination of visual ugliness and human suffering one observed in its poorer areas.[26] Fulda nonetheless voiced enormous enthusiasm both for skyscrapers and for other features of the New York scene. At least some of these tall buildings deserved in his view to be regarded as architectural masterpieces, and the disdain felt toward them by some Europeans was undeserved. Combining features of both houses and towers, structures such as the famous Flatiron Building possessed elements of novelty that would one day enable them to gain wider acceptance than they enjoyed currently. Other aspects of what Fulda witnessed while in New York—Central Park, the subway system, the bright lights that illuminated the city at night, and numerous museums and libraries—all led him to conclude that living in New York as well as visiting it would not be at all disagreeable.[27]

Fulda's travels to urban centers elsewhere quickly led to a realization that New York by no means typified the urban scene in America as a whole. Not located on islands and therefore relatively free from the constraints that forced New Yorkers to build upward instead of outward, they were characterized to a much greater degree by extensive, as opposed to intensive, development. Single-family houses, located on the outskirts of city centers, were therefore much more prevalent, prompting Fulda to observe that only one family typically occupied an amount of space that in a German *Mietskaserne* (rental barracks) would be occupied by ten families. Despite the attractiveness of residential areas outside city centers, the core areas themselves were generally unappealing. Long, straight, broad streets that were lined by buildings which stood in no discernible relationship to one another, as well as by ugly telephone poles, reflected the triumph of utility over beauty, which Fulda deeply deplored. On the other hand, much was being done to improve cities aesthetically. By means of initiatives such as filling in part of Lake Michigan, Chicago was adding to its parkland, and Detroit, Cincinnati, and St. Louis were similarly enhancing opportunities for their inhabitants to enjoy natural surroundings in urban settings. At a time when, in Fulda's opinion, defenders of aesthetic values in German cities were fighting a losing battle, their counterparts in America were steadily and impressively moving forward. Utilitarian and artistic values were by no means mutually exclusive. As for architectural style, there was also a great deal that deserved praise. "Newer monumental buildings," Fulda wrote, such as the federal building in Indianapolis, the public library in Chicago, the state capitol in St. Paul . . . are fully equal in quality to our [Europe's] best architectural creations." And both Washington, D.C., and Boston were especially distinguished for their historic architecture. All in all, American cities were works in progress. "Much that is lacking in them must still be added," Fulda concluded, "and much that is annoying must be eliminated before they can compete with the most beautiful cities in Europe in the eyes of aesthetically trained observers. But following their youthful fermentation they stand on the threshold of adulthood, and they are getting ready to earn the certificate of maturity."[28]

Following a second trip to America, during which he reached the West Coast, Fulda added to his earlier reportage by including brief comments on San Francisco and Los Angeles. The first of these cities impressed him in particular on account of the rapid recovery it had made since the great earthquake of 1906 in ways that echoed earlier accolades for the achievements of Chicagoans after the great fire that had leveled large parts of that city in 1871. As a result of widespread rebuilding, San Franciscans could take pride in having met a huge challenge, even though much of what had been constructed recalled the "stylistic confusion and the same lack of individuality" that marked cities in the Midwest. Los Angeles fascinated him particularly, both on account of its Spanish architecture and on account of the tropical vegetation that was everywhere apparent, to an extent unmatched in Europe, even in Italy.[29]

Arthur Holitscher (1869–1941), who lived in Budapest and Vienna before settling into a career as a journalist in Berlin, expressed himself a good deal more critically than Fulda did, but he too can be characterized as an ambivalent rather than as a fundamentally hostile commentator. Closely linked to satirical and leftist critics of the status quo, with some of whom he collaborated by working on the staff of the magazine *Simplicissimus,* Holitscher was more perturbed than Fulda by America's defects. They figured quite prominently in a report he wrote, that appeared in 1912, about a recent American trip. In it he pointed nevertheless to admirable as well as reprehensible phenomena, or at least to signs of better things to come. He too thus evinced ambiguity rather than certainty about American cities[30]

What first struck Holitscher upon his arrival was a skyscraper skyline of ominous dimensions, comparable to the Egyptian pyramids as causes of shock to those who beheld them. The tall buildings of Manhattan differed from their predecessors by virtue of the advertisements that were plastered to their exteriors and also by virtue of the holes in their walls made by their many windows, which made them look like giant sieves closely packed next to one another. Like the Egyptian pyramids, they seemed to be inimical to humanity. "One cannot imagine," he complained, "that human beings, with eyes, noses, and hair on their heads, spend their lives inside them." He wrote in a similar vein about his impressions as he gazed out the windows after his arrival at his hotel. Here he saw small buildings overshadowed by much larger ones: "these monstrous perforated boxes, these rectangular, vertically erected sieves, gray and stupid, with five-story billboards and advertisements for everything possible on their roofs." Upon ascending a skyscraper, he found the city to be even uglier than when it was viewed from below, many of the tall buildings themselves having been constructed "absurdly," with box-like upper portions on top of lower stories that had been designed in the style of Greek temples and still higher elevations with Renaissance cornices. Thoroughly degraded by the frightening experience of zooming up and down in such buildings, a new type of American, "the skyscraper type," was destined to become "the national idiot."[31]

Holitscher, who at various points expressed strong sympathies for U.S. socialists and other critics of American society,[32] clearly regarded the built environment as a physical expression of inequitable relationships among social classes. The masses of ordinary Americans with whom he sympathized suffered, both inside and outside the places where they worked, at the hands of the arrogant capitalists who were supplying the economic demand for the buildings he detested. This was the case not only in New York but also in Chicago, about which he wrote in similarly disparaging terms. Chicago, "the most awful city in the world," elicited particularly derogatory comments

Das Bügeleisen *Times-Building*

Two of the early New York skyscrapers: on the left, the famous Flatiron Building; on the right, the headquarters of the New York Times. Source: Arthur Holitscher, Amerika heute und morgen: Reiseerlebnisse (Berlin: Fischer, 1912), 51.

The illustrator here combines criticism with humor, depicting an imaginary New Yorker—or visitor—who is overwhelmed by the buildings that surround him. The caption reads, "Ten stories . . . fifty . . . a hundred!" Source: *Arthur Holitscher,* Amerika heute und morgen: Reiseerlebnisse *(Berlin: Fischer, 1912), 47.*

with regard to disparities between wealth and poverty, which Holitscher explicitly tied to the city's architecture: "Like the newest of its skyscrapers, the wealth of [some of] its individuals rises at a dizzying speed; [and] just like endless areas . . . outside the center, consisting of wood and filth, the misery and the poverty of the masses spreads horribly far and wide." On the one side there were tall buildings that reflected the pursuit and the accumulation of great amounts of money by big businessmen; on the other, lowlier ones that reminded the perceptive observer of widespread hardship among many of the people whom these capitalists employed.[33]

Along with these denunciations, Holitscher also expressed more positive sentiments, indicating strong hopes for a better future. The tremendous energy by which he felt himself surrounded while in the midwestern metropolis evoked not only disdain for exploitative employers but also approbation for less privileged citizens—women as well as men—whose enthusiasms pointed toward making the society they inhabited more equitable. Educators made an important contribution in this regard. To be sure, unlike liberal reformers, Holitscher was rather critical of Hull House, the famous settlement house that had been established in Chicago in 1889 by Jane Addams. He regarded it as a well-intended but ineffective attempt to substitute cultural philanthropy for more far-reaching efforts to bring about social change. A visit to a Chicago public school, however, prompted Holitscher to write, "The American school is not an institution in which children are stuffed with erudition. . . . It is a tool with whose help children are turned into citizens. . . . Children from all foreign lands become, in this 'melting pot,' the hard metal of the future America, which is the hope of the world." Favorable commentary on such institutions as child courts and on such places as public parks further helped to suggest the presence of movements whose members zealously pursued social amelioration in urban settings. Still, it must be emphasized that what Holitscher found most hopeful in the American city was the way in which it could serve as a staging ground for social revolutionaries. Echoing a number of other Germans who, as members of the Social Democratic Party, had looked to organized workers in America to some day play a leading role on the world stage, Holitscher expressed similar faith in the redemptive, radical potentialities that inhered in urban America. The greatest virtues of the American city lay in the ways in which it stimulated and facilitated the efforts of groups of city dwellers who sought to overcome its widespread inequities.[34]

Ambiguities also appeared in Holitscher's writing about San Francisco, about which he was much more critical than Fulda was. To be sure, he too expressed astonishment over the rapidity with which the city had emerged from the devastation of 1906. It was "a newly born city," in which "the breath of active energy blew up and down every hill and through every street." Holitscher dwelled more extensively, however, on urban corruption than on urban renewal. Citing misdeeds that had been brought to light by the crusading journalist William Randolph Hearst, he sought to show that the structural integrity of both pre- and post-1906 construction had been undermined as a result of bribery of public officials. The theme of corruption was thus joined to earlier emphasis on capitalistic exploitation. On both counts, conditions in American cities cried out for change. Fortunately, the cities also fostered forces that pointed toward structural transformations.[35]

Cultural Wars between the World Wars

After the hiatus in voyaging overseas that inevitably marked the period of international war between 1914 and 1918, Germans resumed their transatlantic travels, visiting America during the years of the Weimar Republic with a frequency substantially in excess of anything that occurred earlier.[36] Although visitors do not generally travel to places which they find entirely unattractive, the history of the recent conflict among nations cast a long shadow over much of what Germans wrote about the American scene, pushing many of them toward critical views of a country they believed had illegitimately caused their country's military defeat. Despite the large number of Americans of German descent who lived in the United States, and despite Woodrow Wilson's promises to keep America out of the military hostilities, the United States had finally supported Germany's opponents, and its intervention had proved to be decisive in bringing about German defeat. The combination of its military activities during the war and its failure, in German eyes, to honor after the war the promises for a peace of reconciliation that had seemed to inhere in Wilson's "fourteen points" made America a prime target for hostile recriminations. In the aftermath of U.S. victory and German defeat, criticism of the United States from a political standpoint became inextricably intermixed with growing misgivings about American society and culture. These were clearly paralleled by a rising tide of animosity that was directed against urban civilization in general. Indeed, the notion that big cities embodied a modern *Zivilisation* that was both emotionally and morally inferior to more traditional (and more fundamentally German) *Kultur,* which Oswald Spengler did so much to popularize in his widely read *Decline of the West,* emerged in the 1920s and persisted up until at least 1945 as a keynote of German thought.[37] As both Berlin and Chicago joined New York in the ranks of the largest agglomerations of inhabitants in the western world,[38] it therefore seemed to make good sense for antidemocratic and antimodernist conservatives—many of whom expressed a pronounced dislike for their own capital—to denounce the urban milieu in America as a spiritual and a cultural wasteland. Increasing challenges by American exporters, among whom industrial capitalists as well as agricultural producers figured prominently, came together with a perceived process of "Americanization" that seemed to point toward ongoing cultural as well as economic conquests. Following earlier U.S. military victories, they too heightened the sense that Europe was under siege, and they frequently intensified feelings of defensiveness that were coupled with hostility.[39]

There was, to be sure, a strand of cultural commentary that asserted itself throughout the 1920s, according to which much in the American city still deserved sympathy and praise, if not indeed adulation, just as much in the United States more generally should be emulated, not rejected. Exponents of modernism, a hallmark of the impulse toward cultural experimentation that marked much of the German scene during roughly the first half of the interwar period, found much to admire in urban centers overseas. Germans, as they sought to build a more democratic and a more liberal society of their own after the end of the imperial regime, still had much to learn, in this view, from the lifestyles and the surroundings of American city dwellers. One such author was Alfred Kerr, a Jewish theater critic and essayist who, with the publisher Paul Cassirer, had helped to found the artistic journal *Pan* in 1910. In a book that appeared in 1923, Kerr expressed unreserved pleasure in contemplating New York's skyscrapers, its architecture more generally, the lights on Broadway, and many other features of the urban scene. New York was not simply a center of commerce and materialism. It was a center of culture too, and it certainly had a sensitive "soul." Works written by modern architects such as Werner Hegemann and Richard Neutra (who had migrated to America in 1923) reinforced such predilections. Many socialists (who continued to believe that their ideals were destined to triumph sooner in America than in Europe) as well as representatives of business and industry (who admired American progress in the areas of the economy and technology) also expressed positive views of urban or at least industrial developments in the United States.[40]

Such sympathies were, however, rejected, both on the left and on the right. Leftist anti-Americanism came to the fore quite loudly in Arthur Holitscher's account of a return visit to the United States, which contained all of the bitterness and little of the optimism that had suffused his earlier report.[41] In the meantime, however, readers could already have encountered strongly *conservative* anti-Americanism in an enormously popular book written by the author Adolf Halfeld. His volume of 1927 on "America and Americanism," which stands out as perhaps the most widely read of all the America books of the 1920s, contained strident denunciations of urbanization and urban life in the United States, which one can easily categorize as place-specific examples of Spenglerian antimodernism. Having spent many years in the United States, Halfeld had acquired little if any affection for his host country. Far from it. America in general and the American city in particular, in his opinion, stood out as areas where the evils of contemporary civilization as opposed to traditional culture—money as the basic measure of value, materialistic rationalism, selfish individualism, and the loss of respect for old traditions—were plainly and painfully evident. Negative commentary on urban America thus buttressed a radically conservative assault on modernity, which America was thought to symbolize, more generally.[42]

Halfeld made clear the sources of his concern by beginning his work not with an analysis of America itself but instead with an introductory overview of "the Americanization of Europe." Here he anxiously indicated a variety of ways in which the New World was impinging on the one from which it had spun off. Since the United States had tipped the balance against the Central Powers in 1918, Halfeld complained, Europe had suffered further encroachments on its autonomy as a result of a whole host of additional developments. These tendencies pointed toward a grim future unless Europe could find ways to defend itself from the American threat. The fact that Americans produced 90 percent of the world's films was having particularly deleterious consequences.[43] The exportation of American cinema worked to promote not only culturally superficial entertainment and customs but also dehumanizing forms of technology and commerce, for which they served as misleading but powerful advertisements. Mass entertainment went hand in hand with Fordism, or the spread of techniques of industrial production in order to rationalize and maximize the output of manufactured goods in ways that "drilled many millions of human beings into a straitjacket," depriving them of any sense of free will. Such developments boded ill for the United States as well as for Europe. While they helped Americans, at Europe's expense, in their quest to make money, they threatened the spiritual and social health of America itself in ways that could be clearly discerned if one looked closely at developments occurring in that unhappy land.[44]

Halfeld regarded the cities as places where human beings who lacked spiritual individuality had gathered in environments that inflicted upon them further cultural and psychological damage. Something was lacking in the cities' layouts and buildings, for which "all of the luxury, the massiveness, the kitsch, the flickering lights, and the purely technical nervousness of surface life" could not compensate. To be sure, there were some buildings that had been designed by outstanding architects, such as Chicago's Louis Sullivan. But there was no unity, no harmony, no linkage among various structures. The skyscrapers, Halfeld wrote, had no style that could enable them to stand as visually adequate expressions of the concentrated density in which they were located. As the cities expanded, growing by leaps and bounds as a result of "an extremely arbitrary building frenzy," the discrepancies in them between commercial structures and palatial villas that oozed wealth on the one hand and the haunts of the poor on the other remained as glaring as ever. Commercial billboards several stories high added throughout urban areas to the European observer's belief that he was contemplating a scandalous scene. Gas stations and office buildings whose linear simplicity stood as symbols of a "bulky civilization" (not a graceful *Kultur*) were intermixed with pretentious banks and public buildings that had been designed according to all sorts of borrowed styles—neoclassical, neo-Renaissance, and so on. These structures were surrounded by standardized housing that, in Philadelphia, reminded Halfeld of prison buildings. In Washington too, incongruity was the (dis)order of the day, as the triumphal avenue that linked the White House and the Capitol proceeded past ordinary buildings that were quite ugly, in the immediate vicinity of areas inhabited by poor blacks and Chinese. And so it went, each city basically resembling the rest, all displaying "the same spirit of clumsy megalomania" and none expressing any distinctiveness. Sinclair Lewis's Main Street was the dismal norm, not just in the Midwest but also elsewhere. Even Broadway amounted to little more than a Main Street in an exaggerated form.[45] A built environment marked in its residential areas by apartment houses did not necessarily entail material poverty. The "residential factory" (*Wohnfabrik*) offered its inhabitants all sorts of luxuries, from apartments with bathrooms and dining rooms to areas for sports on their roofs. It tended nonetheless to harm its inhabitants by channeling them into impersonal, conventional lifestyles, as a result of which they increasingly became "mass human beings" (*Massenmenschen*). Urban architecture diminished both cultivated individuality and feelings of attachment to particular places in which Americans resided, which all tended to resemble one another in ways that exacerbated a sense of "homelessness" (*Heimatlosigkeit*).[46]

Urbanization worsened the lives not only of America's city dwellers but also of its farmers, in ways that threatened the well-being of the country as a whole. The decline of the agrarian sector as farmers' children migrated to the urban centers further contributed to an overall sense of rootlessness. Referring to rural Americans as "the flesh and blood of the race," Halfeld also expressed the fear, widespread among conservatives, that migration from the countryside to cities was leading to demographic damage. Birthrates and physiological health among those born there were, he warned, much worse than they were among farmers and residents of small towns.[47]

Although Halfeld entered once again into literary combat as an anti-Americanist in 1941,[48] during the years that immediately followed the Nazi seizure of power in 1933 his leading role as a published critic of American society passed to another German writer, Colin Ross (1885–1945). Having obtained a doctorate in economics, the Austria-born Ross turned to journalism. He reported on war in the Balkans in 1912, on revolution in Mexico in 1914, and on his many trips to other parts of the world in the 1920s and 1930s. Clearly sharing a number of the basic judgments and prejudices that were to help bring about Adolf Hitler's declaration of war against an America that Hitler regarded as too degenerate to withstand German power,[49] Ross sought to expose ugly "truths" behind the "facade" of American strength during what he referred to portentously in 1935 "America's fateful hour." Having traveled to the United States several times and having lived with his family for an extended period in Chicago, he asserted vigorously that his own attitudes toward the country had alternated between hatred and love. He also sought to make clear, however, that America was experiencing terrible difficulties and that its confidence and its standing in the world were being correspondingly diminished. Its problems had in part resulted from its own mistakes as a nation, in particular the decision by Woodrow Wilson to lead it into war against Germany. They had to be seen largely, however, as outgrowths of domestic developments, which were particularly evident in its big cities. Here, under the impact of the Great Depression, hopelessness, conflict, and disorder had eclipsed earlier evidence of confidence based on steady progress.[50]

Regarding Chicago, where Ross was residing when he finished writing his book, Ross expressed some ambivalence. Inhabitants of the city had, he observed, performed heroic labors during the preceding decade in the area around their waterfront, removing messy rail lines that had obscured their view of Lake Michigan and replacing the space these tracks had once filled both with fabulous highways and with greenery. Still, immediately next to Chicago's parks, one encountered the same dark slums, with their indescribably filthy streets, that had marred the face of the city two decades earlier. Despite the fact that twenty times as many murders were committed in their city as in all of England, Chicagoans still had a right to feel proud. And yet the prognosis for the future was poor. What had been hailed by the organizers of an exhibition held in 1933 to mark the hundredth anniversary of Chicago's founding as "The Century of Progress" had suddenly, it seemed, come to an end, as the onset of the Great Depression began to dash the earlier confidence of the city's inhabitants. The conclusion of the exhibition itself, which was spoiled by widespread violence and destruction, as lawless mobs sought to seize whatever they could, underlined the shakiness of the belief that freedom and happiness for all could be counted on to proceed hand in hand. Neither in Chicago nor anywhere else in the United States

Chikago
Die Michigan Avenue, eine der herrlichsten Straßen der Welt.

Chikago
Es sieht aber auch vielfach so in Chikago aus

This pair of photographs highlights the sharp contrasts between urban splendor and urban poverty, pointing to the latter as a way of undermining the belief that the growth of cities and social progress went hand in hand. The caption for the one at the top refers to Chicago's Michigan Avenue as "one of the most splendid streets in the world." The second caption asserts, "But a lot of Chicago looks like this." Source: *Colin Ross,* Amerikas Schicksalsstunde: Die Vereinigten Staaten zwischen Demokratie und Diktatur *(Leipzig: Brockhaus, 1935), 41.*

was such optimism justified. Particularly in big cities, the presence of millions of unemployed men who wanted to work showed that freedom could mean simply the freedom to starve. It was indicative of this situation that in Chicago what had begun as a celebration of progress ended in an orgy of destruction.[51]

Ross's comments on New York, the city of "Babel," were still more pessimistic. While the skyscraper skyline received praise in Ross's prose, pictures in his book told a different story, conveying a distinct impression of the incompatibility between skyscraper culture and spiritual culture. Other aspects of New York were even more repellent. To be sure, the magnificence of the city's soaring towers might temporarily distract the visitor in the short run from other aspects of the urban scene. "One sees already during the ride to a hotel the repulsive filth and trash of this city, the horrid residential areas of the poorer classes; but one hardly notices all of that, because one's gaze is continually drawn upwards toward the amazing skyscrapers." Ross, however, had had the opportunity to look more closely, and what he had seen made a largely negative impression on him. What repelled him was not simply the sort of poverty he observed in "the unpleasant areas on the East Side, in which Poles, Jews, and Italians jostle[d] against one another in the midst of grime." More generally, unlike the older cities of Europe, New York lacked "organic" unity. It was a city of conflicting extremes, its lack of balance and stability accentuated and intensified by the destructive influence of "corrosive intellect." It was a "whirlpool of brain power," in which were concentrated all of America's most influential publishing houses and periodical publications," but what they fostered was dissension rather than "a great, enduring, unifying idea." New York also served as the headquarters of America's financiers, whose "criminal speculation" had brought the entire country to the brink of catastrophe, spreading destructiveness from the nation's largest city to the United States as a whole. Consideration of these forces led Ross to conclude that America's greatest metropolis constituted "the strongest evidence against the overly large city, against jamming masses of people together on one piece of ground."

In addition to anti-intellectualism and anticapitalism, blatant racism asserted itself unmistakably in Ross's assessment of New York's prospects.

Neuyork
Der versunkene Gott.

This photograph, titled "The Submergence of God," shows how Trinity Church was surrounded by commercial dwellings that literally overshadowed it to an extreme degree. Although, as a National Socialist, the author of the book in which it appeared held no brief for Christianity, he used the contrast the picture conveyed as a means of strengthening his attack on what he regarded as the materialistic sterility that marked urban America. Source: *Colin Ross,* Amerikas Schicksalsstunde: Die Vereinigten Staaten zwischen Demokratie und Diktatur *(Leipzig: Brockhaus, 1935), 81.*

New York lacked unity not only because of the tenor of its intellectual life and the selfish pursuits of men of wealth but also because of its ethnic diversity. It was an "inorganic heap of buildings" in large part because it sheltered representatives of "all races, all nations, [and] all languages." Having been brought into existence by "the international idea of civilization and progress," New York—like the United States more generally—faced the threat of disintegration as a result of the worldwide resurgence of nationalism, which pointed toward the end of the belief that American cities could assimilate their ethnic minorities. In such passages, criticism of the United States went hand in hand with Nazi beliefs in the deleterious effects of racial mixing. Places like New York, with their large numbers of both Jews and Blacks, were inevitably subject to the threats of internal disunity and decay. These threats posed pressing challenges for New York in particular but also for the United States as a whole, whose largest city stood out as a site and a symbol of disunity and tension.[52]

As indicated earlier in this essay, the combination of anti-Americanism and anti-urbanism expressed in the works of interwar writers such as Adolf Halfeld and Colin Ross was much less evident after the Second World War than it had been before it. Charges by intellectual exponents of Nazi ideology and other critics of "civilization" that American cities embodied ominous forces of cultural and social decay and destruction had been intimately intertwined with still more vicious impulses that emanated from the ranks of the accusers and the political leaders whom they supported. These impulses had led to a war that destroyed many German but no American cities—a war at whose end, be it noted, Colin Ross took his own life. Anti-Americanism, anti-urbanism, and ipso facto harsh criticism of the American city could never function in German life in the same way in which they had functioned for many Germans during the quarter century that preceded the end of the Second World War. But what occurred in the realm of German thought about American cities after the 1930s is a topic for another essay.[53]

NOTES

1. Biographical information about all of these individuals except for Adolf Halfeld can be found in the *Deutsche Biographische Enzyklopädie,* ed. Walther Killy and Rudolf Vierhaus, 10 vols. (Munich: Saur, 1995–99).

2. See the following works, all of which illuminate German views of America: David I. Barclay and Elisabeth Glaser-Schmidt, eds., *Transatlantic Images and Perceptions: Germany and America Since 1776* (New York: Cambridge University Press, 1997); Frank Trommler and Elliott Shore, eds., *The German-American Encounter: Conflict and Cooperation between Two Cultures, 1800–2000* (New York and Oxford: Berg, 2001); Dan Diner, *America in the Eyes of the Germans: An Essay on Anti-Americanism,* trans. Allison Brown (Princeton: Markus Wiener, 1996); Peter J. Brenner, *Reisen in die neue Welt: Die Erfahrung Nordamerikas in Deutschen Reise- und Auswanderungsberichten des 19. Jahrhunderts* (Tübingen: Niemeyer, 1991); Alexander Schmidt, *Reisen in die Moderne: Der Amerika-Diskurs des deutschen Bürgertums vor dem Ersten Weltkrieg im europäischen Vergleich* (Berlin: Akademie, 1997); Ulrich Ott, *Amerika ist Anders: Studien zum Amerika-Bild in deutschen Reiseberichten des 20. Jahrhunderts* (Frankfurt a. M. and New York: Lang, 1991); Alf Lüdtke, Inge Marßolek, and Adelheid von Saldern, eds., *Amerikanisierung: Traum und Alptraum im Deutschland des 20. Jahrhunderts* (Stuttgart: Steiner, 1996); Earl R. Beck, *Germany Rediscovers America* (Tallahassee: Florida State University Press, 1968); Peter Berg, *Deutschland und Amerika 1918–1929: Über das deutsche Amerikabild der zwanziger Jahre* (Lübeck and Hamburg: Matthiesen, 1963); Philipp Gassert, *Amerika im Dritten Reich: Ideologie, Propaganda und Volksmeinung 1933–1945* (Stuttgart: Steiner, 1997). For the views of Britons and Frenchmen, see Richard Rapson, *Britons View America: Travel Commentary, 1860–1935* (Seattle: University of Washington Press, 1971) and Jacques Portes, *Fascination and Misgivings: The United States in French Opinion, 1870–1914,* trans. Elborg Forster (Cambridge: Cambridge University Press, 2000). There are many interesting remarks about European views of America in Hartmut Kaelble *Europäer über Europa: Die Entstehung des europäischen Selbstverständnisses im 19. Und 20. Jahrhundert* (Frankfurt a. M.: Campus, 2001). A more specialized work, which contains several good essays, is Michael J. Wala and Ursula Lehmkuhl, eds. *Technologie und Kultur: Europas Blick*

auf Amerika vom 18. Bis zum 20. Jahrhundert (Cologne: Böhlau, 2000). See also, Philipp Gassert, "Amerikanismus, Antiamerikanismus, Amerikanisierung: Neue Literatur zur Sozial, Wirtschafts- und Kulturgeschichte des Amerikanischen Einflusses in Deutschland und Europa," *Archiv für Sozialgeschichte* 39 (1999): 531–61. The most recent treatment of this theme on a broad scale is Egbert Klautke, *Unbegrenzte Möglichkeiten: Amerikanisierung in Deutschland und Frankreich (1900–1933)* (Stuttgart: Steiner, 2003), which has the advantage that it treats German views in tandem with French ones, pointing to similarities that transcended national boundaries.

3. For treatment of ideas on both sides of the Atlantic, see Andrew Lees, *Cities Perceived: Urban Society in European and American Thought, 1820–1940* (New York: Columbia University Press, 1985). On Germany in particular, see Klaus Bergmann, *Agrarromantik und Großstadtfeindschaft* (Meisenheim am Glan: Hain, 1970); Clemens Zimmermann and Jürgen Reulecke, eds. *Die Stadt als Moloch? Das Land als Kraftquell? Wahrnehmungen und Wirkungen Der Großstädte um 1900* (Basel: Birkhaüser, 1999); Ralf Stremmel, *Modell und Moloch: Berlin in der Wahrnehmung deutscher Politiker vom Ende des 19. Jahrhunderts bis zum Zweiten Weltkrieg* (Bonn: Bouvier, 1992); Peter Fritzsche, *Reading Berlin: 1900* (Cambridge: Harvard University Press, 1996); and Andrew Lees, *Cities, Sin, and Social Reform in Imperial Germany* (Ann Arbor: University of Michigan Press, 2002). On images of cities in America, see Morton and Lucia White, *The Intellectual versus the City: From Thomas Jefferson to Frank Lloyd Wright* (Cambridge: Harvard University Press, 1962); David Hamer, *New Towns in the New World: Images and Perceptions of the Nineteenth-century Urban Frontier* (New York: Columbia University Press, 1990; and Bayrd Still, *Mirror for Gotham: New York as Seen by Contemporaries from Dutch Days to the Present* (New York: New York University Press, 1956).

4. Brenner, *Reisen*, 272–98.

5. Hugo Münsterberg, *Die Amerikaner*, 2 vols. (Berlin: Mittler, 1904).

6. For statistics on individual cities, see Adna Weber, *The Growth of Cities in the Nineteenth Century* (New York: Macmillan, 1899), 450; on developments in Germany as a whole to 1890, see ibid., 80–93 (esp. 90); on the United States, ibid., 20–43. Although Germany was more heavily urbanized overall

than was the United States (45.7 percent) in 1910, it had reached its level of 60 percent from a base in 1849 of 28.3 percent, whereas America had risen since 1850 from a level of only 15.3 percent. In other words, while city dwellers in Germany had approximately doubled as a percentage of their country's population, city dwellers in America had tripled as a percentage of the American population. See Lees, *Cities Perceived,* 4.

7. See Andrew Lees, "Between Anxiety and Admiration: Views of British Cities in Germany, 1835–1914," *Urban History* 36 (2009), 42–66.

8. Lees, *Cities Perceived,* 88–91. See in particular Julius Faucher, *Vergleichende Kulturbilder aus den vier Europäischen Millionenstädte: Berlin, Wien, Paris, London* (Hannover, 1877) and Robert Springer, *Berlin: Die Deutsche Kaiserstadt* (Darmstadt, 1878), 4–6.

9. Friedrich Ratzel, *Städte- und Culturbilder aus Nordamerika* (Leipzig: Brockhaus, 1876). I have relied on the U.S. edition, *Sketches of Urban and Cultural Life in North America,* trans. Stewart A. Stehlin (New Brunswick: Rutgers University Press, 1988), which contains an excellent introduction by Stehlin. See also Woodruff D. Smith, *Politics and the Sciences of Culture in Germany, 1840–1920* (New York: Oxford University Press, 1991), 207–13, 219–29, and Andrew Lees, "Das Denken über die Großstadt um 1900: Deutsche Stellungnahmen zum urbanen Lebensraum im internationalen Vergleich," *Berichte zur Wissenschaftsgeschichte* 15 (1992), 143. For Ratzel's treatment of American cities after he had become a professor, see Friedrich Ratzel, *Politische Geographie der Vereinigten Staaten von Amerika, unter besonderer Berücksichtigung der natürlichen Bedingungen und wirtschaftlichen Verhältnisse,* 2nd ed. (Munich: Oldenbourg, 1893), 315–42.

10. Ratzel, *Sketches,* 3–5.

11. Ibid., 5–8. He wrote with regard to New York, "The Americans are right when they say that appropriately broad streets are a fundamental prerequisite of a big city" (28).

12. Ibid., 6, 35–36.

13. Ibid., 36–53, 92–111, 119–26, 243, 284.

14. Ernst von Hesse-Wartegg, *Nord-Amerika, seine Städte und Naturwunder, sein Land und seine Leute,* 4 vols. (Leipzig: Weigel, 1880). A second edition was

published in 1888. References here are to this edition. Mention of Ratzel's work appeared at the outset of the first edition. It did not appear in the later one.

15. Ibid., I, 1–2, 7, 8–20.

16. Ibid., 4, 32–41.

17. Ibid., 136–38, 146–51.

18. Ibid., 142, 145.

19. Ibid., II, 34–49. See also Ernst von Hesse-Wartegg, *Chicago: Eine Weltstadt im amerikanischen Westen* (Stuttgart: Union, 1893) and Ernst von Hesse-Wartegg, *Amerika als neueste Weltmacht der Industrie: Bilder aus Handel, Industrie und Verkehr in den Vereinigten Staaten* (Stuttgart: Union, 1908), 227–270. On perceptions of the rebuilding of Chicago after the great fire by Chicagoans, see Carl Smith, *Urban Disorder and the Shape of Belief: The Great Chicago Fire, the Haymarket Bomb, and the Model Town of Pullman* (Chicago: University of Chicago Press, 1994).

20. Ibid., III, 47–58.

21. See Lees, *Cities, Sin, and Social Reform*, 23–71.

22. I am much indebted to Alexander Schmidt, "Metropolis–Die Erfahrung der Großstadt," in his *Reisen in die Moderne*, 242–66, which masterfully surveys both German opinion and European opinion more generally.

23. Ludwig Fulda, *Amerikanische Eindrücke* (Stuttgart: Cotta, 1906). An unchanged edition appeared in 1907, a considerably expanded one in 1914.

24. Schmidt's references to the fourth edition indicate more negativity than I detect in the first one, on which I have mainly relied. See Schmidt, *Reisen*, 41, 79, 94, 166, 190, 194, 217, 221, 251, 274, 276, 278, 283, 289, 294.

25. Fulda, *Amerikanische Eindrücke*, 22–23.

26. Ibid., 29–30.

27. Ibid., 23, 33–34, 35, 36, 37.

28. Ibid., 38–45, 51.

29. Ibid., 3rd ed., 253–57.

30. Arthur Holitscher, *Amerika heute und morgen: Reiseerlebnisse* (Berlin: Fischer, 1912). See also Holitscher, *Mein Leben in dieser Zeit* (Potsdam: Kiepenheuer, 1928) and Ott, *Amerika ist anders*, 127–52.

31. Holitscher, *Amerika heute,* 38, 41, 43, 59.

32. Ott, *Amerika ist anders,* 129.

33. Holitscher, *Amerika heute,* 63, 64, 293, 294–95.

34. On Hull House, see ibid., 321–25; on other aspects of Holitscher's views of Chicago, see Ott, *Amerika ist anders,* 141, 142, 144, 150. For views of America by socialists, see R. Laurence Moore, *European Socialists and the American Promised Land* (New York: Oxford University Press, 1970), 25, 101, 104; and Werner Kremp, *In Deutschland liegt unser Amerika: Das sozialdemokratische Amerikabild von den Anfängen der SPD bis zur Weimarer Republik* (Münster and Hamburg, 1993).

35. Holitscher, *Amerika,* 255–58.

36. Beck, *Germany Rediscovers America,* 289–306, contains an impressive listing of both books and periodical articles from the years between 1918 and 1932. For biographical information about approximately three hundred individuals whom he mentions in the main body of his work (a number of whom wrote after 1945), see 311–22. For discussion of economic and industrial concerns, see Mary Nolan, *Visions of Modernity: American Business and the Modernization of Germany* (New York: Oxford University Press, 1994). For treatment of literary figures, in addition to Ott, *Amerika ist anders,* 163–242, see Erhard H. Schütz, *Kritik der literarischen Reportage: Reportagen und Reiseberichte aus der Weimarer Republik über die USA und die Sowjetunion* (Munich: Fink, 1977) and Theresa Mayer Hammond, *American Paradise: German Travel Literature from Duden to Kisch* (Heidelberg: Winter, 1980), 71–187.

37. Spengler's work, originally published as *Der Untergang des Westens,* 2 vols. (Berlin, 1918–22), appeared in English translation between 1926 and 1928. On Spengler within the context of the overall discourse in Weimar Germany about cities, see Lees, *Cities Perceived,* 269–78.

38. Berlin, with 4.3 million inhabitants, and Chicago, with 3.4 million, both outstripped Paris (2.8 million) by 1940. New York, with 7.5 million, remained well ahead of those three cities. Greater London remained the largest city of all, but its growth, like that of Paris, had been much less rapid. See Lees, *Cities Perceived,* 5.

39. On the theme of Americanization during the interwar years, see Klautke, *Unbegrenzte Möglichkeiten,* 153–268.

40. Alfred Kerr, *New York und London, Stätten des Geschicks: Zwanzig Kapitel nach dem Weltkrieg* (Berlin: Fischer, 1923), 25–33, 86–89; Werner Hegemann, *Amerikanische Architektur und Stadtbaukunst* (Berlin: Wasmuth, 1925); Richard Neutra, *Wie baut Amerika?* (Stuttgart: Hoffman, 1927); Berg, *Deutschland und Amerika*, 96–136. On the views of admirers of American industry, see Nolan, *Visions of Modernity*, 17–107.

41. Arthur Holitscher, *Wiedersehn mit Amerika: Die Verwandlung der U.S.A.* (Berlin: Fischer, 1930).

42. Adolf Halfeld, *Amerika und der Amerikanismus: Kritische Betrachtungen eines Deutschen und Europäers* (Jena: Diederichs, 1927). On Halfeld during the Weimar years, see Diner, *America*, 55–56, 69–71, 73–34; and Berg, *Deutschland und Amerika*, 136–41.

43. See Thomas J. Saunders, *Hollywood in Berlin: American Cinema and Weimar Germany* (Berkeley: University of California Press, 1994).

44. Halfeld, *Amerika*, x–xvi.

45. Ibid., 106–10.

46. Ibid., 110–11.

47. Ibid., 169–70. On the theme of urbanization as a threat to Germany's demographic and physiological health, see Lees, *Cities Perceived*, 142–49.

48. Adolf Halfeld, *USA greift in die Welt* (Hamburg: Broschek, 1941).

49. On views of American society held by Nazis and in Nazi Germany, see Gassert, *Amerika im Dritten Reich*, 87–103, 232–46; and Philipp Gassert, "Nationalsozialismus, Amerikanismus, Technologie: Zur Kritik der amerikanischen Moderne im Dritten Reich," in Wala and Lehmkuhl, eds., *Technologie und Kultur*, 147–72.

50. Colin Ross, *Amerikas Schicksalsstunde: Die Vereinigten Staaten zwischen Demokratie und Diktatur* (Leipzig: Brockhaus, 1935; 12th ed., 1942). See also Colin Ross, *Fahrten- und Abenteuerbuch* (Berlin: Gutenberg, 1930) and Colin Ross, *Unser Amerika: Der deutsche Anteil an den Vereinigten Staaten* (Leipzig: Brockhaus, 1936).

51. Ross, *Amerikas Schicksalsstunde*, 49–50, 51–52, 55–60.

52. Ibid., 76–80.

53. On perceptions, see, in addition to works cited in note 2, Alfred L. Cobbs, *The Image of America in Postwar German Literature* (Berne: Lang, 1982). On post-1945 "Americanization," see Kaspar Maase, *Bravo Amerika: Erkundungen zur Jugendkultur der Bundesrepublik in den fünfziger Jahren* (Hamburg: Junius, 1992); Anselm Doering-Manteuffel, *Wie westlich sind die Deutschen? Amerikanisierung und Westernisierung im 20. Jahrhundert* (Göttingen: Vandenhoeck & Ruprecht, 1999); and Alexander Stephan, ed., *Americanization and Anti-Americanism: The German Encounter with American Culture after 1945* (New York: Berghahn, 2005). See also Angela Linke and Jakob Tanner, eds., *Attraktion und Abwehr: Die Amerikanisierung der Alltagskultur in Europa* (Cologne: Böhlau, 2006).

PART 3

Gender and Travel

Travel, Gender, and Identity

George and Anna Ticknor's Travel Journals from Their 1835–36 Journey to Dresden

Thomas Adam

George and Anna Ticknor were the embodiment of old Boston. Both came from old Brahmin families with long family trees that stretched back to the early days of English colonization. And although both came from well-off families, George Ticknor was born into one of modest means. He graduated from Dartmouth College and passed the bar exam in 1813, but quickly became bored at the prospect of a career as a lawyer. In 1814, he decided to pursue academic studies at the famous University of Göttingen (Germany). He left Boston for Europe in mid-April 1815—at a time when Europe was in uproar again because of Napoleon Bonaparte's return to power in France (his famous 100 days). Ticknor spent the next two years in Göttingen. Already in November 1816, the president of Harvard University, John T. Kirkland (1770–1840), offered him a teaching position in modern languages and literatures upon his return. After Ticknor returned from Europe in June of 1819 (he had continued traveling in Europe, including France, Spain, and Portugal, from the end of his stay in Göttingen until then), he was formally introduced at Harvard as the Abiel Smith Professor of the French and Spanish Languages and Literatures and Professor of Belles Lettres on August 10, 1819.[1]

In 1821, Ticknor married Anna Eliot. Nine years younger than Ticknor, she was the daughter of the wealthy Boston merchant Samuel Eliot (1739–1820), founder of the Eliot Professorship of Greek at Harvard.[2] Anna was "an intelligent woman who fully shared her husband's taste for letters and society. Beneath a conventional façade, she was an independent and witty spirit, with a pungent style of writing and conversation and ready

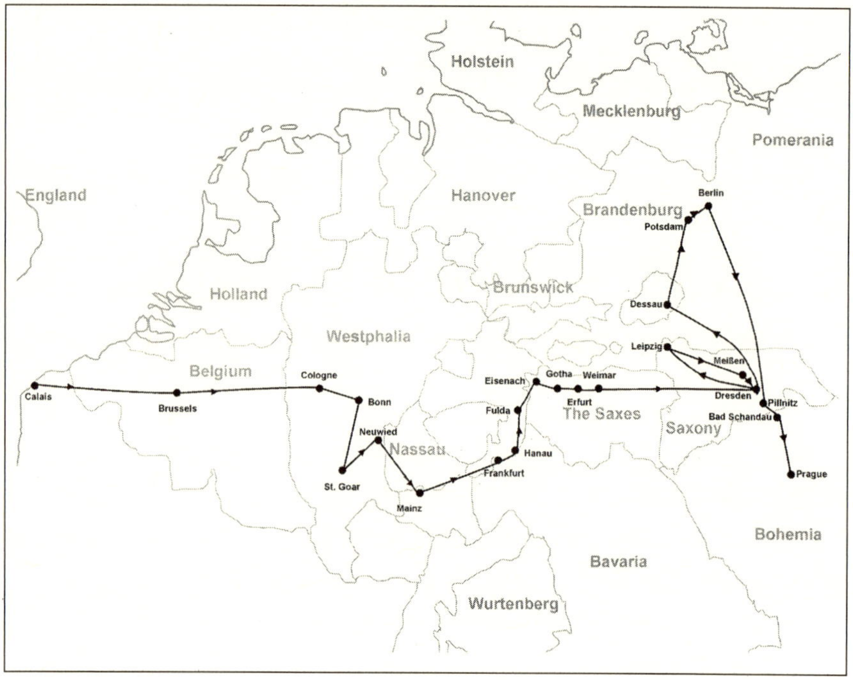

Map of George and Anna Ticknor's travel route, 1835–1836. Based on William C. Woodbridge's map of central Europe of 1837. Courtesy of the David Rumsey Map Collection (www.davidrumsey.com).

affection."[3] And although George Ticknor's father was not poor, it was this marriage to Anna Eliot that provided for a comfortable life. Her significant inheritance of about $85,000 and the very modest legacy left to George by his father allowed the couple to live in comfort.[4] They "bought a house on fashionable Park Street, where they held court for many years to fashionable and literary Boston."[5] The couple had four children, two of whom died in early childhood.

During his sixteen years of teaching at Harvard, Ticknor restlessly attempted to reform the college, inspired by what he had encountered in various German high schools and universities.[6] Resistance to change deeply frustrated him and seemed to have contributed to his resignation in 1835. Freed from professional duties, Ticknor planned a second extensive European journey with his wife and two children.[7] And it is this second journey that is at the center of the following discussion. On June 25, 1835, after a three-week voyage, George and Anna Ticknor arrived with their two daughters, twelve-year-old Anna Eliot (Nannie) and two-year-old Eliza Sullivan (Lizzy) in Liverpool. After a few weeks of traveling in England, Wales, Ireland, and Scotland (June 25 to October 25), the Ticknors headed via Calais and Brussels to Dresden.

They stayed in Dresden for most of the time in the period from November 20, 1835, to May 11, 1836. During this time, both Anna and George Ticknor wrote extensive travel journals about their encounters with Dresden society and the cityscape.[8] They thus provide us with two parallel narratives that allow for a comparison of male and female perception of an alien culture and society and the reflection of these (possibly different and possibly gendered) perceptions in their travel writing. The Ticknor's parallel writing gives us a unique opportunity to test assumptions about the distinct ways in which women and men perceived an alien environment experienced while traveling and the distinct and gendered ways in which they produced travel narratives.

Gender in Travel Writing

Mary Wollstonecraft contended in 1792 that "[a] man, when he undertakes a journey, has, in general, the end in view; a woman thinks more of the incidental occurrences, the strange things that may possibly occur on the road; the impression that she may make on her fellow-travellers; and, above all, she is anxiously intent on the care of the finery that she carries with her, which is more than ever a part of herself, when going to figure on a new scene; when, to use an apt French turn of expression, she is going to produce a sensation."[9] Based on an in-depth analysis of George and Anna Ticknor's travel journals, this chapter will discuss the basic question whether "women's travel accounts differ from those written by men in any fundamental way," and whether there is "a way in which travel writing is inherently gendered."[10]

There are several assumptions about the distinct nature of female and male travel writing, which can easily be summarized. First, some scholars have suggested that women's travel writing "is less directed, less goal-oriented, less imperialistic, and more concerned with people and place."[11] Elizabeth Bohl points to Mary Wollstonecraft's *Letters Written during a Short Residence in Sweden, Norway and Denmark,* in which the author was deeply concerned with the material conditions of existence and less with the scenery and landscape. Wollstonecraft recorded "the material conditions of everyday life, the ways in which beings adapt to their surroundings, and what, exactly they live on."[12] Second, with an eye on Victorian female travel writers, Jane Robinson suggested that part of "this difference must lie in the nature of the journey itself. Women have rarely been *commissioned* to travel, and so their accounts tend not to be prescribed by the need to satisfy a patron or professional reputation (except the professional reputation every writer who travels—as opposed to traveller who writes—is obliged to uphold.) Women can afford to be more discursive, more impressionable, more *ordinary.*"[13] Jane Robinson and Sara Mills "both emphasize the wealth of detail in women's travel accounts, along with a tendency to write about relationships, and both contrast this with the more public discourse of male travelers."[14]

Third, several scholars point to the "textual turbulence" in female travel narratives, which is said to result from the breaking down of borders between the public and private sphere in the experience of women as travelers and as travel writers. Such claims, however, are the result of an adherence to an oversimplified model according to which women were confined to the private sphere. Throughout the nineteenth century, women were active in the public sphere doing charitable and philanthropic work, organizing associations for religious, philanthropic, and social purposes, and engaged in social reform debates and projects.[15] Leaving the home and even one's country for the purpose of traveling abroad, thus, might not have been seen as a violation of nineteenth-century standards of social conduct especially when women traveled in the company of their families. Both traveling and writing about this experience provided women with another venue for the assumption and extension of their position in the public sphere in their hometowns as well as in the cities of their destination. Women's travel and women travelers during the eighteenth and nineteenth century have all too often been treated as exceptional occurrences for the small number of women who were able to travel. One should not forget, however, that those women enabled to travel were not just different from other women but also from most men since travel was a privilege for members of the leisure class.[16] This is not to underestimate the challenge for female travelers—traveling alone or in company of their husbands and family—to renegotiate the boundaries between private and public sphere during traveling and at their destination.[17]

Fourth, gender-specific perceptions and modes of travel resulted, according to Catherine Barnes Stevenson, in different forms of narrative. Women seemed to have given preference to writing "a series of letters home to a predominantly female audience interested in both the everyday domestic life and the writer's psychological reactions to a new environment. The loose, accretive, epistolary form serves as an ideal vehicle for leisurely descriptions of diverse subjects—scenery, flora and fauna, housekeeping problems, food, politics, and local culture. Furthermore, the author of an epistolary travel account can easily slip from narrative to description, to personal rumination, to political commentary."[18]

Fifth, travel writing—and nineteenth-century travel writing in particular—has also been conceptualized as a type of autobiographical narrative superimposed on a travelogue. Travel writing was thus not just about what a traveler saw and how he or she saw it, travel narratives were also expected to offer some insight into the psyche of the author and the author's dealings with the challenges of travel and fitting into an alien environment. This increased importance of the personality of the traveler marks, according to Stevenson, the progression from eighteenth-century travel accounts that focused on sights and customs to nineteenth-century travel books that offered insights into the "relationship of men and women (including the traveler) to their environment."[19] Stevenson further argues that studying "the differences between male and female autobiography provide a valuable perspective on the narrative structures chosen by travellers of the opposite sex. Men, these studies suggest, write formal, distilled autobiographies in which the primary concern is an objective evaluation of the significance of the whole life (or journey). Women, in contrast, produce more private, fragmented, episodic autobiographies (often in form of a diary or series of letters) which impose no overarching design on their lives or travels. Women tend to record, to surrender to experience; men to judge, to schematize experience."[20] Yet, Sara

Mills and Shirley Foster also caution us not to overemphasize and overgeneralize specific traits of female travel writing. They warn of an essentialist view in which it appears "self-evident that Western women travelers write in a qualitatively different way from men."[21] Class and race are as equally important as gender and had an impact on the traveler and the text she produced. For Kristie Siegel it is self-evident that gender affected genre, but it seems "impossible to construct a set of commonalities that would cut across lines of race and class."[22] Foster and Mills therefore demand "to formulate more complex models of gender difference, in order to move away from simple polarization of gender difference, towards a multi-layered analysis where gender is sometimes the most salient feature in the production of a text and, at other times, is mediated through other factors."[23]

The more recent turn toward postcolonial studies caused scholars of travel writing to focus on the processes in which European travelers produced images and narratives about the non-European world and about Europe that deeply influenced Europeans' perception of the world.[24] In this process, female travelers seemed, as Foster and Mills suggest, to have been subjected to discursive constraints as much as their male counterparts. Discourses on colonialism and imperialism structured the thinking of Europeans and, thus, determined "that certain elements are perceived as noteworthy and that they are classified in certain ways. Thus, even the way that one perceives a landscape, despite the fact that it feels as if it is a simple unmediated process of looking, is already mediated through discourses of aesthetics and imperialism which will determine that certain tracts of land are designated as landscape rather than others, and that the viewer experiences certain emotions in relation to particular geomorphological features."[25]

Anna and George Ticknor's Travel Journals

Saxony occupied a central place in the collective admiration of upper-class Americans for continental Europe's advanced cultural and social life throughout the nineteenth century. Dresden's museums and Leipzig's university attracted many well-off men and women from New England in pursuit of cultural and social advancement. John Quincy Adams, James Fenimore

Cooper, Washington Irving, and John Lothrop Motley were among those tourists who were drawn to Dresden by its reputation as the "Florence on the Elb."[26]

The Ticknors were among the first Americans to discover Dresden's rich cultural and social life. By presenting Dresden society as of superior character to any other city on the continent north of the Alps, the Ticknors became trendsetters and thus contributed to the growing attraction of the city among future generations of American travelers. By the 1860s, Dresden's museums had achieved such fame among Americans that William Cullen Bryant (1794–1878), in 1869 at the occasion of the founding of the Metropolitan Museum of Art, felt compelled to remark in his speech to his fellow New Yorkers that "the little Kingdom of Saxony, with an area less than that of Massachusetts, and a population but little larger, possesses a Museum of the Fine Arts marvelously rich, which no man who visits the continent of Europe is willing to own that he has not seen."[27]

The Ticknors succeeded in spreading the word about Dresden's cultural attractions even without publishing their extensive travel accounts in book form.[28] Both Anna and George Ticknor wrote their travel journals during their journey and sent them home to friends and family as extended letters. From Anna Ticknor we know that she wrote her travel logs "rapidly, for my time was quite as much filled as my strength would bear, and about once a month, sent home the sheets, to serve as letters to my sisters, and several friends. I had therefore not much opportunity to look back and consider defects."[29] In the course of time, these letters seem to have become the object of semipublic publication for the educated and wealthy circles in Boston. Already George Ticknor's travel logs from his first journey to Germany had been the object of much public admiration. Shortly after Elizabeth Peabody (1804–1894) had moved to Boston, she wrote to her sister about her reading of George Ticknor's 1815–1817 journals, which she seem to have been given to read by George Ticknor. Peabody informed her sister that these journals had been "lent to many people since his return," who concurred that it was "the most interesting work of the kind they ever saw."[30]

And although both George and Anna Ticknor wrote these journals with the frequency that is usually reserved for a diary, their journals defy an easy categorization since they lack the characteristics that are so typical for autobiographical texts. While we certainly learn about what George and Anna Ticknor did during their stay in Saxony, we are completely left in the dark with regards to how they felt about their extended stay and about the people they met. Both George and Anna's journals exhibit a certain distance between the authors and their journals. Intimate feelings, personal information, and secrets told only to diaries were not included in these travel journals, nor are descriptions of repetitive actions that provide the structure for the day. Both authors seem to have suspended writing when personal problems such as illness and homesickness occurred. When after more than a month of silence, Anna Ticknor continues her travel journal on March 25, 1836, she gives as reasons for this interruption (the last entry dates February 20) that "much other writing occupations and real absence of events, have combined to prevent my continuing my journal."[31] However, she also was stricken by the sudden death of several acquaintances, including the wife of Wolf Heinrich Friedrich Karl Count of Baudissin (1789–1878), a close friend of the Ticknors whom they had visited on the night of February 20. Several of his nieces had contracted whooping cough and scarlet fever. They died within days and infected the Countess Baudissin who also died from the disease. One can only imagine that the Ticknors must have been afraid for the lives of their two girls. They already had lost two children. Yet, Anna Ticknor simply and coldly remarked in her travel journal that Countess Baudissin's death "is sincerely regretted by many in society."[32] She continues to write, "though such events should benefit, as well as grieve us, I will not dwell here upon the circumstances."[33] Both Anna and George Ticknor worked very hard on keeping personal feelings from their travel journals. This resulted in the production of a text that often appears cold and distant. These journals, thus, do not open a window to the authors' souls. Both George and Anna Ticknor simply stopped writing in their journal when emotional problems emerged. During his earlier journey to Göttingen in 1815–1817, George Ticknor apparently became homesick and instead of turning to his travel journal, he gave up writing for close to three months.

If one follows Jane Robinson's implicit distinction between writers who travel and produce (published) travel literature and travelers who write and produce (unpublished and published) travel reports, the Ticknors' travel journal would fall into the latter category. That distinction should, however, not make one believe that travel reports are of lesser value than travel literature. George and Anna Ticknor's travel logs seem to possess even greater value since both authors produced them parallel yet independent of each other. These travel journals seem to be the only known case of truly parallel travel writing by husband and wife. Both wrote about their encounters and experiences with the societies they visited. Sometimes their travel journals reflect different experiences, as when George Ticknor spent time visiting Prince Johann (1801–1873) and Anna Ticknor stayed "home" in their hotel room. At other times, both write about the same experience: the court ball they attended together, the stroll through Dresden they shared, or the friends they visited together for an evening of conversation and games. It seems as if both sets of travel journals were written independently, without much interaction between authors in form of referencing the other by disputing (or agreeing with) the other's view. There is no evidence to suggest that Anna and George exchanged their travel logs or even read them to each other. Both sets of journals seem to offer a unique opportunity to compare male and female travel writing and to discuss the question whether travel writing is inherently gendered.

Both George and Anna Ticknor's travel journals are characterized by a remarkable similarity in tone and intention. Both authors intended to produce a narrative that offered the reader a positive impression of Saxony's culture and social life and the social life of the aristocracy in particular. The reader learns a great deal about Dresden's nobility and the cultural life, including museums and art galleries, from reading these journals. However, Anna Ticknor did not exclusively report about court life. In contrast to her husband, she also offered some insights into the life of the common people. A memorable passage from her journal refers to an observation she made from her room in the hotel: "A day or two ago, I saw a sight which seemed to cap the climax of the degradation of our sex here; which was a woman drawing an empty coal cart without the small assistance of a dog; and a *man* sitting *in the cart,* entirely at his ease, with his arms folded in great dignity. I hoped for his character's sake that something was the matter with him."[34]

Such observations are entirely absent from George Ticknor's travel journals. They are, instead, filled with entries about life at court and meetings with members of Dresden's aristocracy and educated elite. George Ticknor showed little interest in the common people of Saxony, although he once interviewed a woman in Stötteritz about her experience of the Battle of the Nations (1813).[35] Yet, in this exceptional case, he had merely wanted to collect an eyewitness account of a historic event and was not concerned with her as an individual. He did not preserve any of the dialogue with her (nor of any other commoners in the journals) nor did he provide her name to convey authenticity but merely summarized her answers. Anna, on the other hand, tended to comment on her impressions about the common people of Dresden—albeit from a safe distance, such as from behind the window of her hotel room or the windows of their carriage.

George and Anna Ticknor preferred to socialize with the nobility and the educated elites, and thus were able to provide in their travel narratives firsthand accounts of dinner parties with noblemen and poets. Descriptions of common people and their behavior were always the result of observation from a safe distance but did rarely result from direct encounter by staying or talking with these commoners. For that reason, it was not always possible to make sense of something they saw, since information was missing. Anna Ticknor did not know why that woman was dragging the cart with the man sitting inside and she did not inquire about it either. Social status and distinction prevented both Ticknors from direct encounters with the common people.

The aforementioned journal entry should not make one believe that Anna disliked Dresden. In fact she found much to compliment, as her journal entry for January 15, 1836, makes clear:

> I am constantly more and more struck with the pleasant and excellent character of this agreeable little city. I have not yet seen any thing in the streets or houses painful or revolting; no rags or misery, no half clothed children, no ill-tempered mothers or attendants, witching and dragging children, no idle loungers, no intemperance. On the contrary, every body is warmly and thoroughly clothed, the

> children particularly so, their nice little wadded dresses and warm cloth or velvet caps looking as comfortable as possible. The poorest I have seen are dressed with regard to warmth, though the materials are of the cheapest kind. I have seen but one really ragged person since I have been in Saxony. The good temper of all is equally striking and agreeable. . . . The good-humoured smile accompanies the greeting of the heaviest loaded market women, and the workmen along the ways, the porters and roughest looking people I have seen pause to speak and smile with little children of their own degree; I never see children quarrelling with each other or teasing smaller ones or creatures. I have never yet detected a sour or a sulky look, even, amongst them, and though not a deep observer, I am a very minute one.[36]

One of the most fascinating instances in this parallel travel writing is the observation of the court ball Anna and George Ticknor attended on the night of January 10. Both wrote about the event at some length in their journals.[37] The ball was part of the carnival season that stretched from Christmas to Lent and was filled with many parties at court and in private homes. While Anna Ticknor's entry for that day begins with the morning and at least briefly—in one short paragraph—mentioned the preparations for the night, George Ticknor's entry for the day starts with the beginning of the ball. Both complain that although the event was to start at six and they arrived just a few minutes late, they were nearly the last guests to arrive. And while George Ticknor reflects on the organization of the event, the dances, and his conversations, Anna Ticknor provides much more detail with regard to the dresses of the attending women, the food, and the decoration of the palace. In George Ticknor's entry, there is virtually no color, while Anna Ticknor praises the tasteful dresses of the princesses. Both notice the amazingly large quantity of silver dishes and silverware as well as the abundance of diamonds in the dresses of the royal family. George Ticknor wrote: "The quantity of silver must have been immense—for the plates were all of silver for the whole four hundred and fifty persons, and were changed at least four times for each and sometimes six or seven times."[38] It appears that in general,

George Ticknor rarely used colors to describe people, objects, or places in his travel journals. Even when they visit the Green Vault—a famous museum in Dresden with all kinds of valuable and colorful art objects and treasures—George Ticknor is very reluctant to describe the collection's colors. Sometimes looking through George Ticknor's eyes feels like watching an old black-and-white movie. Looking through Anna Ticknor's eyes, by contrast, feels like watching a film in which trees are green, fields are golden, and people have rosy cheeks.

Anna Ticknor's description of the court ball undoubtedly focused on details which seem to have appeared to her husband as insignificant. Both accounts, however, refer to the central figure of the evening in some detail and provide a rather satirical account of the old king's desire to dance at the ball. King Anton, who was born in 1755 and thus eighty-one years old, opened the ball with a "dance." For George Ticknor, Anton was a poor old man who was prevented from falling only by "the great skill of his partner."[39] Anna Ticknor was less reluctant and expressed: "It was a strange and painful sight to see the old king attempting to dance the quadrille. He has always been excessively fond of dancing, and was determined it should be said he had danced after he was eighty. He got through without falling, which seemed wonderful, but he had a gentle, careful partner."[40] Both agreed that watching King Anton's attempt at dancing was painful and both wrote nearly identical phrases in their travel journals. This is a very rare moment in which Anna and George Ticknor's writing appeared coordinated or at least similar.

The eye for details separates George and Anna Ticknor's travel journals. Beyond the details, there are also clear differences in the way George and Anna Ticknor composed their journals. George frequently conducted background research and relied on secondary sources to provide factual descriptions in his journal. As he stated himself in a note added to the front of the journals in 1868, "I prepared myself by reading ample accounts of all the universities, high schools, cities and distinguished people we were to visit. I took plentiful notes of them, which I plentifully used in my Journal before I got back."[41] Yet, in his journals, George Ticknor did not always name his sources. Sometimes he referred to books he carried around, and sometimes it is not clear from where he received his information. Anna Ticknor, by contrast, though she occasionally referred to a book she had read on a topic, does not seem to have conducted much background research. This different level of preparation and not gender resulted in different narratives—a more factual and in-depth account in the case of George Ticknor and the more detailed, colorful, but superficial one in the case of Anna Ticknor.

George Ticknor's most extensive and detailed journal entries deal with institutions of higher learning and culture. His descriptions are always informed by published sources, interviews with individuals working at these institutions, and his own observations. Reading about these institutions before and after he visited them and before he wrote about them in his journals mediated and shaped his perception and thus his journals. The resulting journal entries are the result of negotiations between his three sources: books, interviews, and his own senses. Anna Ticknor, in contrast, trusted her eyes and ears more than printed materials that were easily available to her. The image of Saxony created by George Ticknor, thus, necessarily differs from the image created by his wife. However, in both cases, perception was severely limited by the preconceptions acquired by George Ticknor in the preparation of his visits from what he read and in the case of Anna Ticknor by her language and social communication deficiencies.

Another difference is that George Ticknor seems to have maintained his journal with a higher degree of continuity overall, writing frequent, short entries whereas Anna wrote less often and more at once. Anna wrote a total of 281 pages for the time of her stay in Dresden from November 20, 1835, to May 11, 1836 (172 days). Her travel journal contains sixty-eight separate, dated entries. Sometimes she wrote daily entries several pages in length, and at other times there were large gaps between postings. For example, there are no entries from February 20 to March 25. The shortest entry is about a page in length, and the longest is thirty-one pages (April 26). For the same time span, George wrote a total of eighty-two entries comprising 144 pages. Three summarizing entries are of significant length—the longest is a general entry on Dresden written in April and covering twenty-four pages—but many are just one paragraph long, indicating that in some periods he committed himself to writing on a daily basis.

The Ticknors stayed at the Hotel de Rome on the Neumarkt in Dresden (building to the right labeled "Stadt Rom"). Courtesy of the Sächsische Landesbibliothek, Dresden.

The differences in the quantity of writing might also be connected to the arrangements of social life in Dresden. While traveling resulted in a temporary breakdown of the borders between public and private spheres, these borders could be renegotiated and reestablished at the destination of travel. The Ticknors stayed in one of the most exclusive and centrally located hotels in downtown Dresden—the Hotel de Rome on the Neumarkt. Here they created a home away from home that reestablished a private sphere to which they could return from their encounters with Dresden society and from their excursions into the near environment of the city and to distant places such as Berlin. George Ticknor described the living arrangements as following:

> We have engaged in the *Hotel de Rome,* a suite of six excellent rooms opening into each other, and another one quite near them for my manservant; the principal parlor being five and twenty feet by twenty, and the whole very comfortable, and I have engaged a nicer

> carriage than I could get in London with a coachman and footman so that we have capital quarters to live in, an excellent table to ourselves; and five servants of our own, besides the attendance at the Hotel, which is more prompt than I have yet found anywhere else. Mrs. T. thinks we are better off than we were at the Clarendon. Perhaps we are, though we do not dine from plate—certainly we are better off than we were at Dublin or anywhere else except London since we came from home. Our rooms are on the Neue Market—a very neat, lively square, the pleasantest in Dresden, and exactly opposite the great Picture Gallery and the collection of Casts; near the Palace and the Theater; and, as to the society, in a position that seems to be about central.[42]

George Ticknor was often invited to court and to the homes of other residents alone, leaving Anna Ticknor and the two children at their home in the hotel. Such arrangements had an influence on the production of her travel journal. Left to herself, she had more time to reflect about events and encounters but at the same time she was excluded from various social encounters. Yet, this situation allowed her to observe people outside her hotel rooms through her window. Anna Ticknor's experience, in general, was entirely dependent on her husband since he determined all aspects of this journey. For example, when they traveled to Berlin from Dresden in May 1836, Anna wished to continue on to Hamburg to visit a friend, Elizabeth Gossler, but "Mr. Ticknor would not consent to do it."[43] Moreover, whereas George was fluent in German and spent many evenings socializing with his Dresden friends, Anna lacked proficiency in the German language and spent a good deal of time alone. Yet she never complained about her social isolation in her journal.

Anna and George Ticknor shared a view of Saxony, in which this small kingdom at the center of Europe became the epitome of civilization. In both author's journals, Saxony was represented as a well-organized constitutional monarchy, in which all people were happy. The Ticknors, further, began to identify with Saxons, whom they apparently regarded as a mirror image and, to a certain degree, an even better version of Americans. After reading the

Ticknors' glorifying descriptions of Dresden, one is left with the impression that Saxons represented, at least with regard to culture and education, the future of America. In the Ticknors' eyes, Saxon farmers were educated and possessed libraries, and the rulers were enlightened and engaged in social and political reform. More importantly, Saxons had reached their "civilized state," at least in George Ticknor's (apparently badly informed) mind, without violence and revolution.

When the Ticknors traveled from Dresden to Berlin in May of 1836, Anna Ticknor saw a correlation between civilized society and geography. In her view, Saxony's rich soil and rolling hills made for a civilized population. Prussia's sandy and barren flatlands, by contrast, predisposed the people there to a state of wretchedness. Since, in her eyes, "a people's fortunes were determined by the soil on which they lived," American travelers could hardly expect to find prospering communities in such a wasteland: "the soil is very poor, and cultivation seems to have been given up, as hopeless. The few cottages and people, we saw, looked wretchedly poor."[44] This Prussian soil was not conducive to produce an advanced civilization and thus represented a counter-model to Saxony's culturally rich and enlightened state. Returning to Saxony, Anna Ticknor wrote: "I have felt a certain satisfaction that every mile brought us nearer to Saxony, and, when we had absolutely passed the barrier, I found or imagined that I found immediately a great difference in the appearance of the people, as well as in the cultivation of the country. There is good reason for it, however, for the soil in this part of Saxony is vastly superior to what we have seen in the adjacent part of Prussia, and the people are notoriously contented with their rulers."[45]

Interestingly, the project of building a train connection from Leipzig to Dresden—the first long-distance train connection in Germany, which provided a significant push for industrialization of the region—is not mentioned in either Anna or George Ticknor's travel journals. Preparations for the project had already begun in 1835. Construction started on March 1, 1836. Yet the Ticknors steadfastly ignored this great project, one that would fundamentally change Saxony's society and landscape, as much as they ignored all other signs of advancing industrialization. For the Ticknors, Saxony was to be a romantic and premodern heaven for the arts, culture, and education. Nature and society were to be harmonious and untouched by modern destructive life. Traveling to Saxony was, thus, traveling back in time.

Conclusion

The Ticknors' travel journals offer a unique opportunity to test whether "women's travel accounts differ from those written by men in any fundamental way," and whether there is "a way in which travel writing is inherently gendered."[46] Anna Ticknor, however, is not the typical female traveler that catches the eye of feminist researchers, since she did not travel alone and since she did not produce travel writing of literary quality. However, it is exactly this situation, with a husband and wife traveling together, visiting the very same places and spaces, and writing separately and independently about their impressions, that make these travel journals such an impressive and unique source to explore our guiding question.

Anna and George Ticknor believed that Saxony was the epitome of modern civilization. Mingling with people who belonged to the upper class (and the nobility in particular), and keeping members of the lower classes at a safe distance, both Anna and George Ticknor's travel journals clearly reflect social stereotypes that were so typical for members of the elite. The Ticknors were able to extensively travel in Europe because of their socio-economic position in Boston society. It was, however, not only this socio-economic position that determined the perception of what they saw and how they saw it, but also their adaptation of social stereotypes held by Saxony's social elites that determined the travel experience of both Ticknors. Yet, Anna and George Ticknor's eyes seem to have focused on different aspects and elements of Saxon society. George Ticknor saw and wrote about exclusive social circles, his contact with the royal family and with educated elites of Dresden, as well as the many museums, art galleries, and cultural establishments he visited. Anna Ticknor saw and wrote about these sights too, but in addition noticed smaller things such as colors of dresses and places. She also observed the common people and was concerned with the well-being of women and children. Her eyes caught more detail but did not lose sight of the main events. Her writing was incidental in that she did not prepare for what she would encounter, while George Ticknor's writing was strategic, since he first read about an institution or place, then visited it, and afterward wrote about the place, integrating his own observations into information he had garnered from reading secondhand accounts.

Both George and Anna Ticknor shared many social experiences about which both separately wrote in their travel journals. Their entries, however, lack human emotions even in the face of death and disaster, as well as failing to describe recurring actions that provide a structure for the days and journals. Beyond a factual account of what both authors did during their stay in Dresden, the reader can barely find an autobiographical dimension to these journals. The Ticknors' journey to Dresden was planned and structured by George Ticknor alone. He decided that the family would stay for six months in Dresden and even refused to change his plans when Anna Ticknor suggested a trip to Hamburg. This context should not make one believe that Anna Ticknor hated Dresden and Saxony. She quickly joined her husband in his limitless adoration for Saxony, and Dresden in particular. Even more than her husband, Anna Ticknor made the argument that Saxony had reached a higher level of civilization because of its pleasant landscape (rolling hills) and its rich soil.

How different or how similar are George and Anna Ticknor's travel journals? They both wrote the journals during the journey on a nearly daily basis. Neither account offers insight into the author's emotions. Both writers intended these texts to become at least semipublic documents. Only an eye for detail and the occasional but distanced inclusion of the common people set Anna Ticknor's travel journals apart from those of her husband.

Acknowledgment

I would like to thank Gisela Mettele for her ideas and suggestions that shaped my thinking about the differences and similarities between Anna and George Ticknor's travel journals. While I seem to have an eye for similarities, Gisela was better equipped to point me to the differences.

NOTES

1. For George Ticknor's biography, see David B. Tyack, *George Ticknor and the Boston Brahmins* (Cambridge, Mass.: Harvard University Press, 1967). For his travels, see Thomas Adam and Gisela Mettele, eds., *Two Boston Brahmins in Goethe's Germany: The Travel Journals of Anna and George Ticknor* (Lanham, Md.: Lexington Books, 2009). See also the first chapter in this book, by Ashley Sides, which is based upon his master's thesis: Ashley Sides, "What Americans Said about Saxony, and What This Says about Them: Interpreting Travel Writings of the Ticknors and Other Privileged Americans, 1800–1850," master's thesis, University of Texas at Arlington, 2008.

2. Anna Eliot Ticknor, *Samuel Eliot* (Boston: Boston University Press, 1869), 183–84, 199–200.

3. Tyack, *George Ticknor,* 89.

4. Ibid., 90.

5. E. Digby Baltzell, *Puritan Boston & Quaker Philadelphia* (New Brunswick: Transaction Publishers, 1998), 42.

6. Adam and Mettele, *Two Boston Brahmins in Goethe's Germany,* 58–61; Tyack, *George Ticknor,* 110.

7. See also the first chapter in this book, by Ashley Sides, for a more detailed treatment of American travel to Germany—and to Saxony in particular.

8. These journals are published (although selectively) in Adam and Mettele, *Two Boston Brahmins in Goethe's Germany,* 87–231.

9. Mary Wollstonecraft, *A Vindication of the Rights of Woman: With Strictures on Political and Moral Subjects* (London: Printed for J. Johnson, 1792), 128–29.

10. Susan Bassnett, "Travel Writing and Gender," in Peter Hulme and Tim Youngs, eds., *The Cambridge Companion to Travel Writing* (Cambridge: Cambridge University Press, 2002), 227.

11. Kristi Siegel, "Intersections: Women's Travel and Theory," in Kristi Siegel, ed., *Gender, Genre, & Identity in Women's Travel Writing* (New York: Peter Lang, 2004), 5.

12. Elizabeth A. Bohl, *Women Travel Writers and the Language of Aesthetics, 1716–1818* (Cambridge: Cambridge University Press, 1995), 152.

13. Jane Robinson, *Unsuitable For Ladies: An Anthology of Women Travellers* (Oxford: Oxford University Press, 1994), xii.

14. Bassnett, "Travel Writing and Gender," 227; Sara Mills, *Discourses of Difference* (London: Routledge, 1991), 21.

15. For a reevaluation of the place of women in nineteenth-century society, see: Thomas Adam, *Buying Respectability: Philanthropy and Urban Society in Transnational Perspective, 1840s to 1930s* (Bloomington: Indiana University Press, 2009), 126–52; Benjamin M. Baader, *Gender, Judaism, and Bourgeois Culture in Germany, 1800–1870* (Bloomington: Indiana University Press, 2006); Kathleen D. McCarthy, *American Creed, Philanthropy and the Rise of Civil Society, 1700–1865* (Chicago: University of Chicago Press, 2003); Jean H. Quataert, *Staging Philanthropy: Patriotic Women and the National Imagination in Dynastic Germany, 1813–1916* (Ann Arbor: University of Michigan Press, 2001).

16. William W. Stowe, *Going Abroad: European Travel in Nineteenth-Century American Culture* (Princeton: Princeton University Press, 1994), 4–8, 11.

17. Siegel, "Intersections: Women's Travel and Theory," 5.

18. Catherine Barnes Stevenson, *Victorian Women Travel Writers in Africa* (Boston: Twayne Publishers, 1982), 9.

19. Ibid., 6.

20. Ibid., 9–10.

21. Shirley Foster and Sara Mills, *An Anthology of Women's Travel Writing* (Manchester: Manchester University Press, 2002), 3. Sara Mills, *Discourses of Difference: An Analysis of Women's Travel Writing and Colonialism* (London: Routledge, 1991), 30.

22. Siegel, "Intersections: Women's Travel and Theory," 5.

23. Foster and Mills, *An Anthology of Women's Travel Writing*, 4.

24. Mary Louise Pratt, *Imperial Eyes: Travel Writing and Transculturation* (London: Routledge, 2008).

25. Foster and Mills, *An Anthology of Women's Travel Writing*, 5.

26. Eberhard Brüning, "'Saxony Is a Prosperous and Happy Country': American Views of the Kingdom of Saxony in the Nineteenth Century," in Thomas Adam and Ruth Gross, eds., *Traveling between Worlds: German-American Encounters* (College Station: Texas A&M Press, 2006), 20–50; Anja Becker, "For the Sake of Old Leipzig Days . . . Academic Networks of American

Students at a German University, 1781–1914," PhD thesis, University of Leipzig, 2006; Sides, "What Americans Said about Saxony."

27. *A Metropolitan Art Museum in the City of New York: Proceedings of a Meeting Held at the Theatre of the Union League Club, Tuesday Evening, November 23, 1869* (New York: Printed for the Committee, 1869), 9. This document is stored on George Comfort deposit reel 4276 T 6814 (microfilm) at the Smithsonian Archives of American Art.

28. The first publication of excerpts from George Ticknor's travel journals occurred only after his death. George S. Hillard and Anna Eliot Ticknor, eds., *Life, Letters, and Journals of George Ticknor,* 2 vols. (Boston: James R. Osgood and Company, 1876).

29. Adam and Mettele, *Two Boston Brahmins in Goethe's Germany,* 218.

30. Letter of Elizabeth Peabody to Mary (Peabody) dated June 12, 1822 (Peabody Family Papers, Sophia Smith Collection, Smith College, Northampton, Massachusetts).

31. Mrs. Ticknor Journals, September 1835 to November 1836, 678 (March 25, 1836).

32. Ibid., 679.

33. Ibid.

34. Adam and Mettele, *Two Boston Brahmins in Goethe's Germany,* 194.

35. Ibid., 49.

36. Ibid., 193.

37. Ibid., 118–19 (George Ticknor) and 190–93 (Anna Ticknor).

38. Ibid., 119.

39. Ibid., 118.

40. Ibid., 191.

41. Quoted in Steven Allaback and Alexander Medlicott Jr., *A Guide to the Microfilm Edition of the European Journals of George and Anna Ticknor,* (Hanover, N.H.: Dartmouth College Library, 1978), 3–4.

42. Adam and Mettele, *Two Boston Brahmins in Goethe's Germany,* 105.

43. Ibid., 218.

44. Sides, "What Americans Said about Saxony," 86–87.

45. Adam and Mettele, *Two Boston Brahmins in Goethe's Germany,* 224.

46. Bassnett, "Travel Writing and Gender," 227.

The Women of Palestine in American Women's Travel Writing

James Ross-Nazzal

In no city on earth, perhaps, is woman found in greater variety than in the "City of the Great King." The fair ruby-lipped Circassian and the sable daughter of Ham, the fur-clad Russian and the semi-nude Bedawy of the desert, the graceful Greek and the clumsy Copt, the modest Armenian and the brazen Fellahah, the haughty inmate of the harem and the oppressed Jewess, "from every nation under heaven." But, however widely they all differ in blood, manners, customs, and appearance; they more or less resemble each other in at least this common point— they are the abject slaves of the "lords of creation."

—Sarah Johnson Barclay, 1857

This chapter focuses on the travel writings of fifty-one American women who ventured to Palestine between 1832 and 1899. These Americans seemed to have spent much time observing and writing about Palestinian women. While the way Palestinian women dressed seemed to preoccupy the American travelers the most, they did not limit themselves to shallow, cursory, or trendy observations. American women discussed such important topics as Palestinian women's social positions in the family in Palestinian society at large. In several instances American women, such as Kate Kraft and Clara Moyse Tadlock, called for the need to hold a woman's rights convention in order to address the inequalities between the sexes. American women travelers also detailed the place and function of Palestinian women in the public sphere, from weddings to funerals. They recorded instances of physical abuse, the inequality of Palestine's divorce laws and customs, and the nearly total lack of support for women's education.

The current historiography is replete with travel observations by American and British women about foreign women. For example, Mary Suzanne Schriber notes that "American women . . . look at the female 'other' through two windows: difference and doubling."[1] American women, in other words, see themselves as able to enter spaces usually off-limits for male travelers, such as the kitchen and the harem. Thus, American women, according to Schriber, weighed the culture and politics of foreign women against their own in order to argue that American culture and politics were better for women than foreign models. She sees "doubling" by American women as first showing signs of sympathy with their foreign counterparts, but then justifying the lot of foreign women as being what all women have to expect out of life "even as it betrays the trace of superiority of the American Woman."[2] Hilton Obenzinger notes that American women traditionally exhibited in their published travelogues empathy with Palestine's women, especially American women who "were often given greater access to female realms."[3]

Following a similar line of thought, Brigitte Georgi-Findlay notes that American women travelers to the American West were able to identify with the struggles of American Indian women, but were unable to pose solutions because they saw the "plights" of Indian women as part of the way the world simply worked. "By turning the lens on Indian women's complicity in their own victimization, she effectively prevents the critical identification of white and Indian women's common oppression and deflects attention away from the relations of unequal power between whites and Indians."[4] However, many American women were sympathetic to the condition of Palestinian women, and did offer suggestions and advice as to how their lives could be made better.

Additionally, Judy Mabro notes that American women who ventured into the Middle East tended to pass moral judgments on polygamy, the harem, and immorality of foreign women, as well as their inability to be good mothers, and their lack of education.[5]

As I will show, however, the American travelers in this study did not seem to be simply interested or concerned with telling their potential readers about the condition or status of Palestinian women. They seemed to be truly motivated in correcting what they believed to be problems facing Palestinian women. More often than not, American travelers blamed the poor status of Palestine's women on the fact that Palestine was not as modern as the United States. Ideas of progress were often couched in religious terms in which American female travelers would measure progress by assessing how Christian their subjects were. While these travelers noted the sad condition of Palestinian women, they often overstated the degree of female equality in the United States. In their writings they argued that American women were equal to American men on all levels. This may suggest that American female travelers held different degrees of perceived inequality. This was, as Mabro notes, not just an American phenomenon since European women too tended to believe they were more equal than they really were: "When travelers in North Africa and the Middle East told the people they met about the perfect equality to be found in Western marriages they may have believed it at that time or were making a generalization based on a limited experience. In reality, much of the criticism they leveled at the societies they visited could also be leveled at their own."[6] This is an important element in understanding the points of view expressed by American women. As Mabro notes, most European women were torn between identifying with their race and identifying with their gender.[7] In the end, European women sided with their race and thus "adopted a condescending tone" toward non-European women.[8] The views expressed by American women in this study seem to challenge the finding of Mabro on European women's treatment of Middle Eastern women.

American women were surprised that Palestinian women were not equal to Palestinian men. Yet, the travelers did not specifically blame Islam, Judaism, or Arabic or Turkish customs and traditions for the plight of Palestinian women. Rather, they simply held responsible the husbands and fathers of Palestinian women, as the quote at the beginning of this chapter suggests—thus boiling down the problem to a basic one of patriarchy. This undermines the argument of Schriber and Georgi-Findlay who believe that American women both acknowledged the plight of foreign women yet believed that there was nothing that could be done about it because their lot was natural.

Palestinian Women in Family, Religion, and Society

American women travelers, except for Cora Agnes Benneson, identified the ethnic or religious background of each of the Palestinian women they wrote about. This may suggest a relative informal level of engagement with her subjects, especially where "neutral" does not mean "objective." Benneson, an Illinois attorney, retold a story about a young Palestinian mother who offered to sell her baby to the author. This story is unique for two reasons. First, this is the only time in which the ethnicity or religion of the subject of the story was not revealed. Second, this is the only instance I have come across in these travel accounts that explicitly references the selling of babies in Palestine.

Shortly after arriving in Jaffa, Benneson visited Miss Arnott's mission school. Arnott, a British subject, operated one of many schools established to convert Jewish girls to Christianity. Two of the students, Anesa and Sophia, volunteered to act as Benneson's guides and translators while Benneson was in Jaffa. The little girls took Benneson one day for a walk along the shore. They stopped to talk to "a Syrian woman" who was sitting on the beach, watching her six children play in the sand. "You have a pretty baby," Benneson said to the woman, referring to the youngest child. "Yes," the Syrian woman replied, "wouldn't you like to buy it?"[9] Benneson asked how much for the child and the woman responded "forty-five dollars." Anesa said to Benneson, "Don't take it at that price. She has asked you too much."[10] Then Benneson and the girls left the beach after that exchange, presumably without the baby.

I find this story interesting for several reasons. Was the "Syrian woman" Arab or Jewish? She could have been either. If the Jewish girls from Miss Arnott's school spoke only English and Hebrew then the "Syrian woman" was probably Jewish. If the girls spoke Yiddish they were probably immigrants from Europe, spoke other languages, and would probably not have referred to the mother as "Syrian." On the other hand, if the girls also spoke Arabic, then it was possible that the mother was an Arab. In either case, what is most interesting is the sense that selling one's baby in late-nineteenth century Palestine was not considered outside the social norm by the "Syrian woman," or even by the two schoolgirls. Anesa's problem with the transaction was not that it was taking place, but that the mother was simply asking too much for her child.

Additionally, if the little girls realized that the "Syrian woman" was asking too much for her baby, they may have known what was an acceptable price for a child of that age. In other words, Anesa may have witnessed other sales of babies or at least been aware of the fact that the selling of babies took place. In either instance, this story suggests that the selling of babies was a culturally or socially acceptable practice. Benneson, of course, seemed shocked at the potential transaction. As Mabro points out, however, American female travelers tended to note the "deplorable" condition of motherhood throughout the world.[11]

This story also indicates a sense of the lack of cultural uniqueness or national identity on the part of the "Syrian woman." If she was willing to sell her child not only to a stranger but to a foreigner, one who would more than likely raise the child to speak a foreign language and embrace foreign customs and traditions, what does that say about this "Syrian woman's" cultural identity? Maybe economics and not culture was the fulcrum on which this woman's world turned.

Altogether, these American travelers identified five different ethnic or religious categories of Palestinian women: Muslim, Jewish, Christian, Bedouin, and Druse. Approximately 75 percent of their writings focused on Muslim women. Only five American female travelers referenced Jewish women. Christian women were discussed three times. Bedouin women were twice investigated and Druse women were discussed only once. Druse are an ethnic, religious, and linguistic minority in the Middle East. Religiously, they accept the ancient writings found in the first five books of the Christian bible. Ethnically they are separate from Arabs or Jews, and their language is also distinct from Arabic or Hebrew.

Marion Harland was the only woman in this examination who wrote about Druse women, and she focused on their attire. Harland visited the home of a Druse family. She noted that the matriarch of the family wore "pink calico trousers, very wide and full, a short jacket of the same material, of a deeper red, and a veil of coarse white cotton, pinned tightly around her forehead and falling down her back."[12]

Harland did not tell her readers how she determined this family was Druse. She never wrote about their customs, traditions, or beliefs. Besides noting the dress of the Druse mother, Harland observed that she placed cushions on the bare floor for everyone to sit upon and that the mother had several babies around her, none of which looked "plump" or "robust."[13]

Bedouin are Arabs who historically embraced a pastoral, nomadic lifestyle. In Palestine, Bedouin were Arabs, Muslims, and spoke Arabic. They lived in the rural parts of Palestine, especially along the Jordan River. Bedouin women were also rarely the focus of travelers' accounts. Louise Griswold and Dr. Sarah Furnas Wells were the only two travelers in this group who wrote about Bedouin women. Mrs. Stephen Griswold wrote about Bedouins as if they were a monolithic entity: "The Bedouin Arab" was the usual way she described Bedouins. "Their women are made to do the drudgery, and are the slaves of the men," wrote Griswold. Not only did she believe that Bedouin women were second-class citizens, but that horses were more important to their husbands than their wives. "The Bedouin Arab often thinks more of his horse than of his wife," Griswold recalled. "Give him a piece of bread and he will share it with his horse." She was also not impressed with their cultural strategy of applying henna tattoos: "They paint and tattoo their faces, making themselves as hideous as the South Sea Islanders."[14] As Mabro notes, it was not unusual for European travelers to denote Middle Eastern women as "slaves."[15]

Wells had even less to say about Bedouin women, which was particularly disappointing, as she noted in her introduction that being a female traveler necessarily permitted her to gain new insights regarding the state and condition of women abroad. In this case, Wells limited her insights to the dress of a Bedouin woman who wore "a dark blue cotton robe" similar to those worn by "the peasant women" in other parts of Palestine. The major difference between the dress of Bedouin women and of those other peasant women, as Wells noted, was that Bedouin women wore either crimson or white veils versus the black veils donned by non-Bedouin women. Wells also observed that

Bedouin women wore rings on their fingers and toes, and bracelets on their arms, "both above and below the elbow." Their hair tended to be braided in order to support their earlobes, which were "weighted down with jewelry."[16] While Wells promised her readers new and interesting details into the lives of "oriental women," in the case of Palestine's Bedouins she provided nothing particularly insightful.

American female travelers wrote slightly more about Christian women than either Bedouin or Druse women. Additionally, the travelers ignored dress while focusing on the social position of Christian women, the differences between Christian and Muslim women (besides the obvious religious distinctions), and education among Christian women of Palestine. Susan Brewer Thomas, a patron of women's religious education in the pre–Civil War South, based her sentiments about the social position of Christian women in Palestine on their religious customs. She believed that Christian women "of the East" were at the bottom of the social and religious ladder in society (the same level as their Jewish and Muslim counterparts) because Arab Christian women took no active part in their religious worship. Thomas saw the duty of Arab Christian women to be the same as their American Christian counterparts—to raise healthy, Christian, patriotic children. Yet she saw that women in Palestine were prevented from being what she called the "guardian spirit[s]" who guided their children to "elevated thought, and noble aspirations for a higher life." In a sense, it seems that Thomas saw women's lack of participation in church services as an indication that they lacked any beneficial or instructive position within the family.[17] As Brewer had been a proponent of American women's education, and of American women taking active roles in their churches, this may be a clear example of how at times travel writings can be more about home than places abroad.[18]

Harland focused her investigation and analysis around the differences between Arab-Christian and Arab-Muslim women and Christian women's education. "It is not an expression of superior intelligence alone that characterizes the Christians, but a general alertness of bearing and play of countenance, a sort of self-respectfulness," wrote Harland. She attributed this to the fact that Muslim women believed they had no souls, and so would not be able to go to heaven. Christian Arab women held that they were more accountable to God than to their husbands, thus they tended to not only be more happy in the thought of eventually going to Heaven, but also to be more independent than their Muslim counterparts.[19] Similarly, Mary Allen told her readers that Muslims did not believe that women had souls and therefore could not enter heaven, and that Muslim men further felt justified to routinely mistreat their wives and daughters because "the Mohammedan religion recognizes woman as a mere animal."[20] Of course, Harland's and Allen's attitudes towards Muslim and Christian Arabs may support Mabro's findings. Mabro notes that European travelers tended to view religious evolution on a continuum, with Christianity being at the pinnacle of evolution while Islam was at the other end.[21]

Likewise, Harland attributed the look of intelligence, alertness, and self-respect upon the faces of Arab-Christian women to their level of education. "It is rare to find a Moslem woman of twenty who can read or write," noted Harland. "It is rarer to meet with a Christian woman of any age among the respectable middle classes who cannot."[22] In other words, Harland did not simply believe that all Christian women were more educated then their Muslim counterparts. Instead, she assumed that respectable Christians were educated. Thus even though an Arab might be Christian, she could not have that look upon her face of intelligence and self-respect unless she was educated. For Harland, respectability equated education. To be a respectable middle-class Christian Arab necessarily meant, and was a result of, education.

Along the lines of their treatment of Arab-Christian women, American female travelers simply scratched the surface of the lives of Jewish women of Palestine. Those few who did write about Jewish women tended to focus on their social position, religious status, and their dress. Just as Susan Brewer Thomas believed Arab-Christian women held low positions in society due to their inability to take an active role in their religious services, so did she conclude about the social status of Jewish women: "The glory of Jewish women . . . is departed, and their condition is dark and hopeless. It was with the deepest sympathy that we looked upon the social condition of women, lost to all that is noble, refined, and intellectual, in her Mohammedan paradise. A veil, thicker and darker than that which covers her face, enwraps her soul, excluding her from sight all that is beautiful and lovely in the social world."[23]

Regarding religion, several women supported Thomas's assertion that Jewish women did not participate in religious practices. "The women are not allowed to participate in the service, or even to sit in the body of the synagogue," recalled Sarah Barclay Johnson, "but are allotted a place in the gallery, which is partitioned off by lattice work."[24] This maybe more of an indication of Johnson's lack of information of the religio-cultural strategies of Jews more than it is an indictment of the position of Jewish women in Palestinian society. Her mother, Julia A. Barclay, also focused on the religiosity of Jewish women: "the matrons, maids, and damsels of Israel are possessed of the deepest religious feeling." She also believed that nearly all Jewish women could read. She never explained to her readers how she had come to that conclusion but she did suggest that it had something to do with their religious convictions.[25] Barclay was a Protestant missionary. It is possible that she spent some time converting or preaching to Palestine's Jews. If so, they would probably have been Jewish women rather than a mixed group. British missionaries predated American attempts at conversion by at least a decade, thus it is not impossible that, at a minimum, the efforts of British missionaries to convert the local population resulted in raising the literacy rates, as it was important to be able to read the Bible.

Ellen Clare Miller echoed the sentiments of Johnson and Thomas regarding Jewish women's position in religious services and customs. She was in Jerusalem during the Christian season of Lent, which corresponded with the Jewish Feast of Purim. During Purim, Miller visited two synagogues. In the first she noted one hundred people "all dressed alike in high fur-bordered hats, and dressing-gowns like coats." They recited prayers from the Book of Esther and banged sticks or bones whenever they read the name "Haman." She wrote about a similar scene in the second synagogue she visited that day. In neither synagogue did she notice any women participating in the festivities. Thus, Miller concluded "that woman among the Jews is incapable of" taking part in Judaic religious customs and traditions.[26] Again, some Jewish women were allowed to participate as equals in their religious ceremonies, and so it is possible that these American female travelers witnessed orthodox services in which men and women would have been segregated.

American travelers talked about the dress of Middle East women more than any other subject, thus suggesting the importance American women placed upon dress in society. As Florence Hartley wrote in *The Ladies' Book of Etiquette, and Manual of Politeness,* "A lady is never so well dressed as when you cannot remember what she wears."[27] With Jewish women it was no exception. Clorinda Minor, the American who attempted to establish colonies of converted Jews to await the Second Coming, simply noted that Jewish women did not veil, like their Muslim counterparts, yet "their persons were entirely wrapped in the universal white garment of this land."[28] While Minor related that Jewish women were not veiled, Thomas noted just the opposite about Jewish women in Palestine.[29]

Arab Muslim Women

While these American travelers gave more examples of Jewish women than they did of Christian, Bedouin, or Druse women of Palestine, what they wrote about these women pales in comparison to the sheer volume that they wrote about Arab Muslim women. Education, religion, physical abuse, divorce, the harem, weddings, funerals, social position, and, of course, the dress of Muslim women, were just some of the topics covered by thirty-two American female travelers. In other words, nearly two-thirds of these women talked about Palestinian Muslim women. Therefore, it is clear that the subject of Muslim women most caught the attention of the American travelers in this inquiry, much more so than Arab-Christian women, Jewish women, or any other ethnic or religious group of Palestinian women.

Sometimes these American travelers relayed rather cursory or seemingly unimportant facts about the lives of Palestine's Muslim women to their American readers. For example, Mrs. D. L. Miller noted than some women of the town of Sulem were washing clothes in a most strange fashion. Yet she never told her readers just how unusual their clothes washing was. Instead she said that she doubted the women used soap because the water did not indicate so.[30] She was the only traveler to even acknowledge this seemingly basic task—that of washing clothes in public. It seems to be that in a period before widespread electricity and washing machines, there would be many examples of authors writing about that drudging task. Interestingly enough, Miller was the only one, and certainly not in any detail, to mention this typical nineteenth-century woman's job.

While examples of beggars are numerous in most of these travel accounts, there was only one reference to Muslim women begging for money. Again, Mrs. D. L. Miller noted that in the village of Sulem, where "great piles of manure and filth were seen on the main streets," a woman approached her, holding a baby in her arms, and asked for money, "Backsheesh for baba," said the woman. Miller gave her "a few coins" and off she went. A few minutes later a younger woman appeared with the same baby in her arms asking Miller for money for her baby. "No doubt the women thought showing her baby was paying business," thought Miller, "therefore placed the child in the hands of others to help along the enterprise."[31]

Miller's recollection suggests several things about Palestinian society in the late 1880s and early 1890s. No other American female traveler mentioned stopping off in this town, yet by the actions of the woman with the baby it should be apparent that there had been some previous interaction between foreign visitors and the local population. She spoke broken English, according to Miller. While she could have learned English from a missionary, it is also possible that she learned just enough to beg for money, or had lived in a more cosmopolitan place where English was more likely to be spoken than in this Palestinian town.

A few other travelers also noted seemingly inconsequential activities of Muslim women at that time that may offer us a glimpse into Palestinian society. For example, in Shiloh, Thomas noted a group of "Mohammedan women and children, dressed in gayest costumes, amusing themselves by dancing, swinging, and other sports, in the merriest moods."[32] Likewise, Cora Agnes Benneson noted a group of Muslim women near Elisha's Fountain "in festive costume . . . singing, clapping their hands gleefully and dancing in a ring."[33] While the activity is certainly benign, and the lack of detail provided by the authors suggests the lack of importance the authors felt toward the dancing, it is nonetheless significant. These accounts suggest that

Muslim women were not always veiled in public, that the lives of Muslim women were not always dreary and dowdy, and that Muslim woman, against the conventional wisdom of the time, could indeed be seen in public without male chaperones and performing rather public, emotional displays. Certainly these two incidents of public festivities suggest a certain level of freedom and choice among Muslim women in Palestinian society at that time.

Sarah Barclay Johnson, a Protestant missionary, noted the importance of Muslim women veiling while in public. She noted, however, that Muslim women were permitted to be unveiled in their private spaces, such as in their gardens. She told her readers that all of the muezzins were always selected from a group of blind men "in order to prevent them from seeing the women who may be walking unveiled in their gardens below."[34]

Marriages

Some of the American travelers were allowed to take part in, or witness, Muslim weddings and funerals. Mrs. Stephen Griswold was staying at the home of "a wealthy Turkish family" while in Jerusalem in 1868. One evening, she noticed a marriage procession passing beneath her window. In her book she noted that Muslim weddings were usually contractual and that the groom paid a sum of money to his future in-laws who purchased jewels and coins for their daughter to wear on her scarf. Griswold maintained that this became the sole property of the bride. "The jewels can never be taken by law to pay the husband's debts, neither has he the power to dispose of them."[35]

Many years later, Marion Harland told a similar tale about the marriage customs of Palestine's Muslims. She observed that the weddings were usually arranged and that the participants rarely saw each other before the ceremony unless the bride-to-be catches "a glimpse of him [her future husband] through the window."[36]

Harland also noted a disparity in the ages of some of the couples that suggests the difference between cultural ideas toward adulthood between Palestinian Muslims and Americans. "A girl of ten is a child with us," Harland wrote, "a child and nothing more." Yet she heard of a marriage between a ten-year-old girl and a man of seventy. According to Harland, the bride's father could no longer support her so he accepted the dowry of "fifty napoleons." While some would see that as a dowry, others, such as Harland, saw it as nothing less than selling children.[37] In contrast Emile Loyson described the Muslim strategy of the dowry as beneficial for women. She even thought that Muslim women might have been in better economic situations then their American Christian counterparts because the dowry was no longer a widely practiced strategy in late nineteenth-century American society. "The Islamic practice of the dowry is to ensure that women have some wealth of their own if they get divorced or become widowed," Loyson noted. "Christian women, on the other hand, were at the discretion of their husbands regarding dowries or gifts from the brides' parents."[38]

Johnson also noted attending a Muslim wedding in which she called the participants "mere children." The groom was twelve while the bride was nine. Yet she noted that such arrangements were not uncommon in Palestine.[39] Marrying at a young age, however, was not limited to Muslims. Barclay recalled attending a Jewish wedding in which the groom was thirteen and the bride was only eleven.[40] Clara Moyse Tadlock noted that people "in these countries" often married by the age of ten.[41] Finally, Jane Eames wrote that she witnessed a "Turkish" wedding ceremony in Palestine in which the groom was ten and the bride "not quite nine."[42]

The Muslim wedding ceremony that Harland witnessed began by the guests going to the bride's house. She noted that the women marched together and men marched in their own group toward the bride's house. Upon reaching the gates the men waited outside while the women entered the house and brought the bride outside, carried upon a white altar while she sat on a chair. The bride was wearing a white dress with a pink veil. "I thought white the bridal garment all over the world?" Harland asked the bride. She replied, "Not with us. Pink she must wear, or the marriage will not be fortunate."[43] Each of the women in the processional was given a lighted candle. According to Harland this was a tradition to ensure that each woman would live to see her children get married. Harland was not impressed, however: "Of course, that is all superstition, but the Mohammedans are very, very superstitious."[44] Interestingly enough, Harland never seemed to remind her reading audience of any of the American wedding ceremony superstitions such as throwing rice at the couple for hopes of fertility, or the bride throwing her bridal bouquet at a group of single women with the idea that the woman who caught the bouquet would be assured of being married before the year ended.

Like others before, Harland saw the dowry as a way to buy a bride and not as a means for the bride to establish permanent personal property or movable wealth that was outside of the control of her husband. She believed, however, that Christian Arabs did not engage in any sort of dowry practice but that only Muslims did so. One Palestinian woman in attendance even suggested to Harland that Muslim men got married over and over again as a way of making a living.[45]

While Harland gave her readers more editorializing and little substance about the actual ceremony, Lucia A. Palmer provided little critique and much detail about the Muslim wedding she attended. The first three days of the ceremony consisted of feasting and festivities at the groom's house, according to Palmer. The bride was not present, however. She remained at her father's house "with closed eyes and face turned toward the wall." At the stroke of midnight after three days of feasting at the groom's house, all the guests proceeded toward the bride's home, "headed by a band of music composed of flutes, tambourines, and a Turkish drum."[46]

The bride walked out of her father's house, under a canopy of red silk, accompanied by a few female friends. Once at the place where the final ceremony transpired, the women were ushered into a separate room where they sat along the walls. A few men entered and sat in chairs in the middle of the room while a band played music. The singer, "a large Abyssinian woman," was reported to have the "finest voice in Jerusalem." Then small cakes and other desserts were passed to the guests. About nine hours after this party commenced, the groom entered, followed by male relatives, all of whom presented the bride with gold coins.[47]

The bride was dressed in purple and gold. She wore a crown of flowers and her veil was red, dotted with gold. Her hands were stained with henna, and she wore strings of gold coins around her neck that reached her waist. Palmer noted that these coins were part of her dowry and were the one thing that was truly her own; "they could not be taken from her even to pay the debts of her lord and master."[48] The bride walked to the center of the room and there met with the groom who removed her veil while she kept her eyes closed. At the stroke of midnight (twenty-four hours after the bride was escorted from her father's house), the groom ushered her out of the building, thus ending the official ceremony. After the newlyweds departed, coffee was served to the remaining guests. Palmer knew it was time to leave. "When coffee is served in the Orient it is an indication that the visit or interview is finished."[49] Unlike Harland, Palmer never criticized the ceremony or traditions of the Muslim couple.

One thing that all three of these accounts have in common is their lack of noting any type of joy or happiness by the bride and groom or their immediate family. While these weddings seemed to lack emotion by the main participants, Muslim funerals, according to the travel accounts of those American ladies who witnessed them, were full of emotion.

Funerals

Sarah Barclay Johnson, in the mid 1850s, was the first American female traveler to write about a Muslim funeral in Palestine. She noted that four men carried a wrapped corpse with a turban placed on top. Women preceded the corpse. According to the author they were topless, their hair was "disheveled and flowing over their shoulders, and their faces and breasts were bruised." The women flung their arms into the air, shrieked, and sung "their doleful death-songs." They also tore out their hair and threw dust on their heads. Following the half-naked women singers was a group of musicians and veiled women who were "near relatives of the deceased." Barclay concludes her description by saying that the funeral did not end upon placing the body in the ground. Veiled women, the deceased's relatives, made daily visits to the grave site "to utter their piercing death songs, and deposit a plate of sweetmeats on the gravestone as a way of reconciling angels to the wicked deeds committed during the lifetime of the deceased."[50]

Over thirty years later, Clara Moyse Tadlock described a Muslim funeral quite differently than the one portrayed by Johnson. Tadlock witnessed a funeral for a small boy. "A dozen blind mourners chanted as they followed the bier, while others filled every pause with wailing and lamentation," she reported. A tent was placed over the grave, in which the child's mother held the boy one last time. The coffin was quickly buried and on top of the fresh grave was placed myrtle. The blind mourners, who Tadlock noted were being paid to mourn for the family, began to recite passages from the Koran as all but the mother slowly departed the gravesite. Family members "had a pleasant little picnic" near the grave, while the mourning "was carried on by proxy with due earnestness and zeal." There were no men present, save the blind mourners, therefore the women family members removed their veils at the "picnic."[51]

Griswold was the only traveler to write about a Muslim wedding as well as a Muslim funeral. Her observations are important because Western historiography lacks examples of Westerners witnessing these traditionally important events. Griswold noted that the mourners were not members of the deceased's family, as Johnson had noted a decade earlier. Griswold believed that the family hired the mourners, akin to the belief of Tadlock. "The amount paid them is regulated by their ability to wail and mourn," noted Griswold. She also remarked that the hired mourners wore bottles under their eyes in order to catch their tears, and they cried fast or slow depending on how much they were paid. "All this seemed a very foolish and barbarous custom," concluded Griswold, who thus referred to them as "ignorant Mohammedans."[52]

A fourth description of a Muslim funeral came from Cora Agnes Benneson, the Illinois lawyer who traveled abroad to study foreign law codes and how they impacted women. Benneson only mentioned that near Bethlehem, by the Tomb of Rachel, stood a small cemetery used by Muslims. She saw a number of women holding hands, standing in a circle around two graves. The women had placed a few baskets of food and money on the graves "as offerings to the dead." The women moved around the graves, "dancing and wailing." Standing in the center of the circle was a young girl. According to Benneson's account, the girl's parents were buried in those two graves.[53]

While these four views of Muslims funerals and mourning customs display striking differences, there are also some similarities. First, it is apparent that women played the prominent role of the mourners. The only men in any of the accounts were the four who carried the corpse in the first recollection and the blind mourners in Tadlock's report. Second, it is clear that emotions were more readily displayed at these funerals than at the weddings discussed earlier.

The Turkish Bath

While women played a prominent role in Muslim funerals, as shown in the four examples above, probably the place where women played the most visible roles was in the so-called Turkish baths and the harems. Sarah Barclay Johnson wrote a ten-page chapter on her experiences and the encounters of Muslim women at the "Turkish bath," as she called it. "Oriental women frequently spend the entire day at the bath," reported Johnson. One of her Muslim friends, Turfendah, invited her to spend the day at the bath of a mutual friend's house. Upon knocking at the door, they were met by the homeowner's slaves.

Slavery

There are very few accounts of Western observations regarding slavery in Palestine. Sarah Barclay Johnson was one of the travelers who spoke quite often of slaves, although not about the institution of slavery itself. She also did not note if the "slaves" were male or female. Johnson simply acknowledged their existence in passing, as if the institution of slavery was common enough that she did not have to report it in any detail. She never used the term "servant," only "slave."[54] Were these actually slaves, or was Johnson editorializing by using the word? Her accounts of the situations are too brief to draw any concrete conclusions from them. Nevertheless, it should be remembered that she lived between 1837 and 1885. Sarah Barclay Johnson published her account in 1858, three years before the Confederate troops fired on Fort Sumter. She was from Virginia, where slavery was thriving in the 1850s. It would not be unreasonable to suggest that Johnson supported slavery, and thus found no reason to critique the "peculiar institution" at a time when the United States was slowly being torn apart over the issue.

Also, slavery was still practiced in the Middle East when Johnson traveled to Palestine.

While the slaves removed the turban from Turfendah's head, their host offered them coffee and a smoke from her "chibouque," a blown-glass and ceramic communal pipe. The women, presumably naked, lay on towels and rugs spread across the marble floor as the slaves placed more logs on the fire to increase the level of steam in the room. A number of slaves "were engaged in pouring hot water on the crouching figures of women and girls of every age," wrote Johnson. She "trembled as [she] saw one of the dreaded specters approaching [her] with a vessel holding a gallon of smoking hot water." Johnson called the experience something akin to being parboiled.[55] Again, I find it interesting that Johnson rarely noted the gender of the slaves. Were some of them male eunuchs? She never did tell her readers.

Next, one of the slaves covered Johnson with soapsuds and scrubbed her with a horsehair brush. Johnson referred to this slave as "my torturer" who probably "imagined herself scrubbing the floor, rather than a human being." After that, each woman was given a "joint-cracking, limb-stretching, body-shaking" massage. Johnson decided not to engage in that process. She also noted that slaves were dyeing the host's hands with henna. Upon being dressed, the ladies enjoyed sherbet, coffee, pipe smoke, "and goblets of the most delicious lemonade." Johnson recalled that she spent the entire afternoon at that bath.[56] She never did describe what the women talked about, if anything.

It is quite probable that the unnamed woman who hosted the daylong bath in this story was an upper-class woman. One could not expect to find such a private bath and slaves in every Muslim home in nineteenth-century Palestine. Nonetheless, the idea of taking all day to bathe, keeping in mind what Johnson said about the propensity of "Oriental" women to spend all day in their baths, is an interesting contrast with the observation made by Harland about poorer women: "Home washing is an unknown luxury. Four times a year, parents and children treat themselves to a plunge at the public bath."[57] Certainly that could not be true of practicing Muslims who ritualistically washed before their five daily prayer sessions. In this sense, it seems that Johnson was not trying to compare prayer-washing with steam bathing, but the two observations do suggest the disparity within Palestinian society.

The Harem

A few American travelers were permitted to observe for themselves what daily life was like for Muslim women in a harem. Sarah Barclay Johnson gave a rather detailed account of the day she and her entourage spent in the company of a wealthy Jerusalemite Muslim women from the Bashkatib family. She was greeted by the hostess's slaves, and was handed a pipe and coffee. She noted that the woman of the house could read and write, and that she was rather conversant in the Koran "and other text-books of Mohammedan faith."[58] They spent the day sampling all sorts of dishes, from "confections prepared from rose leaves and apricots, transparent jellies and soups composed of a variety of nuts. Cucumbers scooped out and filled with rice and minced meat, were a favorite dish; and another, almost as popular, was a bowl of minute cylinders of dough, dried in the sun, and then mixed in a sauce of butter and sugar." In fact, Johnson observed that the hostess frequently fed her morsels of food with her own hands. It was "intended as a mark of great honor," recalled Johnson. After the eating and being fed, musicians and dancing women performed for the group.[59]

While Palestinian women tended to be the object of these American women, in this case the tables were turned and it was Johnson who became the object of curiosity by Arab women. The focus of everyone's attention, according to Johnson, was her Western dress. Upon the hostess's insistence, Johnson and some of the Muslim women exchanged clothes. Large mirrors were brought into their room. Also, the Muslim women wanted Johnson to tell them about the status and position of American women in the United States. "Great was their surprise on hearing of the liberty enjoyed by their Western sisters," noted Johnson. Interestingly enough, Johnson spoke to them in Arabic.[60] She never told her reading audience how or when she had learned to speak Arabic. This is one of the rare examples I have uncovered of the American traveler attempting to converse in anything else but English, Spanish, or French with the Arabic inhabitants of Palestine.

Johnson did not tell her reading audience specifically what she discussed with the Muslim women in the harem. However, she may have used the opportunity to proselytize about Protestant Christianity as well as American culture. "I left them," Johnson wrote, "feeling more grateful than ever for the light I enjoy, and the hope of a blissful immortality, and ardently desiring to share with them my own glorious civil and religious privileges, which would at once release them from the leading cause of their degradation—the tyranny exercised over them by their husbands."[61]

Mrs. Stephen Griswold's account of her visit to a harem begins with the lady of the house meeting Griswold at the front door with a pair of pearl-laden slippers to wear. "There was no particular ceremony of introduction," recalled Griswold, "further than the information that I was a lady from America. This is Oriental etiquette." She noted that the women were dressed in "flowing robes, silk girdles, full trowsers [*sic*], and fancy turbans." The hostess escorted Griswold to her private chamber—a huge room with a polished floor that resembled marble. Pink lace and silk covered the chairs. A "Nubian woman" brought out sherbet, "a kind of lemonade—flavored with rose," which was followed by coffee and cigarettes.[62] This description is interesting, as it suggests a difference between Western and Middle Eastern perceptions of private space.

Not unlike Johnson's experience, the Muslim women were most interested in examining Griswold's dress. "The inspection of my garments was next in order," wrote Griswold. "These they examined thoroughly, even to the buttons on my dress, and were much interested in trying on my gloves." These Muslim women were also interested in trying on Griswold's clothes. Yet, unlike what transpired in the Johnson story, Griswold refused the invitation to exchange clothes. Nevertheless, Griswold did note that the Muslim women were impeccably gracious and cordial. "One of the characteristics of the East is hospitality, and there is no lack of social politeness," she recalled.[63]

Clearly, in these two accounts American women tended to make positive and gracious comments about their Muslim hosts. Mabro notes that Western female travelers were torn between supporting their race and supporting their gender when describing the condition and status of Middle

East women. More often than not, Mabro argues, female travelers tended to support their race.[64] While American women did grapple with supporting their race or their gender, as the examples discussed here indicate, American women could also support their class. These travelers tended to place positive characteristics upon their Palestine counterparts when those women exhibited wealth (such as those who controlled harems) and social graces, or demonstrated glimpses of perceived "Western" culture such as smoking. In other words, maybe it is most accurate to argue that American female travelers at times supported their race, their gender, and their class as opposed to arguing that women limited themselves in their support of just one of these.

In the first two incidents described above, the Muslim women simply did no work, at least according to the American travelers, which would not have been strange, at least during the initial reception of guests. Tadlock noted that when she visited a harem "of a wealthy Muslim," the women were busy sewing—a common activity among women. One woman acted as an interpreter between Tadlock and the woman of the house. The author did not, however, mention what they talked about. What little information Tadlock provided her readers was rather cursory. For example, she noted that the Muslim women were dressed in wide trousers. One had a complexion of bright brown, wore her hair in braids, and wore much gold over a long dress of purple silk and velvet. In her hair she sported a net, "such as was worn in America a few years ago," Tadlock remarked.[65]

Just as in the previous stories, cigarettes and coffee circulated among the women. On a table the hostess placed plates of candy, fruits, nuts, "and sugar-coated parched peas looking like pills." Tadlock seemed to like the communal eating in which no utensils were present. In fact, she thought that eating with one's fingers increased the sociability of the afternoon. Finally, with the second round of coffee, Tadlock knew it was time to depart.[66]

American women, as the examples above suggest, tended to portray positive qualities of the harem. For them, it was a place to relax and be pampered. In this sense, the way in which American women described their experiences in the harem supports Mary Russell's observations on British women's views of the harem in which they saw it as "a safe and desirable haven."[67] For example, Lady Montagu wrote that she "was offered a place of honour, seated upon white satin cushions, and deducted that Turkish ladies led a life of uninterrupted pleasure."[68] Dianne Sachko Mcleod argues that European women tended to view the harem in more political terms—as a symbol of female autonomy. For European women, the harem was a symbol of Middle Eastern women's ability "to refuse conjugal sex, to own property, to enter into contracts and to divorce their spouses."[69] However Mabro's analysis indicates that European women tended to be hostile toward the harem, not unlike their male European counterparts, thus the historiography is inconsistent.[70] It is clear from this study that American female travelers treated the harem at worst neutrally, and at best by ascribing positive characteristics to it. Overall, descriptions of the Middle Eastern harem were important parts of a Westerner's travel account because, as Shirley Foster points out, men were prevented from entering that women-only arena, and thus this may have been one way for women to differentiate their travel experience from those of men.[71]

Divorce

The three stories by American women visiting Muslim harems certainly do not paint accurate pictures for the reader of what life was like for average Muslim women in Palestine. But American women travelers also wrote about everyday events and conditions such as divorce, physical abuse, religion, and education.

Accounts of divorce are rare among the travel writings of these fifty-one American women. In one case, Sarah Barclay Johnson told her readers how divorce laws in Palestine were written to favor husbands. She recalled one "man" who divorced his wife before either had reached twelve years of age because he saw another woman that he wanted to marry, so he simply purchased her.[72] This suggests that females had no power to prevent a divorce from taking place. It is also interesting because of Johnson's use of the word "buy" in reference to obtaining a new wife. While Johnson could be talking about the dowry, it is also possible that she believed that dowries were euphemistic purchases, because, as Johnson wrote, "love, of course, is a plant that will thrive in no such soil."[73]

Some American women believed that divorce rates in Palestine were high because Palestinian women had no rights in society. For example, Johnson observed that Arab husbands, when they became angry with their wives, even in the presence of Western guests, would hurl "any missile at them which may chance lie in their way, beating them with sticks, and otherwise causing the blood to flow." She also noted how some women would kill themselves to end their suffering while others were driven to kill "their cruel masters."[74] Harland recounted a conversation she had with a Muslim woman who believed her husband treated his animals better then he treated her. "[H]e beats the donkey less," said the woman to Harland.[75]

Education

With rare exception, the American travelers noted that Muslim women were not allowed to seek—or simply did not have—any type of academic education. Education was certainly not widely available to American women, however it seems that many of the women in this study had some sort of formal education, from schooling at girls' academies to university degrees. Johnson blamed Muslim women's lack of access to education on culture and tradition, not on the women's lack of desire: "The education of Oriental women is not entirely neglected, but strongly reprobated by public sentiment." She also noted that a lack of a formal education was not limited to poor Muslim women: "Among the rich and poor, in the family of the Effendi and the Fellah, she is alike ignorant." According to Johnson, Muslim women were taught only the most basic "womanly" tasks such as how to cook "and administer to the every whim of her *doting* husband!"[76] This shows the variation in American women's observations on the status of Palestinian women in society. First, Johnson was the only traveler to note that illiteracy was widespread: it was not limited to the lower classes. Second, it is possible that Johnson believed that Palestinian women would be able to begin to change their plight if they could only learn to read, which indicates that she believed that if women could not read it was because their husbands prevented the basic education, which was probably correct. Overall, these examples indicate that middle-to-upper-class American Protestant women could support women regardless of class in the realm of education. In other words, these female travelers held the notion that education for women (regardless of class or status) was something positive and possibly reflective of a modern society.

Likewise, Marion Harland noted the general lack of formal education among Palestine's Muslim women. "It is rare to find a Muslim woman of twenty who can read and write," she wrote. She also told the story of a wealthy Muslim father who took his daughter to a Christian missionary school in order to be taught how to sew, enjoy music, and read. He did not, however, want his daughter to be taught how to write. "Women who can write will bring dishonor upon their families by sending love-letters to men who are not chosen by their parents to be their husbands," the Muslim father allegedly said to the Christian missionary.[77]

Similarly, Sarah Lanman Smith, the wife of a distinguished Protestant missionary, noted as early as the 1830s that women had "no books, and no means of moral or intellectual improvement. It is considered a disgrace for a female to know how to read and write, and a serious obstacle to her marriage, which is the principal object of her parent's heart. This abhorrence of learning in females exists most strongly in the high classes."[78] Accounts that highlighted spousal abuse and editorialized about the plight of Middle Eastern women who were prevented from obtaining an education may be more reflective of the worries and trepidations of the authors. As Terry Caesar points out, travel writing may have been more about the concerns and fears at home than the actualities of abroad.[79]

Religion

American women portrayed the Muslim women they met and talked about as devoted believers and true to their religious convictions. "These depraved creatures are very religious," Johnson noted, "as far as bodily exercise goes, strictly observing their many feasts and festivals, and devoting much of their time to prayer." She even believed that their five-times-a-day praying should be an example for American Christians, "which, if imitated to but a limited extent, would prove a blessing not only to ourselves, but reflexly [*sic*] to them."[80] This certainly supports the argument that travelogues were more about the culture or wishes of the travelers than of the places traveled to and the cultures experienced, as this example could be an editorial against what Johnson believed to be a problem in American society: a lack or a lessening in public displays or expressions of Christian religiosity.[81]

Julia A. Barclay, the mother of Sarah Barclay Johnson, also noted a deep level of religiosity among Muslim women: "We had nearly two dozen of these Moslem ladies in our conversation room on one occasion, and just as soon as the muezzin announced the hour of prayer, they all spread their shawls, sheets, or mattings on the floor, and most devoutly engaged in their imposing worship."[82] In fact, Barclay believed that Christian women in the United States were not as punctual "in attending to their religious duties" as were Muslim women.[83] For the most part, though, American women travelers painted a dark picture of the lives of Muslim women in Palestine. According to the observations of some American women, the only escape for Muslim women from physical abuse and social inequality was suicide or becoming immersed in religious practices. Yet these Americans were usually sympathetic to the plights of Muslim women and offered suggestions to alleviate their problems in Palestinian society.

Dress

American women typically focused their observations of Muslim women on their dress and deportment. These women tended to generalize based on specific instances. For example, the way in which the Muslims were dressed in Jericho was how all Muslims dressed, or so some of these Americans believed. For example, Emily Severance noted that all Muslim women "were very poorly dressed," wearing a string of coins around their faces and being heavily tattooed, or wearing nothing but white clothing, including silk veils.[84] Most other travelers identified the dress of Muslim women as a white sheet and a white veil. "The women looked more like a species of white bat than anything else," noted Eleanor V. Hutton.[85]

White was not the only color noted, however. Sarah Barclay Johnson described Muslim women wearing blue dresses, and many others noted that Muslim women wore nothing but black clothes. Mrs. Stephen Griswold, for example, painted a dark, sinister, and untrustworthy picture of Muslim women based on their attire: "A dark colored cloak is thrown over their heads falling to their feet. A piece of black cloth hangs from beneath their eyes tapering to a point below their chin, or sometimes falling to their knees. This forms kind of a mask and is ornamented with gold coins. Some of the women who do not wear them have their faces tattooed, and wear gold rings fastened through the upper or under lip. They have khol [*sic*] about their eyes, and stain their finger nail with henna, all of which they consider an addition to their charms."[86] Next to the description, Griswold provided a drawing entitled "Woman of Jaffa." The woman is dressed from head to feet in a black garment. She is wearing shoes, however, which was unusual, at least according to the descriptions provided by other American travelers. She sports a black veil, which is connected to her black scarf by what appears to be a string of coins. In her right hand she holds a round, covered container, ornamentally decorated along the sides, with a crescent on top as a kind of handle. She is also wearing a bracelet on her right wrist, and with her left hand she is holding a handful of the black dress, possibly to prevent it from dragging on the ground. Besides her hands, the only other visible body part is her eyes, which are cast over her left shoulder and look rather piercing.[87]

One American traveler liked the way Muslim women dressed. Susan Brewer Thomas noted that Muslim women in Jerusalem were dressed "in gay Oriental style," with veils tossed over their shoulders, "exhibiting fine faces with lustrous black eyes." She also observed the extensive use of henna to tattoo the face and hands, and recalled that Christian Arab women also used henna to tattoo their faces and hands.[88] Thomas believed that Palestinian women dressed rather simply, yet gracefully. "Their costume is said to have undergone little or no change since the days of Naomi and Ruth," believed Thomas.[89]

While Thomas imagined that the manner in which some women dressed had not changed in nearly nineteen hundred years, others less romantic believed the lack of change was an indication of their stunted growth as a civilization and as women. For example, Sarah Lanman Smith noted that not only were the "weak-minded Syrian females" generally inattentive to their personal hygiene needs, but that their manner of dress was neither neat nor tasteful: "Their apparel is precisely such as the Apostle recommended that Christian females should avoid. It is emphatically and literally the outward adorning of plaiting the hair, and wearing of gold and costly array."[90]

Mary Thorn Carpenter naively believed that matters were improving for the women of Jerusalem because some had begun to adopt Western garb. "A group of native women are the vanguard of civilized dress in Jerusalem," Carpenter noted, "having inclined favorably towards as pretty a rose and blue satin umbrella as one can see on the Riviera. The parasol forms a hopeful leaning towards European dress, and forestalls a not far distant day of independence for these Asiatics who have adopted so great an innovation over the ideals of a simple, worn-out past."[91]

Conclusion

It is apparent that most of these authors saw the manner of dress among Palestine's women as generally backward and outdated; one even found it counter to what is described as proper in the New Testament. American female travelers touched upon the existence of physical abuse, gender inequality, and inequality in laws, especially regarding divorce. They observed and reported to their reading audiences that Palestine's women generally lacked even the basic tenets of a formal education and were generally treated as second-class citizens. Furthermore, in one instance an American noted that a Muslim woman believed that her husband treated his animals better than he treated her. What hope did these seemingly oppressed women have? Many

American women believed the root of this inequality lay in the custom of plural marriage. Sarah Barclay Johnson had a different idea, and she presented it in a chapter titled "An Appeal in Behalf of Oriental Females."

Johnson, the American traveler who wrote more about the status, position, and plight of Arab women in Palestine than any of her fellow travelers, concluded her book with a chapter that sought to address the problems that plagued Palestine's women as well as solutions to those problems—at least as she saw them. Johnson argued that American women were best suited to help their Palestinian counterparts because America "is renowned for her liberal principles . . . it is yet more justly celebrated as the arena on which woman is allowed the freest exercise of all the functions of her exalted mission."[92] In other words, she believed that American women were in the best position to help bring equality to Palestinian women because American women were the freest women in the world.

Women were simply not as appreciated anywhere in the world as they were in the United States, according to Johnson. She believed that she could correctly estimate "woman's character and condition" in Palestine because she had spent three years traveling throughout the Middle East. In other words, she was a self-appointed expert. Johnson concluded that she was most appropriate to lay out a plan that would help ameliorate the "degraded state" of women in Palestine, more so than any of her American male travelers, past or present.[93]

First, Johnson addressed some basic problems faced by women in Palestine, as she saw them. She was concerned with slavery, not only with the issue of slavery itself but that slave women were used to spy on the wives and daughters of their head of the household: men pitted women against each other, that was her primary concern. She argued that this strategy also resulted in Palestinian women being nearly invisible in society because women in general and wives in particular were not considered socially better than slaves. According to Johnson, men were not allowed to even acknowledge the existence of women—even of their own sisters or wives—as they passed them in the streets or else it would be considered a sin. Regardless of whether women were actual slaves or not, in the end, according to her beliefs, as Johnson reported, all women were treated as slaves.

Johnson believed that another thing preventing Palestinian women from achieving equality was the custom of "buying" wives—something akin to slavery in Johnson's mind. Possibly because she saw the "purchase" of wives as nothing but slavery, she argued that women did all the manual labor in Palestine while the "brutal husband spends the livelong day lounging in the idle group at the gathering-place of the village."[94]

After outlining the "civil and social disabilities of woman in the East," Johnson argued that their "mental and moral servitude" was equally lacking, possibly suggesting that Palestinian women were not properly channeling their natural skills and talents toward bettering their families and society. In a nutshell, Johnson called for an increase in Christian missionary activity and intensification in the number of American women financially supporting those missionaries in order to improve the position of Palestinian women. While she suggested that the problems of Palestine's women resulted from the attitudes of Palestinian men, her solution was nothing less than a call to Christianize the masses as the only way to alleviate the problems facing women in Palestine. Johnson's suggestion reflects the general tendency of Western travelers to proscribe Christianity as the cure-all for whatever ailed foreign cultures and societies.[95] Yet Johnson's chapter on Palestinian women was not solely a call to help them. It was also an editorial written for the ears of American women regarding material possessions. Johnson argued that women in Palestine dressed simply and did not adorn themselves with gold and other baubles to the extent that she witnessed in America. Additionally, Palestinian women wore their dresses until they fell apart, observed Johnson, as opposed to the United States in which women threw their dresses out after wearing them three or four times.[96] Johnson's closing chapter not only addressed some of the problems facing Palestinian women, but also touched upon some problems facing American women, at least as Johnson believed. In this sense, Johnson's account supports the arguments of William Stowe and Marilyn Wesley who argue that travel texts are as much about home as they are about places abroad.[97]

In all, these authors tended to see the women of Palestine as clearly unequal in society and the home. They recorded incidents of domestic abuse, inequitable divorce laws, and questionable social traditions such as plural marriages. Moreover, they tended to draw connections among those three characteristics of Palestinian society, believing that one necessarily caused the others and thinking that the extinction of one would break the chain of inequality. Additionally, their narratives suggest that Palestinian women were not to blame for their status in society and within the family—that men controlled their lives and that men were to blame for the terrible condition in which Palestinian women found themselves. The tendency for American women not only to feel the plight of Palestinian Muslim women but also to prescribe solutions to improve their status in society tends to challenge Mabro's argument with regard to British women travelers who in the conflict between supporting their gender or their race, typically supported their race over their gender.[98]

Overall, American female travelers believed that a basic inequality existed between men and women in Palestine. While in Bethlehem, D. L. Miller noted that the lives of Muslim women were no different from their Christian counterparts in Palestine. All women of Palestine, according to Miller, lived a life of "degradation and slavery," though she did not provide examples or explain how this was so.[99] Likewise, Miller was not sure why Muslim women were not equal to men; however, she felt blessed "in being allowed to live in a land where women are on an equality with men and not beneath them, as is the case in Palestine."[100] Like some other American female travelers, Miller asserted that American women enjoyed equality to American men at a time when American women in reality lacked full political, economic, and social equality. Nonetheless, this could support Mabro's idea that European women tended to view foreign cultures as different and thus wrong because foreigners were not Protestant Christians.[101]

Kate Kraft, however, believed that Muslim women were not equal to men because they were forced to marry at such a young age. "Each of these females is taken as a wife by the time she attains the age of thirteen or fourteen, by some filthy Mussulman [*sic*] boor."[102] Similarly, Tadlock concluded that Muslim women were not equal to Muslim men because of the culturally acceptable practice of plural marriage. She called them slaves, not wives.

She believed, however, that poor Muslim women had a better life, relatively speaking, than their upper-class counterparts because poor husbands could not afford to wed other women. Also, Tadlock noted that the wives of poor Muslim men tended to go about their duties unveiled and were not so rigidly segregated as their more wealthy counterparts.[103] Bertha Spafford Vester, a long-time American resident of Jerusalem, also believed that the root cause of the inequality between Muslim men and women was the strategy of plural marriages. She pointed out, however, that Muslim women typically feared that their husbands would take multiple wives.[104]

If the root of sexual inequality was the practice of plural marriage, what, according to these American travelers, could be done to correct the inequality? Not surprisingly, the answer was Christianity. Both Sarah Barclay Johnson and E. C. Miller suggested that Christianizing the population would necessarily result in bringing equality among men and women. Johnson had already noted a positive change in some Muslim men's perceptions of women and attitudes toward them, due to the increasing Western and Christian influences such as travelers, the establishment of missionary schools, and the creation of other social activities such as sewing bees.[105]

In their pursuit to understand the reason for the inequality between Muslim women and men, American travelers found the culprit to be plural marriage. Many in the United States at that time denounced the Mormon practice of plural marriage, especially decision makers in Washington, D.C., who prevented Utah from becoming a state until the leaders of the Mormon church denounced the tradition. Perhaps expressed opinions of American female travelers were more a reflection of general fears that pervaded nineteenth-century American society than a true reason for the inequality of Muslim men and women.

Appendix A: The American Women Travelers, Chronologically

Name	Year(s) Abroad
Kirkland, Elizabeth	1832
Smith, Sarah Lanman	1835
Livermore, Harriet	1836, 1839, 1845, 1852, 1858
Haight, Sarah Rogers	1839
Minor, Clorinda	1849–1850
Paine, Caroline	1850
Minor, Clorinda	1851–1855
Barclay, Julia A.	1851–1853
Johnson, Sarah Barclay	1851–1857
Eames, Jane Anthony	1854
Thomas, Susan Brewer	1857–1858
Severance, Emily A.	1867
Griswold, Mrs. Stephen M.	1867–1868
Floyd, Theodocia Chandler	1867–1886
Hale, Susan	1868
Hale, Lucretia Palmer	1868
Miller, Ellen Clare	1868–1869
Clement, Clara Erskine	1869 (also in 1882)
Kraft, Kate	1869
B., Miss S.	1871
Snow, Eliza	1872–1873
Baldwin, Mary. B.	1873–1877
Adams, L. L.	1874
Wells, Sarah Furnas	1874–1875
Grant, Julia Dent	1877–1878
Straiton, Marie and Emma	1880
Wallace, Susan E.	1881
Bainbridge, Lucy S.	1881
Wood, Mattie Sisson	1881
Hale, Susan	1882

(*continued*)

Name	Year(s) Abroad
Vester, Bertha Spafford	1882–1949
Little, Anna P.	1883
Jessup. Mrs. Henry H.	1885
Ninde, Mary L.	1885
Leland, Lilian	1885
Elliot, Sarah Barnwell	1886–1887
Green, Lenamay	1887–1888
Wallace, Susan E.	1888
Knight, Susan G.	1888
Tadlock, Clara Moyse	1889
Benneson, Cora Agnes	1890
Champney, E. Williams	1892
Miller, Mrs. D. L.	1892
Holyoke, Maria Ballard	1893
McMillan, Lizzie	1893
Hutton, Eleanor V.	1893
Harland, Marion	1893
McMillan, Lizzie	1893
Carpenter, Mary Thorn	1894
Loyson, Emilie	1895
Allen, Mary S.	1896
Palmer, Lucia A.	1897
Bottome, Margaret	1897
Muhr, Fannie	1897
Beckman, Nellie Sims	1899

NOTES

The quote in the epigraph is from Sarah Barclay Johnson, *Hadji in Syria* (New York: Arno Press, 1977), 297. This is a reprint of the edition published by J. Challen, Philadelphia [no date].

1. Mary Suzanne Schriber, *Writing Home* (Charlottesville: University Press of Virginia, 1997), 81.

2. Ibid., 83.

3. Hilton Obenzinger, *American Palestine* (Princeton: Princeton University Press, 1999), 51.

4. Brigitte Georgi-Findlay, *Frontiers of Women's Writing* (Tucson: University of Arizona Press, 1996), 179.

5. Judy Mabro, *Veiled Half-Truths* (London: I. B. Tauris, 1991), 6.

6. Ibid., 16.

7. Ibid., 13.

8. Ibid., 164.

9. Benneson never noted if the "Syrian woman" spoke English, as her account suggested, or whether her words were translated into English.

10. Cora Agnes Benneson, "Palestine To-Day," *Unitarian* 5, no. 1 (January 1890), 16.

11. Mabro, *Veiled Half-Truths,* 6.

12. Marion Harland, *Under the Flag of the Orient* (Philadelphia: Historical Publishing Company, 1897), 69.

13. Ibid.

14. Mrs. Stephen S. Griswold, *A Woman's Pilgrimage* (Hartford, Conn.: Published by the author, 1871), 307.

15. Mabro, *Veiled Half-Truths,* 197.

16. Sarah Furnas Wells, *Ten Years' Travel* (West Milton, Ohio: Morning Star Publishing Company, 1885), 209.

17. Susan Brewer Thomas, *Travels in Europe, Egypt, and Palestine* (Philadelphia: J. B. Lippincott, 1860), 315.

18. On the argument that travel writing is more about home than places abroad, see, for example, Terry Caesar, *Forgiving the Boundaries* (Athens: University of Georgia Press, 1995), 5–6; and Schriber, *Writing Home,* 9.

19. Harland, *Under the Flag of the Orient,* 236.

20. Mary S. Allen, *From East to West, or, The World as We Saw It* (Chicago: Free Methodist Publishing House, 1898), 73.

21. Mabro, *Veiled Half-Truths,* 23.

22. Harland, *Under the Flag of the Orient,* 236. Julia A. Barclay also noted the rarity of a literate Muslim woman; see *The Jerusalem Mission* (New York: Arno Press, 1977), 276 (reprint of the 1853 edition published by the

American Christian Publication Society, Cincinnati, edited by David Staats Burnet).

23. Thomas, *Travels in Europe, Egypt, and Palestine,* 315.

24. Johnson, *Hadji in Syria,* 270.

25. Barclay, *The Jerusalem Mission,* 276.

26. Ellen Clare Miller, *Eastern Sketches* (New York: Arno Press, 1977), 122 (reprint of the 1871 edition published by W. Oliphant, Edinburgh, Scotland).

27. Florence Hartley, *The Ladies' Book of Etiquette and Manual of Politeness* (Boston: Lee and Shepard, 1873), 21.

28. Clorinda Minor, *Meshullam!* (New York: Arno Press, 1977), 64 (reprint of the 1851 edition published by the author).

29. Thomas, *Travels in Europe, Egypt, and Palestine,* 315.

30. Mrs. D. L. Miller, *Letters to the Young* (Mount Morris, Ill.: Brethren's Publishing Company, 1896), 215.

31. Ibid., 216.

32. Thomas, *Travels in Europe, Egypt and Palestine,* 323–24.

33. Benneson, "Palestine To-Day," *Unitarian,* May 1890, 229.

34. Johnson, *Hadji in Syria,* 237.

35. Griswold, *A Woman's Pilgrimage,* 262–63.

36. Harland, *Under the Flag of the Orient,* 88.

37. Ibid., 89.

38. Emile Loyson, *Through the Lands of Islam* (Chicago: Open Court Publishing Company, 1905), 321–22.

39. Johnson, *Hadji in Syria,* 191.

40. Ibid., 193.

41. Clara Moyse Tadlock, *Bohemian Days* (New York: John B. Alden, 1889), 362.

42. Jane Anthony Eames, *Another Budget,* 2nd ed. (Boston: Ticknor and Fields, 1855), 372.

43. Harland, *Under the Flag of the Orient,* 95.

44. Ibid.

45. Ibid., 98.

46. Lucia Palmer, *Oriental Days* (New York: Baker and Taylor Company, 1897), 194.

47. Ibid., 196–97.

48. Ibid., 198.

49. Ibid., 199.

50. Johnson, *Hadji in Syria,* 33–34.

51. Tadlock, *Bohemian Days,* 40, 341.

52. Griswold, *A Woman's Pilgrimage,* 232–33.

53. Benneson, "Palestine To-Day," 285–86.

54. Johnson, *Hadji in Syria,* 287.

55. Ibid., 207, 208, 209.

56. Johnson, *Hadji in Syria,* 210, 211, 212.

57. Harland, *Under the Flag of the Orient,* 69.

58. Johnson, *Hadji in Syria,* 215.

59. Ibid., 216–18.

60. Ibid., 218.

61. Johnson, *Hadji in Syria,* 219.

62. Griswold, *A Woman's Pilgrimage,* 263–64.

63. Ibid., 268.

64. Mabro, *Veiled Half-Truths,* 12–14, 164.

65. Tadlock, *Bohemian Days,* 360–61.

66. Ibid., 362.

67. Mary Russell, *Blessings of a Good Thick Skirt* (London: Collins, 1986), 118.

68. Ibid., 119.

69. Dianne Sachko Mcleod, "Cross-cultural Cross-dressing: Class, Gender, and Modernist Sexual Identity," in *Orientalism Transposed: The Impact of the Colonies on British Culture* , ed. Julie F. Codell and Dianne Sachko Macleod (Hants, England: Ashgate, 1998), 63.

70. Mabro, *Veiled Half-Truths,* 2.

71. Shirley Foster, *Across New Worlds, Nineteenth-Century Women Travellers and their Writings* (London: Harvester Wheatsheaf, 1990), 16.

72. Johnson, *Hadji in Syria,* 219.

73. Ibid.

74. Ibid., 221.

75. Harland, *Under the Flag of the Orient,* 239.

76. Johnson, *Hadji in Syria,* 224 (emphasis in original).

77. Harland, *Under the Flag of the Orient,* 237.

78. Sarah Lanman Smith, *Memoir of Mrs. Sarah Lanman Smith* (Boston: Perkins & Marvin, 1839), 316.

79. Caesar, *Forgiving the Boundaries,* 5–6.

80. Johnson, *Hadji in Syria,* 223.

81. For example, see Schriber, *Writing Home,* 9; Marilyn Wesley, *Secret Journeys* (Albany: State University of New York Press, 1999), xiv, xvii; and Mabro, *Veiled Half-Truths,* 51.

82. Barclay, *Jerusalem Mission,* 275.

83. Ibid., 276.

84. Emily A. Severence, *Journal Letters* (Cleveland: Gates Press, 1868), 167, 168.

85. Eleanor V. Hutton. "A Little Visit to Jerusalem," *Christian Union,* June 24, 1893, 1250.

86. Griswold, *A Woman's Pilgrimage,* 220.

87. Ibid., 221.

88. Thomas, *Travels in Europe, Egypt, and Palestine,* 332.

89. Ibid., 299.

90. Smith, *Memoir of Mrs. Sarah Lanman Smith,* 316.

91. Mary Thorn Carpenter, *In Cairo and Jerusalem* (New York: Anson D. F. Randolph and Company, 1894), 187.

92. Johnson, *Hadji in Syria,* 295.

93. Ibid., 296.

94. Johnson, *Hadji in Syria,* 301.

95. Mabro, *Veiled Half-Truths,* 3, 6; Mary Suzanne Schriber, *Telling Travels* (Deklab, Ill.: Northern Illinois University Press, 1995), xxii.

96. Ibid., 301–2.

97. William Stowe, *Going Abroad* (Princeton: Princeton University Press, 1994), xi.; Wesley, *Secret Journeys,* xiv, xvii.

98. Mabro, *Veiled Half-Truths,* 164.

99. E. Miller, *Eastern Sketches,* 150.

100. Miller, *Letters to the Young,* 193.

101. Mabro, *Veiled Half-Truths,* 12–14.

102. Kate Kraft, *The Nilometer and the Sacred Soil* (New York: Carleton, 1869), 275. When the author was in Egypt she called for a woman's rights convention because Egyptian women, unlike their American counterparts, were doing nothing to secure their right to vote (see 184–85).

103. Tadlock, *Bohemian Days,* 346, 347.

104. Bertha Spafford Vester, *Our Jerusalem* (Garden City, N.J.: Doubleday, 1950), 111–12.

105. Johnson, *Hadji in Syria,* 221, 225; Miller, *Eastern Sketches,* 150.

ABOUT THE CONTRIBUTORS

THOMAS ADAM is professor of history at the University of Texas at Arlington where he teaches German and modern transatlantic history. He has published on topics such as philanthropy, intercultural transfers, modern German history and German-American history. His most recent publications include *Buying Respectability: Philanthropy and Urban Society in Transnational Perspective, 1840s to the 1930s* (2009); *Two Boston Brahmins in Goethe's Germany: The Travel Journals of Anna and George Ticknor* (with Gisela Mettele, 2009); *Stipendienstiftungen an deutschen Universitäten, 1800 bis 1950* (2008); and *Germany and the Americas: Culture, Politics, and History*, 3 vols. (2005).

DIETER K. BUSE is Professor Emeritus of history at Laurentian University, Sudbury, Canada. His study *The Regions of Germany* (2005) complements his edited work, *Modern Germany: An Encyclopedia of History, People and Culture, 1871–1990*, 2 vols. (1998). He co-edited *Never Far Away: The Auschwitz Chronicles of Anna Heilman* (2001), *Whose National Security? Canadian State Surveillance and the Creation of Enemies* (2000), *Hard Lessons: Mine Mill in the Canadian Union Movement* (1995); and edited *Parteiagitation und Wahlkreisvertretung: Eine Dokumentation über Friedrich Ebert und sein Reichstagswahlkreis Elberfeld-Barmen 1910–1918* (1975).

ANDREW LEES is professor of history at the Camden Campus of Rutgers, The State University of New Jersey, where he teaches courses on the intellectual and social history of modern Europe and the United States. His most important publications are *Cities Perceived: Urban Society in European and American Thought* (1985); *Cities, Sin, and Social Reform in Imperial Germany* (2002); and *Cities and the Making of Modern Europe, 1750–1914* (with Lynn Hollen Lees, 2007).

NILS H. ROEMER is professor of Jewish studies at the University of Texas at Dallas. His areas of expertise are Jewish cultural and intellectual history and popular culture and cultural memory in particular. He is the author of *Jewish Scholarship and Culture in Nineteenth-Century Germany: Between*

History and Faith (2005) and numerous articles on modern Jewish history. His most recent publications is *German City, Jewish Memory: The Story of Worms* (2010).

JAMES ROSS-NAZZAL is the discipline chair and professor of history in the Women and Gender Studies Program at Houston Community College–Southeast, where he offers courses in U.S. and Mexican American history. His recent publications include *A Pax Americana: The U.S. Veto in the United Nations Security Council on the 'Question of Palestine' 1972–2007* (2008); and "Where is the 'Middle East'" and "Israel's Nuclear Weapons and Deterrence" in *History in Dispute: The Middle East since 1945* (2003).

ASHLEY SIDES earned his B.A. in European studies at the University of Oklahoma in 2001 and his M.A. in history at the University of Texas at Arlington in 2008. His M.A. thesis is entitled "What Americans Said about Saxony, and What This Says about Them: Interpreting Travel Writings of the Ticknors and Other Privileged Americans, 1800–1850." He taught various history and government classes at Fort Worth Christian High School from 2008 to 2010.

FRANK TROMMLER is Professor Emeritus of German and comparative literature at the University of Pennsylvania, where he taught from 1970 to 2007. From 1995 to 2003 he directed the Humanities Program at the American Institute for Contemporary German Studies in Washington. His areas of expertise are nineteenth- and twentieth-century German literature and culture, German-American relations, and cultural politics. Among his numerous publications are *Die Kultur der Weimarer Republik* (with J. Hermand, 1978); *America and the Germans* (1985); *The German-American Encounter* (2001); and *Weimars transatlantischer Mäzen: die Lincoln-Stiftung 1927–1934* (with J. Reulecke and M. Richardson, 2008).

WHITNEY WALTON is professor of history at Purdue University. She is the author of *Internationalism, National Identities, and Study Abroad: France and the United States, 1890–1970* (2010), and *Eve's Proud Descendants: Four Women Writers and Republican Politics in Nineteenth-Century France* (2000). Her publications also include many articles and book chapters on modern French social and cultural history and Franco-American cultural relations.

INDEX

Adams, John, 23
Adams, John Quincy, 16, 23, 194
Addams, Jane, 168
Adams, L. L., 241
Albany, 97
Albert Kahn Around-the-World Scholarship(s), 4, 50, 53, 54, 59–60, 61, 62, 67, 68
Allard, Rachel, 59
Allen, Mary S., 217, 242
Alsace, 53
Altoona, 106
Amalia (Princess), 28; Amalie Heiter (pseudonym), 28
American Exceptionalism, 84, 87
American Expatriate communities, 12, 13, 30
American Federation of Labor (AFL), 100, 107
American Socialist Party, 107
American Field Service Fellowships for French Universities, 56, 64, 66
American Knights of Labor, 93, 96, 107
Americanization, 170, 171
Anthony (Anton, King of Saxony), 28, 200
anti-Americanism, 5, 151, 171, 178
anti-Semitism, 135, 137
Anti-Socialist Law, 86
Antin, Mary, 141
Appiah, Kwame Anthony, 52
Argentina, 134
Arnott, Miss, 213
Around-the-World Society, 61
Austria (-Hungary, Empire of), 11, 17, 20, 22, 27, 30, 132, 133, 156, 173
Aveling, Edward, 2, 83, 89, 92–96, 98, 107, 108

Baden, 23
Bainbridge, Lucy, S. 241
Baldwin, Mary B., 241
Bancroft, George, 3, 13, 24
Barclay, Julia A., 218, 222, 234, 241
Bashford, John, 25
Baudissin, Wolf Heinrich Friedrich Karl Count of, 196
Baumeister, Adolf, 107
Bavaria (Kingdom of), 17
Bebel, August, 84–85
Beckman, Nellie Sims, 242
Benjamin, Israel Joseph, 134
Benneson, Cora Agnes, 213–214, 220, 225, 242
Bergson, Henri, 53
Berkeley, 100
Berlin, 3, 18, 30, 36, 37, 38, 87, 109, 117, 133, 137, 138, 139, 140, 151, 153, 162, 164, 169, 203; University of Berlin, 3
Bethlehem, 225, 239
Bismarck, Otto von, 84, 86, 135, 150
Boerne, Ludwig, 134
Bohl, Elizabeth, 192
Boston, 86, 96, 97, 106, 109, 117, 155, 164, 189, 190, 195, 205
Bottome, Margaret, 242
Brandenburg (Province of Prussia), 38, 40
Bremen, 113
Brooklyn, 101, 106
Brown University, 34
Brussels, 35, 191

Bryant, William Cullen, 195
Buber, Martin, 135
Budapest, 133, 164
Buffalo, 97, 106
Buttler, Nicholas Murray, 55
Buzard, James, 2–3

Caesar, Terry, 7, 233
Calais, 191
California, 83, 87, 99, 103, 118, 156, 159
Calkins, Gary N., 66
Calvert, George Henry, 35
Cambridge (Massachusetts), 97; Harvard University, 55, 66, 155, 189, 190
Canada, 83, 97, 106, 110
Carnegie Endowment for International Peace, 54–55
Carpenter, Mary Thorn, 236, 242
Cassirer, Paul, 170
Caullery, Maurice, 66
Center for Social Documentation, 61
Challaye, Félicien, 60, 61
Champney, E. Williams, 242
Chicago, 86, 88, 100, 106, 110, 117, 149, 152, 153, 159, 163, 164, 165–166, 168, 169, 172, 174–176; Haymarket Massacre, 86; Hull House, 100, 168; Michigan Avenue, 175; slums, 100; World Exhibition, 5
Cincinnati, 92, 106, 163
Clement, Clara Erskine, 241
Cleveland, 100, 106
Cody, Bill (Buffalo Bill), 90; Wild West Show, 90–91, 94
Cogswell, Joseph Green, 3, 13
Cologne, 156
Colorado, 111
Colorado Springs, 106
Concord (Massachusetts), 97; Prison of Concord, 97
Congress of Vienna, 16, 17, 19, 20, 34, 38
Connecticut, 116
Constantinople, 157
Cook, James, 98
Cooper, James Fenimore, 3, 30, 111, 194–195
cosmopolitanism, 52
Coubertin, Pierre de, 52
Czechoslovakia, 63

Dante (Alighieri), 28, 30
Dartmouth College, 189
Davenport (Iowa), 106
David-Weill Travel Scholarship(s), 4, 50, 54, 56, 58, 66–67
Davis, Rebecca, 84
Dayton (Ohio), 106
Debs, Eugene V., 100
Dennery, Etienne, 68–69
Denver, 106
Detroit, 86, 93, 106, 163
Dresden (Florence on the Elbe), 3, 16, 18, 25–26, 29, 30–31, 32, 36, 40, 189–206; Art Gallery, 15; common people, 197, 198–199; Royal Court, 197, 199–200; Green Vault, 200; Hotel de Rome, 202–203; museums, 194, 195; Neumarkt, 202–203; nobility, 197, 198; Picture Gallery (Museum of Fine Arts), 195, 203
Dublin, 203
Duden, Gottfried, 134
Duggan, Stephen P., 55, 56, 57, 62, 66, 67, 68
Duhamel, Georges, 61, 62
Dwight, Timothy, 16, 19–21, 22, 23–24, 27–28, 31, 32–33, 34–35, 37–38

Eames, Jane Anthony, 222, 241
Ebert, Friedrich, 113, 138
Eckartsberg, 17
Elbe (River), 32
Eliot, Samuel, 189
Elliot, Sarah Barnwell, 242

Elsterwerda, 18
Engels, Friedrich, 2, 83, 85, 96–98
England, 3, 12, 13, 15, 19, 33, 39, 40, 85, 93, 191
Erie, 106
Everett, Edward, 3, 13, 16, 18, 35

Fellowships for Americans to study abroad, 56–57
Fitzgerald, John F., 109
Florence, 12, 13
Floyd, Theodocia Chandler, 241
Forster, Georg, 98
Fort Sumter, 225
Foss, Eugene, 109
Foster, Shirley, 194, 231
France, 3, 13, 14, 15, 19, 20, 39, 50, 51, 53–54, 55–56, 61, 62, 63, 64, 66, 67, 70, 189; higher education, 64–66
Frederick (II, King) of Prussia, 35
Frederick August (King of Saxony) I, 27–28
Frederick Augustus II (King of Saxony), 28
Fresno, 106
Fulda, Ludwig, 150, 162–164, 168

Georgi-Findley, Brigitte, 211, 212
German Social Democratic Party (SPD), 2, 85, 86, 107, 111, 113, 114, 168
German Society of America, 162
Germany, 4, 11–13, 53, 63, 99, 101, 102, 106, 109, 111, 115, 154, 162; German universities, 3, 13–14, 39
Goethe (Johann Wolfgang von), 134
Goldberger, Ludwig Max, 5
Gompers, Samuel, 100
Gossler, Elizabeth, 203
Göttingen, 14, 189; University of Göttingen, 3, 13, 14, 16, 189
grand tour (European), 7, 13, 15; cultural education, 30, 39; social elevation, 39, 41
Grant, Julia Dent, 241
Great Britain, 161
Great Depression, 174
Green, Lenamay, 242
Grimes (William C.), 6
Griswold, Mrs. Stephen M., 215, 221, 225, 229, 235, 241
Gutenberg (Johannes), 34

Haight, Sarah Rogers, 241
Hale, Lucretia Palmer, 241
Hale, Susan, 241
Halfield, Adolf, 150, 171–173, 178
Halle, 20, 38; University of Halle, 3
Hamburg, 203
Hannover, 18
Harland, Marion, 214–215, 216–217, 221–223, 227–228, 232, 233, 242
Hartley, Florence, 219
Hearst, William Randolph, 168
Hegemann, Werner, 170
Heine, Heinrich, 86, 134
Herzberg, 36–37
Hesse-Wartegg, Ernst von, 150, 156–161, 162
Hitler, Adolf, 115, 173–174
Hitzel, Edmée, 61
Hoboken, 97
Holitscher, Arthur, 1, 131, 132, 133, 136–137, 139, 140–141, 150, 164–168, 171
Holyoke, Maria Ballard, 242
Homestead, 106, 110
Hovelaque, Emile, 60
Hudson River, 116
Humboldt, Alexander von, 99, 134
Hutton, Eleanor V., 235, 242

Illinois, 100, 213, 225
India, 142
Indianapolis, 106, 164
Industrial Workers of the World (the Wobblies), 100, 107

Institute of International Education (IIE), 4, 50–51, 54, 56, 57, 62, 63, 64, 67, 68, 69, 71; survey of study abroad fellows, 62–64, 66
internationalism, 51–52, 58, 60, 68, 70
Iowa, 118
Ireland, 4, 191
Iriye, Akira, 51
Irving, Washington, 3, 30, 195
Italy, 3, 4, 12, 13, 14, 15, 39, 164

Jaffa, 213, 235
Jericho, 6, 234
Jerusalem, 6, 221, 223, 235, 236, 240
Jessup, Mrs. Henry H., 242
John (Johann, Prince and King of Saxony), 28, 197; Philalethes (pseudonym), 28
Johnson, Sarah Barclay, 210, 218, 221, 222, 224, 226–227, 228–229, 231–233, 234, 235, 237–238, 240, 241
Jordan River, 215

Kafka, Franz, 1, 7, 136, 139, 140
Kahn, Albert, 4, 50–51, 52–54, 58, 62
Kahn Foundation for the Foreign Travel of American Teachers, 54, 56, 57
Kansas City, 95, 106, 110
Kelley, Florence, 96, 100
Kerr, Alfred, 138, 170
Kingston (Ontario), 97
Kirchhoff, Theodor, 159
Kirkland, Elizabeth, 241
Kirkland, John T., 189
Kisch, Egon Erwin, 131, 132, 133, 140
Knight, Susan G., 242
Kompert, Leopold, 134
Kracauer, Siegfried, 132
Kraft, Kate, 210, 239, 241

Lake Placid, 97
Legaré, Hugh Swinton, 35
Legien, Carl, 2, 83, 94, 105–112, 117–119
Le Havre, 13
Leipzig, 16, 17, 18–19, 21–22, 26, 29, 31–32, 204; Battle of Leipzig (Battle of the Nations), 15, 16, 18–19, 21–22, 198; Trade Fairs of Leipzig, 15; University of Leipzig, 3, 31, 194
Leland, Lilian, 242
Lenin, Vladimir Iljitsch, 105
Lewis, Sinclair, 173
Liebknecht, Helmut, 103
Liebknecht, Karl, 2, 83, 98–105, 107, 111, 113
Liebknecht, Wilhelm, 2, 83, 84–92, 93, 94, 98, 107, 114, 115–117
Linforth, Ivan, 59–60
Lissitzky, El, 138
Little, Anna P., 242
Livermore, Harriet, 241
Liverpool, 13
Lombardy, 23
London, 30, 87, 155
Los Angeles, 106, 110, 164
Loyson, Emilie, 222, 242
Luther, Martin, 15, 21, 34–36, 38
Lützen, 17
Lyon, 67

Mabro, Judy, 211, 212, 214, 215, 217, 229–230, 231, 239
Main, Anne, 60
Maine, 89
Manchester (Massachusetts), 99
Mann, Horace, 24, 25, 33
Marx, Eleanor, 83, 89, 92–96, 107, 108
Marx, Karl, 83, 85
Massachusetts, 14, 96, 116, 195
McKeesport, 106
Mcleod, Dianne Sachko, 231
McMillan, Lizzie, 242
Meißen Porcelain, 15–16
Melanchthon (Philipp), 35
Merced, 106

Mexico, 173
Michigan, 93
Michigan, Lake, 163, 174
Mignon, Madeleine, 59
migration, 4–5, 81, 83; German migrants, 87, 89; German migration, 81
Miller, Ellen Clare, 218, 240, 241
Miller, Mrs. D. L., 219–220, 239, 242
Mills, Sara, 192, 193–194
Milwaukee, 86, 88, 100, 106, 109
Minneapolis, 95, 106
Minor, Clorinda, 219, 241
Montagu, Lady, 231
Monterey, 106
Montreal, 97
Mosse, George, 135
Motley, John Lothrop, 195
Muhr, Fannie, 242
Munich, 162
Münsterberg, Hugo, 152

Naples, 157
Napoleon Bonaparte, 3, 12, 15, 18, 22, 32, 39, 189
Napoleonic Wars, 22
Nazareth, 6
Netherlands, 23
Neutra, Richard, 170
New England, 3, 14, 34, 39, 40, 156, 194; New Englanders, 11, 21
New Hampshire, 116
New Haven, 86, 88
New Jersey, 96
New Orleans, 83, 99, 155
Newark, 99
New York City, 1, 86, 87, 89, 93, 94, 95, 97, 98, 99, 100, 105, 106, 108, 117, 135–136, 137, 140, 149, 152, 153, 155, 157–159, 160, 162, 163, 165–166, 169, 170, 176–178; Broadway, 157–158, 173; Brooklyn Bridge, 139; Castle Garden, 157; Central Park, 159, 163; Columbia University 55; Ellis Island, 157; Fifth Avenue, 159; Lower East Side, 135–136, 139, 140, 141, 176; Manhattan, 106, 162, 165; Metropolitan Museum of Art, 195; modernity, 138, 139; schools, 89, 93; skyscrapers, 132, 166–167, 170, 176–177; Statue of Liberty in 98, 139, 140, 162; subway, 163
New Zealand, 134
Niagara Falls, 97, 98, 106, 110
Ninde, Mary L., 242
Nordau, Max, 135

Oakland, 106
Obenzinger, Hilton, 211
Ohio, 96, 116
Olympic Games, 52
Ostjuden (Eastern European Jews), 135, 137, 139–140

Paine, Caroline, 241
Palestine, 6, 7, 131, 132, 139, 141, 210–242; Bedouin, 215–216; divorce 231–232; dress of women, 221, 224, 234–236; education of women, 216, 217, 218, 219, 232–233; funerals, 221, 224–226; harems, 228–231; marriages, 221–224, 237, 240; religion of women, 216–219, 233–234; selling of baby, 213–214; slavery, 226–228, 237, 238, 239; Turkish Bath, 226; women 210–242
Palmer, Lucia A., 223–224, 242
Paris, 12, 30, 53, 66, 139, 141; University of Paris, 54, 64
Peabody, Elizabeth, 195
Penn, William, 91
Pennsylvania, 91, 96
Philadelphia, 88, 106, 153, 155, 156, 159, 160, 172; Franklin Institute, 156; Girard College, 156; University of Pennsylvania, 156; World Exhibition, 5

Pinkerton agency, 86, 91, 110
Pittsburgh, 101–102, 106, 110, 118
Plattsburgh, 97
Port Hope, 97
Portland, 106
Portugal, 19, 189
Potsdam, 35, 36
Prague, 1
Providence, 106
Prussia (Kingdom of), 11, 16, 17, 18–21, 22, 24, 27, 30, 34, 36–37, 38, 135, 204; education, 24; secret police, 85
Pullman, 100

Rathenau, Walter, 142
Ratzel, Friedrich, 150, 153–156, 157
Reformation, 21, 24–25, 34–35, 38
Rhine (River), 23
Rhine Valley, 12–13
Rhodes, Cecil, 52; Rhodes Scholarships, 52
Rio de Janeiro, 157
Robbins, Bruce, 52
Robinson, Jane, 192, 196
Robinson (Edward), 6
Rochester, 106
Rome, 12, 13, 30
Ross, Colin, 150, 173–178
Roth, Joseph, 131, 132, 133, 139–140, 141
Roxbury, 97
Ruhr Valley, 153
Russell, Mary, 230–231
Russia, 20, 27, 101

Sacramento, 106
Salt Lake City, 106
Salomon, Alice, 141, 142
San Francisco, 1–2, 61, 102, 106, 108, 156, 159–161, 164, 168; prostitution, 102
Santa Clara Valley, 106
Santa Cruz, 106
Saxe-Weimar-Eisenach (Grand Duchy of), 25
Saxony (Electorate of), 34, 37
Saxony (Kingdom of), 3, 11–41, 189–206; bitterness between Saxony and Prussia, 18–19; education, 25, 204; education of peasants, 23–24, 204; fertility of Saxon soil, 23–24, 38, 40; image of Saxony, 201; population of Saxony, 24–27, 40, 204; royal family, 27–29; Saxon dialect, 20; Saxon identity, 18–19, 22, 25, 36–37, 40; Saxon cession to Prussia, 18–21, 33–39; Saxony as Prussia's victim, 20–21, 22; Saxon Switzerland, 32–33
Saxony (Province of), 19, 20
Schenectady, 100, 106
Scheu-Riesz, Helene, 141
Schmidt-Gernig, Alexander, 161
Schriber, Mary Suzanne, 211, 212
Scotland, 191
Seattle, 106
Seven Years' War, 22
Severance, Emily A., 234–235, 241
Shakespeare (William), 30
Shiloh, 220
Siegel, Kristie, 194
Siegfried, André, 61
Silesia, 16, 20
Simmel, Georg, 133
Singer, Mendel, 140
Slezkine, Yuri, 131
Smith, Sarah Lanman, 233, 236, 241
Snow, Eliza, 241
Social Crossings, 82
socialism, 84, 86, 97, 102; American socialism, 99–100, 102, 111; socialist writers, 2
Society for American Fellowships in French Universities, 56
Soil and Civilization, 20, 23–24, 38, 204, 206

Sorge, Friedrich, 97
Soukup, Frantisek, 136
Soviet Union, 131, 132, 141
Spain, 13, 19, 189
Spengler, Oswald, 169
St. Louis, 86, 99, 106, 156, 163; World Exhibition, 5
Stevenson, Catherine Barnes, 193
Stötteritz, 21
Stowe, William, 238
St. Paul, 95, 99, 106, 164
Straiton, Emma, 241
Straiton, Marie 241
Struck, Hermann, 132, 133, 137–138
Sulem, 219–220
Sullivan, Louis, 172
Switzerland, 3, 12, 63, 85, 156

Tabor, 6
Tadlock, Clara Moyse, 210, 222, 224–225, 226, 230, 239–240, 242
Tadmor, 38
Tagore, Rabindranath, 60
Taylor, Bayard, 27, 33
Téry, Simone, 50, 70
Theroux, Paul, 7
Thirty Years' War, 22
Thomas, Susan Brewer, 216, 217, 218, 219, 235–236, 241
Thompson (William McClure), 6
Thuringia, 25
Ticknor, Anna (neé Eliot), 3, 7, 23, 25–26, 27, 28, 29–32, 33, 36, 37, 39, 40, 189–206
Ticknor, Anna (Eliot), 30, 191
Ticknor, Eliza Sullivan, 191
Ticknor, George, 3, 13, 14, 16–19, 21–22, 23, 25, 28, 29–32, 33, 35, 37, 39, 40, 189–206
Toledo, 106
Toronto, 97, 106, 110
travel: by steamship, 12; by railway, 12, 88–89, 97–98, 106, 108; educational travel, 4, 50–71; of Jews, 131–143; of the upper class to Europe, 12, 39, 41
travel writing and gender, 191–194, 197–206
Treuenbrietzen, 20, 37, 38
Tucholsky, Kurt, 132
Twain, Mark, 6, 8

United Kingdom, 13, 14, 15, 39
United States, 1, 2, 4, 50, 51, 54, 56, 57, 58, 59, 60, 61, 62, 66, 67, 68, 70, 83, 84–119, 131–143, 149–178, 237; African Americans, 89, 91, 109, 114, 137, 140, 178; big cities, 5, 149, 153; child labor, 93, 100, 101, 102, 103, 116; cowboys, 92–93; education, 89–90, 96, 110, 155–156, 168; image of the United States, 1, 81–119, 149–178; Jews, 89, 131, 178; Native Americans (Indians), 90–91, 94, 103, 111, 113, 114, 134–135; modernization, 2, 5; modernity, 5, 6, 133–137, 138, 149–178; Prohibition, 89, 105, 106, 108–109; slavery, 91, 101, 109, 134; urbanization, 5, 154, 173; women's rights, 89, 90, 93, 113, 116, 141, 212, 228
University of California at Berkeley, 59
University of Heidelberg, 3

Venezuela, 156
Verne, Jules, 53, 103
Vester, Bertha Spafford, 240, 241
Vienna, 139, 164
Virginia, 226
Voltaire, 35

Wales, 191
Wallace, Susan E., 241, 242

Washington D.C., 86, 95, 106, 109, 117, 164, 172, 240
Wawona (California), 111
Weimar, 17
Weimar Republic, 132, 138, 150, 169
Wells, Sarah Furnas, 215–216, 241
Wenger, Beth, 135
Wertheimer, Pierre, 66–67
Wesley, Marilyn, 238
Weulersse, Georges, 59
Wheaton, Henry, 34
Whitman, Walt, 142
Wikoff, Henry, 28
Wilhelm II (Emperor of Germany), 135, 161
Wilmington (Delaware), 99
Wilson, Woodrow, 169, 174
Wittenberg, 21, 34–37, 38
Wollstonecraft, Mary, 191, 192
women travelers, 6, 25–32, 36–37, 189–206, 210–242
Wood, Mattie Sisson, 241
Woringer, Pierre, 67
Wörlitz, 36

Yosemite Valley, 106

Zangwill, Israel, 141
Zilcosky, John, 1
Zionism, 132, 140
Zweig, Stefan, 6, 131, 132, 133, 141, 142

Other Titles in the
Walter Prescott Webb Memorial Lectures Series:

Creolization in the Americas / Buisseret and Reinhardt
African Diaspora / Jalloh and Maizlish
Sacrifice and National Belonging in Twentieth-Century Germany / Eghigian and Berg
Beyond Black and White / Cole and Parker
Manifest Destiny and Empire / Haynes and Morris
Traveling between Worlds / Adam and Gross
Transatlantic History / Reinhardt and Reinhartz
Lights, Camera, History / Francaviglia and Rodnitzky
Catholicism in the American West / Treviño and Francaviglia
Baseball in America and America in Baseball / Kyle and Fairbanks
Assumed Identities / Garrigus and Morris